Alfred Spont

Letters and Papers Relating to the War with France

1512-1513

Alfred Spont

Letters and Papers Relating to the War with France
1512-1513

ISBN/EAN: 9783744689083

Printed in Europe, USA, Canada, Australia, Japan

Cover: Foto ©ninafisch / pixelio.de

More available books at **www.hansebooks.com**

LETTERS AND PAPERS

RELATING TO THE

War with France

1512—1513

BY

ALFRED SPONT

ANCIEN ÉLÈVE DE L'ÉCOLE DES CHARTES

PRINTED FOR THE NAVY RECORDS SOCIETY

MDCCCXCVII

THE COUNCIL
OF THE
NAVY RECORDS SOCIETY
1897-8

PATRONS

His Royal Highness the DUKE OF SAXE-COBURG AND GOTHA, K.G., K.T., &c.

His Royal Highness the DUKE OF YORK, K.G., &c.

PRESIDENT
EARL SPENCER, K.G.

VICE-PRESIDENTS

FANSHAWE, ADMIRAL SIR EDWARD, G.C.B.
LOTHIAN, MARQUIS OF, K.T.
MARKHAM, SIR CLEMENTS R., K.C.B., F.R.S.
NORTHBROOK, EARL OF, G.C.S.I.

COUNCILLORS

BALFOUR, LIEUT.-COL. EUSTACE.
BEDFORD, VICE-ADMIRAL SIR FREDERICK, K.C.B.
BROWNING, OSCAR.
BURROWS, PROFESSOR MONTAGU.
CHAMBERLAIN, J. AUSTEN, M.P.
CLARKE, LIEUT.-GEN. SIR A., G.C.M.G.
CLARKE, LIEUT.-COL. SIR GEORGE, K.C.M.G., F.R.S.
COLOMB, VICE-ADMIRAL.
CORBETT, JULIAN S.
DASENT, JOHN R., C.B.
EDYE, LIEUT.-COL. L.
ELGAR, DR. FRANCIS, F.R.S.
GRENFELL, CAPT. H. H., R.N.
HAMILTON, ADMIRAL SIR R. VESEY, G.C.B.
HOSKINS, ADMIRAL SIR ANTHONY, G.C.B.
LYALL, SIR ALFRED C., K.C.B.
MARKHAM, VICE-ADMIRAL A. H.
MEADE, HON. SIR R., G.C.B.
OVEREND, W. H.
SHIPPARD, SIR SIDNEY, K.C.M.G.
STEVENS, B. F.
TROWER, H. SEYMOUR.
WHARTON, REAR-ADMIRAL SIR W. J. L., K.C.B., F.R.S.
WHITE, SIR W. H., K.C.B., F.R.S.

SECRETARY
PROFESSOR J. K. LAUGHTON, King's College, London, W.C.

TREASURER
H. F. R. YORKE, C.B., Admiralty, S.W.

The COUNCIL of the NAVY RECORDS SOCIETY wish it to be distinctly understood that they are not answerable for any opinions or observations that may appear in the Society's publications. For these the responsibility rests entirely with the Editors of the several works.

INTRODUCTION

' HENRY VII. had been chiefly occupied in securing the permanence of his dynasty, and although sometimes drawn into action abroad, had avoided any serious entanglement in continental politics. His son's policy was the reverse of this, and his reign presents a series of unsuccessful attempts to make England the centre round which European politics were to revolve.'[1]

After two years of apparent indifference, Henry VIII. sent two armies abroad, one to Guelders, under the command of Sir Edward Ponynges, the other to Cadiz, under the command of Lord Darcy,[2] while difficulties arose with Scotland and Denmark about the capture of Andrew Barton, a Scottish privateer. Holinshed's narrative of this affair is as follows :—

[1] M. Oppenheim, *The Administration of the Royal Navy*, p. 45. The chapter of this excellent book on Henry VIII. must be read for the knowledge of naval organisation in those days : shipbuilding, wages, victualling, &c.; all historical students will appreciate the immense amount of information summarised in pp. 45-99. The present collection of documents is purely narrative, and lays no claim to technical teaching; it only completes M. Oppenheim's volume for a very short period.

[2] Brewer, *Calendar of State Papers, Henry VIII.*, vol. i Preface, xl.

viii   INTRODUCTION

'In June the King, being at Leicester,[1] heard tidings that one Andrew Barton, a Scotchman and pirate of the sea, saying that the King of Scots had war with the Portuguese, robbed every nation, and stopped the King's streams, that no merchant almost could pass ; and when he took Englishmen's goods, he bare them in hand that they were Portugal's goods, and thus he hunted and robbed at every haven's mouth. The King, displeased herewith, sent Sir Edward Howard, lord Admiral of England,[2] and lord Thomas Howard, son and heir to the Earl of Surrey, in all haste to the sea, which hastily made ready two ships, and taking sea, by chance of weather were severed. The lord Howard, lying in the Downs, perceived where Andrew was making toward Scotland, and so fast the said lord chased him, that he overtook him ; and there was a sore battle between them. Andrew ever blew his whistle to encourage his men, but at length the lord Howard and the Englishmen did so valiantly that by clean strength they entered the main deck. The Scots fought sore on the hatches, but in conclusion Andrew was taken, and so sore wounded, that he died there. Then all the remnant of the Scots were taken with their ship, called the Lion. All this while was the lord Admiral in chase of the bark of Scotland, called Jennie Pirwine,[3] which was wont to

[1] Henry VIII. did not reach Leicester till the beginning of August, 1511 : 'For the King's offring at the high aulter at his comyng to Leycestre abbey' (3–10 Aug., *R.O., Chapter House Book* 215, p. 131).
[2] This is incorrect. See *post*, p. xxviii.
[3] The Jenett of Purwyn belonged to the King of Denmark ; she had been brought from Copenhagen by Barton without the

INTRODUCTION ix

sail with the Lion in company, and so much did he with other, that he laid him aboard, and though the Scots manfully defended themselves, yet the Englishmen entered the bark, slew many and took all the residue. Thus were these two ships taken, and brought to Blackwall the 2d of August.'

Holinshed seems to be trustworthy in the main points. Edward Howard fitted out some ships in June, July, and August 1511, to defend the merchant adventurers going to Zealand against the rovers of the sea,[1] and some Scotch prisoners were brought to Westminster in September.[2] We cannot ascertain if Howard fitted out two or three ships; but we think that he hired for that purpose John Iseham's

King's licence (Brewer, No. 3718). The King sent a message to Henry VIII. about the middle of July (*R.O., Chapter House Book* 215, p. 129.)

[1] 'Sir Edward Howard his charge.—To Sir Edwarde Howarde opon a warrant for the preparing and rigging of certain shippes to the see for the fast and sure condyteing of the merchants aventurers mense Junii anno iij^{cio} : 200*l*.

'Item to the same Sir Edwarde opon a warrant for the charge of vitaling of iij shippes lately set to the see, and for the wages of maryners and souldeyers being in the same shippes mense Julii anno iij^{cio} : 200*l*.

'Item to the same sir Edwarde opon a warrant for the wages of certain souldeyers for wafting of the shippes of merchant aventurers into Seland mense Julii anno iij° : 100*l*.

'Item to the same Sir Edwarde opon a warrant for the arrerage vitall of certain shippes wafting and defending of the merchaunts against the rovers of the see mense Augusti anno iij° : 117*l*. 9*s*. 9*d*.' (*R.O., Chapter House Book* 1, p. 34). Cf. *ibid. Chapter House Book* 215, p. 122.

[2] 'Paid to William Atclif for vitailling of certain Scotts beyng at th' archbusshope of York's place at Westmynster (Sept.–Nov.)' 150*l*. (*R.O., Chapter House Book* 215, pp. 139, 143, 147). They were released in December 1511 : 'To the lord Dacre and Sir Richard Ratclif by th' ands of William Atclif for the conveyaunce of Scotts that were in th' archebusshop of York's place, 10*l*.' (*ibid*. p. 151).

x *INTRODUCTION*

Barbara and George Harward's Mary Barking.[1] Of the King's ships, the Mary and John and the Anne of Fowey had been hired to some merchants as early as April 1511; the Regent, the Sovereign, the Mary Rose and the Peter Pomegranate left Portsmouth for the Thames in September. The Regent had been built in 1486, on the model of the Colombe, the ship of Guillaume de Casenove, *dit* Coulon or Colomb, Vice-Admiral of France in the time of Louis XI. and Charles VIII. The Sovereign was almost contemporary; the Mary Rose and the Peter Pomegranate were just finished. In October 1511, two barks and two rowbarges were begun, but they were not launched before July or August 1512.

I.—*The Naval Campaign of* 1512.

Henry VIII. was decidedly involved in the international intrigues of the Continent. In December 1511 he joined a league planned two months before by the Pope, Julius II., and the King of Aragon, Ferdinand the Catholic, against Louis XII., King of France. 'The 25th day of January (1512) began the Parliament; it was concluded that war should be made on the French King and his dominions. Whereupon was wonderful speed made

[1] 'To John Iseham and George Harward for the wages, vitaill and tontage for 2 shippes called the Barbara and the Mary Barking (1-8 July 1511) 37*l*. 15*s*.' (*R.O.*, *Chapter House Book* 1, p. 35; 215, p. 126).

INTRODUCTION xi

in preparing all things necessary both for sea and land.'[1]

With the help of Spain, Henry VIII. intended to invade Guyenne and to be master of the sea. The latter view is clearly exposed in the instructions given to Sir Edward Howard, on his appointment as admiral of the fleet (7 April, 1512); he was to cruise in the Channel from Brest (the Trade) to Calais and London:

'Amongst other articles contained in a treaty made and concluded between the King's Highness and his father the King of Aragon, it is provided that the King's Highness for his part shall, before the end of this instant month of April, put in readiness and actually send to the sea the number of 3,000 men, well and sufficiently harnessed, in ships apparelled, dressed and furnished with habillements of war apt and necessary for battle on the sea, to

---

[1] Holinshed. But according to Polydore Vergil there was some discussion in the King's Privy Council about waging war against France: 'Legatus interea Anglus, Cristophorus, legatus, litteris et nuntiis Henrico regi significabat Julium pontificem auxilia ab Anglia expectare, et quo magis sciebat se Pontifici ob delatum sibi Cardinalatus honorem debere, hoc impensius obtestabatur, rogabatque Regem ut ejus salutis rationem haberet. . . . Cristophori studium ita Henricum permovit, ut res ad Consilium delata sit. Multæ et variæ sententiæ in utramque partem dictæ sunt. Rex, ætate florens, ac opibus æque ut viribus præstans, bellum suscipiendum censebat. Nonnulli id e republica fore negabant. . . . Postremo tamen vicit Regis sententia, quam Consiliarii potissimum probarunt, partim ut ne Regii animi alacritas bellandi extingueretur, qui jam tum militarem disciplinam pluris quam ceteras artes faciebat. . . . Ita bellum esse suscipiendum decretum est . . . et post longam disputationem, placuit sociare arma cum Ferdinando Rege . . .' (Polydore Vergil, *Historiæ Libri* 27, Basileæ, 1570, fol., p. 623).

keep and defend the sea after their policies, strengths and powers, from the mouth of the Thames to the Trade, against the courses of outward enemies. Like as the King's said father, the King of Aragon, is by the said treaty semblably bound to defend the sea, with like number of men and ships, beyond the said Trade. The said armies to continue in such defence and tuition of the sea by the space of 6 months. . . . After the fleet shall come to the sea, the Admiral shall take his course, if wind and weather will serve, towards the Trade, for the defence of the sea on that coast, according to the tenour of the said articles, and from thence return, scouring the sea, to and fro, as the case shall require.'[1]

Sir Edward Howard made the following indenture with the King (8 April 1512):—

'The said Admiral shall have under him in the said service 3,000 men harnessed and arrayed for the war, himself accounted in the said number, over and above 700 soldiers, mariners, and gunners that shall be in the King's ship called the Regent. Of which 3,000, 18 shall be captains, 1,750 shall be soldiers, 1,233 shall be mariners and gunners. The said Admiral shall have for the maintaining of himself and his diets, wages, and rewards daily, during the said voyage, 10s.; and for every of the said captains, for their diets, wages, and rewards, daily, during the said time, 18d. except they be of the number of the King's spears, which shall be contented with their ordinary wages. And for every soldier, mariner,

---

[1] Rymer's *Fœdera*, 3rd edit., 1741, vi. 30 b.

and gunner, he shall have every month, during the said voyages, accounting 28 days for the month, 5s. for his wages, and 5s. for his victuals, without anything else demanding for his wages and victual, saving that they shall have certain deadshares, as hereafter does follow.

'The said Admiral shall, before he and his said retinue enter into the ships, make their musters before such commissioners as shall Our Sovereign Lord depute and assign, and immediately after the said musters made, he shall receive wages, rewards, and victual money after the rate before rehearsed, for 3 months then next following, accounting the month as above.

'And at the same time, he shall receive for the coat of every captain and soldier 4s., and for the coat of every mariner and gunner 20d.

'And at the end of the said three months, and when the said Admiral . . shall . . resort to the port of Southampton, and then and there revictual himself and the said army and retinue, he shall make his musters . . and . . receive . . new wages and victual money, after the rate before rehearsed, for the said 3 months then next following.

'And so from 3 months to 3 months continually during the said time.

'The said Admiral shall have . . 18 ships . . in such manner rigged, equipped, tackled, decked, and furnished with ordnance and artillery as to such a voyage and service for the honour of our said Sovereign Lord.'

Ship	Tons		
Regent	1000 tons	50	also 4 pilots borne in the Regent
Mary Rose	500	34½	
Peter Pomegranate	400	28	
John Hopton	400	23½	
Nicholas Reede	400	23½	
Mary John	240	22½	
Anne of Greenwich	160	22½	
Mary George	300	22½	
Dragon	100	22½	
Lion	120	22½	deadshares
Barbara	140	22½	
George of Falmouth	140	22½	
Peter of Fowey	120	22½	
Nicholas of Hampton	200	22½	
Martinet	180	22½	
Jenett	70	22½	
Christopher Davy	160	22	
Sabyn	120	22	

'And for the victualling and refreshing of the said ships with water and other necessaries, the said Admiral shall, over and above the said ships, have 2 crayers, the one being of the portage of 65*l.*, wherein shall be the master, 12 mariners, and 1 boy, and the other crayer shall be of the portage of 55*l.*, wherein shall be the master, with 10 mariners and 1 boy. And every of the said masters and mariners shall have for his wages 5*s.* and for his victual money 5*s.* for every month, accounting the month as above, and every of the said 2 boys shall have for their month wages 2*s.* 6*d.*, and for their victual money 5*s.* And either of the said masters shall have 2 deadshares.

'Also the said soldiers, mariners, and gunners shall have of Our said Sovereign Lord conduct money, that is to say, every of them for every day's journey from his house to the place where they shall be shipped, accounting 12 miles for the day's journey,

INTRODUCTION xv

6*d*. Of which day's journey they shall have credence by their oath. . . .'[1]

Once the muster taken at Blackheath, on 16 April, Sir Edward Howard took an oath at Westminster, in presence of the King,[2] who issued a warrant for the wages of all his spears [3] and had 6,000*l*. sent to John Dawtrey, customer of Southampton, ' for victualling and revictualling of the King's ships and army upon the sea under Sir Edward Howard, and for other necessaries for the same army in time coming.'

Sir Edward Howard cruised for a fortnight in the Channel, chasing the French fishing-boats [4] and plundering every trading ship he met. For instance, some Spanish ships were seized on the ground that the cargo belonged to Genoese and Florentine merchants, friends of the French King and adversaries of the Holy See; the Venetian Consul in London, Lorenzo Pasqualigo, felt anxious for the safety of goods expected from Chio and Candia.[5] Flemings were treated as badly as Spaniards by Sir Edward

[1] Rymer, vi. 31. Cf. the account printed, pp. 3-13.
[2] 'Et memorandum quod 20° die Aprilis, anno præsenti, prædictus Edwardus venit coram domino Rege in cancellaria sua apud Westmonasterium, et recognovit indenturam prædictam ac omnia et singula in eadem contenta, in forma prædicta' (Rymer, vi. 31, col. 2, *in fine*).
[3] 'To sir Edward Howarde, sir Weston Browne, Edmounde Howarde, William Kingston, John Burdet, William Sherbourne, William Sydney, Griffith Don, Robert Mourton, sir John Audeley, Geffrey Gats, William Parr, William Fitzwilliam, Edwarde Nevell, Edwarde Don, Edwarde Cobham, James Delabare, for their hole yere's wages, every of them, at 3*s*. 4*d*. the day, from the 1st of Aprill last passed. Item to Thomas Lucy, 60*l*. 16*s*. 8*d*.— 1,155*l*. 16*s*. 8*d*.' [18-25 April] (*R. O., Chapter House Book* 215, p. 178).
[4] Doc. 10.   [5] Doc. 9, 11.

a

Howard and his captains : Griffith Don, captain of the Mary and John, compelled Jacques Berenghier, of Lille, to serve as a gunner, seized all his goods, and racked him so that he lost one foot ; then he was kept prisoner at Southampton, had his ears slit, and was threatened with hanging, only because he spoke French ! [1]

The English fleet returned to Portsmouth about the middle of May. The Regent was at last ready with 400 soldiers and 300 mariners ; [2] so also were the two landing barges, begun in October 1511, the Rose Henry and the Catherine Pomegranate.

Sir Edward Howard's successful cruise took Louis XII. by surprise, for he had thought that the news of the victory of his army at Ravenna (11 April) and the threatened breach with Scotland [3] would for a while restrain Henry VIII.'s military ardour.[4] His naval preparations were begun in February ; [5] but all that he did was to appoint the Duc de la Trémoille his Lieutenant-General in Normandy (Blois, 12 April),[6] and to conclude a league of mutual aid with James IV., King of Scotland (Blois, 22 May), who confirmed it at Edinburgh on 10 July. Louis XII.'s Ambassador, La Motte, left on the following day for France in Robert Brownhill's ship, convoyed by Robert Barton and David Faulconer. But they were met near Berwick by the English : La Motte was compelled to fly towards Denmark ; ' Faulconer's

---

[1] Brewer, n° 3,417. Cf. two other acts of piracy committed by the English against Alonso de Lalo and François de Haeze (*ibid.*, n°s 3,571, 3,815).
[2] Doc. 8.
[3] Doc. 3, 4, 5, 10.   [4] Doc. 1.   [5] Doc. 2.
[6] P. 17, *note* 2.

INTRODUCTION xvii

ship was drowned, himself taken, sent up to London, and shrewdly handled.'[1] Barton was denied a safe conduct in Zealand by Marguerite of Savoy (Brussels, 27 July), and on returning to Scotland appealed Brownhill 'for flying when Faulconer was taken.'[2]

Henry VIII. was master of the Channel and North Sea. But this was not enough for his pride; he wished to recover Guyenne. The Marquis of Dorset departed from the Isle of Wight on 3 June, and he was guided by Sir Edward Howard until he came against the coasts of the Trade.[3]

Howard remained four days on the spot.

'On Trinity Sunday [6 June] he arrived at Berthram Bay[4] with 20 great ships, and suddenly set his men on land, and there won a bulwark, which the Bretons kept and defended a while; but being overcome, fled out of their hold, and left it to the Englishmen. Then the lord Admiral passed 7 miles into the country, burning and wasting towns and villages, and in returning skirmished with divers men of arms, and slew some of them; and nothwithstanding that the Bretons fought valiantly in defence of their country, yet they were put to the worst, and so the lord Admiral returned to his ships.'[5]

'On Monday [7 June][6] he landed in the morning, and commanded to burn the house of the lord Piersmogun,[7] with the town of Conquet and divers other places, and chased the Bretons into the castle

---

[1] Brewer, n°ˢ 3,322, 3,326. [2] *Ibid.*, n° 3,340.
[3] Doc. 16.   [4] Bertheaume.   [5] Holinshed.
[6] Dated 23 May by mistake.   [7] Hervé de Porzmoguer.

a 2

of Brest; and notwithstanding all the assemblies and shows that the Bretons made, yet they suffered the English peaceably to return with their prey and booty.'

The following day [1] 'the Englishmen took land in Croiton [2] bay, and then the lords of Brittany sent word to the lord Admiral, that if he would abide, they would give him battle. The Admiral rewarded the messenger, and willed him to say to them that sent, that all that day they should find him in that place tarrying their coming. Then, to encourage divers gentlemen the more earnestly to show their valiancy, he dubbed them knights, as Sir Edward Brook, brother to the lord Cobham, Sir Griffith Don, Sir Thomas Windham, Sir Thomas Lucy, Sir John Burdet, Sir William Pirton, Sir Henry Sherborne and Sir Stephen Bull. When the lord Admiral saw the Frenchmen come, he comforted his men with pleasant words, thereby the more to encourage them. The whole number of the Englishmen was not much above 2,500, where the Frenchmen were at the least 10,000; and yet when they saw the order of the Englishmen, they were suddenly astonished. Then a gentleman of good experience and credit amongst them advised the other captains not to fight, but to retire a little and take a strong ground, there to remain till the Englishmen returned toward their ships, and then to take the advantage. And then the captains began to retire: which when the commons saw, they ran all away as fast as they might, supposing that the

---

[1] Dated 1 June by mistake. [2] Crozon.

captains had seen or known some great peril at hand, because they were not privy to the purpose of their captains.

'The lord Admiral seeing what happened, when the night came, returned to his ships. After this the gentlemen of Brittany sent to the Admiral for a safeconduct for divers persons, which they meant to send to him about a treaty. The lord Admiral was of his gentleness content to grant their request. Then certain lords of Brittany took a boat and came to the ship of the lord Admiral, where he was set with all his council of the army about him. The request of the Bretons was that it might please him to surcease his cruel kind of war, in burning of towns and villages; but the Admiral plainly told them that he was sent to make war, and not peace. Then they required a truce for 6 days, which would not be granted; and to their reproof, the Admiral told them that gentlemen ought to defend their country by force, rather than to sue for peace. And thus (making them a banquet), he sent them away.

'And after hearing that there was ships of war in the seas, he coasted from thence along the country of Normandy, still scouring the sea, so that no enemy durst appear. And at length he came and lay by the Isle of Wight, to see if any enemies would appear.'[1]

According to Pasqualigo, Howard had captured 26 Flemish hulks and about 40 small Breton ships. France seemed in a dangerous extremity: Henry had apparently the choice of landing any-

[1] Cf. Doc. 19 and 22 corroborating Holinshed's narrative.

INTRODUCTION

where he liked; but a well-informed spy pointed out the three best places for landing—Lower Normandy, where a part of the French fleet could be burnt in the mouth of the Seine, Rochelle and Fontarabia, for invading Guyenne and Languedoc[1]—and persuaded him to avoid Picardy, Upper Normandy, and Bordeaux, at that time the strongholds of the kingdom.

[1] '[Ilz font] arrester tous les navires tant de Bretaigne que d'aultre part qui [sont] en ce quartier de delà et font aprester tous leurs navires de Normandie à Honnteflou, là où on les répare du tout pour la guerre, et peult estre en nombre de 100 à 120 navires, lesquelles sont tous en l'entrée de la Seine, sans encores point de provision ne de garde, sinon qu'ilz font armer 4 grans navires pour bouter en la mer pour faire le ghet et veoir quelles navires passeront. Et est à présumer, se le roy d'Angleterre à present fust prest de descendre et que il eust armés 10 ou 12 navires avec quelque 5 au 6,000 hommes, et venir avec la haute mer audit enboutement de la Seine, on pourroit facilement bruler tous leursdits navires, à cause que il n'y a encores point d'ordre.
... Et semblablement avoir aultre armée preste pour se joindre avec lesdits navires, après avoir fait leur emprise, et descendre en la Basse Normandie, et pourront facilement piller tout le pays, ... et n'y a en ladite Basse Normandie point grant deffence ne gens qui soient combatans et de faire partout crier franchise à ladite descente, car beaucoup de gens se joindront avec eulx à cause du malcontentement de la réduction des monnoyes, aussy des grans tailles, car à présent on a cru la taille de 4 sous pour livre.
'Et quant à veniren la Haulte Normandie, comme aux pays de Caux et envers Abbeville et le pays de Picardie, on ne seroit point de cest advis, veu la force des villes et aussy que les gens du quartier sont bons combatans, et jà ont mis garde partout . . . et font de nouveau 600 hommes d'armes pour mectre en ce quartier delà, dont M. d'Angolesme est lieutenant général sur la conduicte de M. de la Trémoille. . . .
'Semble que ce seroit le plus seur, après a[voir mis le ffeu] sur lesdits navires et avoir pillé toute la Normandie que toute l'armée se reboutasse en la mer et v[int pour] venir prendre terre à la Rochelle, et pourroit on [peut estre] et que les chaines du avre ne fust tendu, que . . . l'emporteroit, au moins leur feroit on grand dommaige. . . . Et en prenant terre à lad e

INTRODUCTION xxi

Henry VIII. had leisure to mature the plan submitted to him, as he had to wait for the Spanish fleet to be ready, according to the last treaty concluded with Ferdinand the Catholic. In the meantime he strengthened his naval force. Some other ships were fitted out ; such as the Margaret of Topsham (Capt. James Knyvet), the Mary James (Capt. Ant· Ughtred), and the Magdalene (Capt. J. Brigandyne) ; the Lion, needing repair, was replaced by the Henry of Hampton. Thomas Knyvet, appointed captain of the Regent,[1] was entrusted with the revictualling of the fleet.[2] Sir Charles Brandon and Sir Harry

Rochelle, et que l'armée vint descendre à Fontarabie et venir entre en tous . . . Labourt, en Chalosse, en Rivière, en Fezensac et Auch en . . . joignant Toulouse, par ce party pourroit on destruire le [pays] de Languedoc et tout le quartier de Guyenne. Car de venir descendre au quartier de Bordeaux, on [ne seroit point de] cest advis, à cause de la grande garde qui y est et y [est à présent] M. de Longueville, qui a fait grosse provision' (Brit. Mus., MSS. Calig. E 1, fol. 108).

[1] 'Henry, by the grace of God king of Englande and of Fraunce and lord of Irelande, to the tresourer and chambrelains of our Exchequier, greting.

'Forasmuche as our trusty and welbeloved servaunte sir Thomas Knyvet, maister of our horses, hath by our commaundement provided and must provyde certain bisket, bere and other vitaills, and also hoyes for the conveyaunce of the same for the revitailling of our armye upon the see, we therfore woll and commaunde you that of our tresour beyng in your keping ye doo content and paye or doo to be contented and paied unto our said servaunte or his assigners for the charge by him to be bourne and susteyned in that behalf the somme of 50 pounds sterling, withoute any prest or other charge upon him to be set in our pele for the same. And this oure lettres shalbe your sufficient waraunts and discharge in that behalf.

'Yeven under oure pryve seall, at oure manour of Grenewiche, the 12th day of July the 4th yere of our reigne' (Brewer, i. 3308).

[2] Sir Richard Gyldeford, master of the King's armoury and bailiff of Winchelsea, was sent with 100 soldiers on the Regent :

Gyldeford were appointed captains of the Sovereign, with the rowbarge Catherine Pomegranate, and two victuallers.[1]

At the end of July the Spanish fleet was not yet heard of, and Henry VIII. had to do without it. 'Having a desire to see his navy together, he rode to Portsmouth '[31 July–2 August 1512], and offered his captains 'a banquet before their setting forward' (Holinshed).

But Sir Edward Howard was going to find some opposition this time, because Louis XII. had at last made naval preparations. After issuing letters patent for the levy of a land tax, he appointed Pierre Gautier to control the victualling of the fleet in Normandy (Blois, 20 June).[2] About 14 ships were fitted out in that province,[3] and 8 others in Brittany:[4] altogether some 22 men-of-war (5 belonging to the King,[5] 4 to Queen Anne, his wife,[6] the remainder hired[7]), under the command of René de Clermont (Blois, 2 July).[8]

Moreover, the French King withdrew from Lombardy and Genoa, which he had conquered in 1499, to oppose all his naval force to England: Prégent de Bidoux, Knight of Rhodes, French

'Foreasmuche as we have appointed, as ye knowe . . . our ful trusty knight and counsellour sir R. Gyldeford to be emploied . . . 100 men we have asked him to aredye to entre into our ship the Regent' [Greenwich, 5 June 1512] (Brewer, n° 3238).
[1] Brewer, n° 4475. [2] Doc. 17–18.
[3] P. 48, *note* 2. [4] P. 47, *note* 1.
[5] Nefs de Rouen, d'Orléans, de Dieppe, de Bordeaux, Petite Louise, all built since 1507.
[6] Nefs de Morlaix, de Brest, de Rochelle, de Bordeaux. Cf. note about the Cordelière, page 47: it remains doubtful whether she was the nef de Morlaix or the nef de Brest.
[7] The freight was 25 sous-tournois monthly per ton.
[8] Doc. 20.

INTRODUCTION xxiii

admiral in the Mediterranean ('Admiral du Levant'), was summoned to Blois at the beginning of July and ordered to Brittany with his galleys.

Trade was practically stopped in Western Europe : Pasqualigo reports that the cargoes from Candia could not be insured, even at 10 per cent. ; Louis XII. had already declared commercial war with England, by delivering letters of reprisal to some merchants of Rouen (Blois, 8 June) ;[1] he went on later to forbid intercourse of any kind not only with England, but with Spain and Portugal (Blois, 6 Aug.).[2]

Friends and adversaries were indifferently plundered by the French King's captains, Bernardin, Prégent's nephew, near Cartagena, and Hervé de Porzmoguer, captain of the Cordelière, on the coasts of Galicia.[3] But they did but follow the example of Sir Edward Howard's seizing Flemish trading ships and hulks.[4] If the King's captains acted thus, what could be expected of the privateers ?

The French rovers were very numerous. About 80 sailed out of Brest,[5] while a Malouin, Philippe Roussel, in his bark the Rochellaise, made 11 or 12 prizes between Ireland and Scotland, and among them a Spanish vessel, off Kirkcudbright.[6] Roussel was not considered as a pirate, as he was taken into the King's service at the end of the year 1512.

[1] Doc. 12. [2] Doc. 27. [3] Doc. 22, 25.
[4] Ferdinand the Catholic acted likewise : the Florentine John Cavalcanti having, by Henry VIII.'s commission, shipped sulphur and saltpetre from Naples in a Portuguese ship, the cargo was seized on its arrival in Spain by Ferdinand's officers (Letter of Henry VIII., Greenwich, 6 Oct. 1512).
[5] P. 46, *note* 2. [6] P. 42, *note* 3.

Sir Edward Howard was at Portsmouth, waiting for the arrival of the Normandy ships at Brest: they had not arrived there on 2 August,[1] but must have come two or three days later. The English ships, 25 in number,[2] left Portsmouth, and reached, for the second time, the Trade on the eve of St. Lawrence. Their arrival was quite unexpected: the French ships were two or three miles outside the Goulet of Brest, near the shore, and 300 gentlemen with their wives were on a visit on board the Cordelière, for the feast of St. Lawrence.

Had the French a fair prospect of success? The two fleets were nearly equal in number: 22 to 25; but the largest French ship, the Louise, is described as of 790 t., the Cordelière of about 700 t., while the Regent and the Sovereign are said to have been each of 1,000 t. The two fleets seem to have suffered from the same lack of victual: Antoine de Conflans, captain of the Rose and of the Béthune, complained that the food and drink were bad,[3] while part of the soldiers in the Mary James were obliged to remain nine days on land at Portsmouth for lack of victual.[4] Still the Cordelière was pretty well stored: 200 tons of wine, 100 pipes of salt meat and 400 of biscuit. The French were inferior in infantry to the English;[5] but,

---

[1] Doc. 28. A Portuguese chaplain saw in Brest harbour seven of Queen Anne's ships: the Cordelière was still near la Coronna with Porzmoguer.
[2] Without the 26 Flemish hulks and the victuallers.
[3] Doc. 31. [4] P. 61, *note* 2.
[5] 'La Franzese s' intende essere gagliarda, ma non si bene provista di fanterie come quella' (Doc. 68). The Regent had 400 crossbowmen, 100 gunners, 80 soldiers and sailors.

INTRODUCTION xxv

on the other hand, they were well provided with ordnance. The Cordelière had '60 barrels of gunpowder, 15 great brass curtalls, with some marvellous number of shot and other guns of every sort.'[1]

Sir Edward Howard sighted the French fleet on 10 August, about 11 A.M.: he cannonaded René de Clermont's ship, the Louise, and shot away her main mast, while Anthony Ughtred, captain of the Mary James, tried to board the Cordelière, and fired at her successfully with his 6 curtalls. René de Clermont turned back and fled cowardly towards Brest, and only two French ships remained on the spot, the Cordelière and the nef de Dieppe. Rigault de Berquetot, captain of the nef de Dieppe, fought seven hours with five English ships, and was at last rescued, about 7 P.M., by some Guérandais. In the same time, Porzmoguer showed great courage: the Sovereign had joined the Mary James, 'and lay stem to stem to the carrack; but, by negligence of the master, or else by smoke of the ordnance, or otherwise, the Sovereign was cast at the stern of the carrack: with which advantage the Frenchmen shouted for joy. But when Sir Thomas Knyvet, who was ready to have boarded the great ship of Dieppe, saw that the Sovereign missed the carrack, suddenly he caused the Regent (in the which he was aboard) to make to the carrack, and to grapple with her along board. And when they of the carrack perceived they could not depart, they let slip an anchor, and so with the stream the ship turned, and the carrack was on the weather side, and the

[1] Doc. 30.

Regent on the lee side. The fight was cruel between these two ships, the archers on the English side and the crossbows on the French part doing their uttermost to annoy each other. But finally the Englishmen entered the carrack, which being perceived by a gunner, he desperately set fire to the gunpowder, as some say, though there were that affirmed how Sir Anthony Ughtred, following the Regent at the stern, bowged her in divers places, and set her powder on fire. But howsoever it chanced, the whole ship, by reason of the fire, was set on fire, and so both the carrack and the Regent, being grappled together so as they could not fall off, were both consumed by fire at that instant.'[1]

Only 180 men of the Regent and 6 of the Cordelière escaped.[2]

[1] Holinshed.
[2] Holinhed's narrative has been completed by Doc. 30, 33, 36 and 39. Alain Bouchart, a contemporary Breton chronicler, gives the following account : 'Le roy d'Angleterre envoya vers Bretaigne son Admiral accompaigné de plusieurs grans navires, et principallement avoit ung grant navire où estoit ledit admiral d'Angleterre, lesquelz vindrent escumant la mer au long de la coste de Bretaigne. Laquelle chose voyans, les Bretons et François, qui n'estoient pas assez fors pour résister encontre les nefz et navires, et mesmement les gens qui estoient dedans, aussi pareillement que lesdits Bretons et François furent prins à despourveu et non soy donnant garde de Anglois, ce nonobstant, ung vaillant capitaine de mer breton, nommé Primoguet, lequel estoit capitaine d'une grande nef nommée la Cordellière, laquelle nef la Royne de France avoit fait faire en la ville de Morlaix, en la Basse Bretaigne, depuis peu de temps, qui avoit cousté ung gros argent, dont ledit Primoguet, comme ung loyal serviteur, et d'ung grant courage, mostra de quel amour il aymoit les Anglois. Car il partit de Brest tout le premier, et vint crocher par grant hardiesse la plus grant nef d'Angleterre nommée la Régente, qui estoit sans comparison plus grande que la Cordelière. Et quant vint au joindre, y eut plusieurs pièces d'artillerie deschargées d'une part et d'autre, puis vindrent à entrejoindre l'ung à l'autre, et battre et frapper l'ung sur l'autre

INTRODUCTION xxvii

Sir Edward Howard lay that night in Bertheaume Bay, and remained for the two following days in the neighbourhood, burning 27 small ships and capturing 5; on 13th August he landed and took 800 Breton prisoners. Thence he put again to sea and scoured all along the coasts of Brittany, Normandy, and Picardy, taking many French ships and burning such as they could not bring with them. By the end of August the English ships returned, some to Dartmouth, some to Southampton.[1]

The Normandy ships were still at Brest on 1st September, 1512,[2] but left a few days later for Honfleur and Dieppe, as the warrant for the payment of wages to the controller, Pierre Gautier, dated Blois, 22 September, states that his commission is ended.[3]

Henry VIII. seemed quite satisfied with the result of the 'drowning' of the carrack of Brest, as he rewarded with 10*l*. 'the man that brought tidings from

---

d'une terrible sorte. Mais à la fin aulcun de la Cordelière qui estoit en la hune getta le feu dedans la Régente, parquoy le feu print aux pouldres et salpestres, et furent presque tous bruslez, tant d'ung costé que d'autre, et entre les aultres y demoura l'admiral d'Angleterre et ses gens. Le capitaine Primoguet, voyant le feu si près de luy et que n'y avoit aucun remède ne secours, se getta en la mer tout armé, et fut noyé : dont ce fut ung très grant dommaige pour tout le royaulme de France, et signeaument pour toute Bretaigne. Et quant le demourant de ladite armée de France eussent aussi bien fait son debvoir comme Primoguet, les navires d'Angleterre ne fussent point retournées en leur pays dire des nouvelles aux aultres. Et furent ces deux nefs toutes bruslées, sans ce qu'il en eschappast guères de gens.' Polydore Vergil has also given a brief account of the battle in the 27th Book of his *English Chronicles* (ed. 1570, Basileæ, p. 628).

[1] The report of the pilot of the Cordelière and other French prisoners is dated London, 5 Sept. (Doc. 33).
[2] Doc. 3.
[3] Doc. 56.

xxviii *INTRODUCTION*

Sir Edward Howard, knight, Lord Admiral ' (22–29 August, 1512).[1] A few days earlier, before the news had reached the court, Sir Edward Howard had received the reversion of the office of admiral of England held by the earl of Oxford.[2] On 10th October he was granted 66*l*. 13*s*. 4*d*. ' for his goode service upon the sea.'[3]

On the other hand Louis XII. allowed 100 francs to the captain of the *Louise* for the good news brought from Brest : ' l'exécution que avoit faicte nostre armée de mer à l'encontre de nos ennemys.' But Clermont had sent a false report. Three months later Berquetot, the gallant captain of the nef de Dieppe, accused the Admiral of cowardice, and he was supported by all the other captains.[4] Unfortunately Clermont was not sentenced as he deserved, and after having disappeared from court during the year 1513, he was still holding his office in the spring of 1514.[5]

If the naval war had been honourable for the English flag, the expedition of the Marquis of Dorset to Guyenne was a failure and a disgrace. ' Insubordination broke out in the fleet and in the army ; the seamen plundered the victuals when the soldiers were sea-sick.'[6] Moreover Ferdinand the Catholic was too selfish to keep his engagement with Henry VIII., and only wished to gain the kingdom of Navarre. ' No provision had been made for the landing of the English, and no tents for their

---

[1] *R. O., Chapter House Book* 215, p. 199.
[2] *Dict. of Nat. Biog.* xxviii. 11.
[3] Doc. 42. [4] Doc. 43.
[5] Doc. 106. [6] Brewer, preface, p. xl.

shelter. The troops slept out in the fields and under bushes, exposed to incessant rains and the tropical sun of a Spanish sky. The season was pestilential ; the hot wines of Spain increased the evil. Worst of all, no beer was to be had, and the English had not yet learnt to fight without it.' The Marquis of Dorset departed from Spain on Sunday, 30th October, and reached Falmouth on the following Thursday.[1]

Ferdinand's conduct had been treacherous ; he had not for one moment adhered to his arrangements with Henry VIII. His fleet ought to have been ready by the end of April,[2] but it only reached Southampton on 8th September, under the command of Don Juan de Lezcano,[3] when the naval campaign was practically over.[4] However, Lezcano was cheered : after a first reward of 6*l.* 13*s.* 4*d.*, he received 100*l.* ; his son and three other captains, 100*l.* ; 300*l.* were 'distributed among the whole army.'[5] After three months' stay, Lezcano returned to Spain at the end of December.[6]

On the other hand, Louis XII. endeavoured to decide the Kings of Denmark and Scotland in his favour.[7]

Louis XII. urged James IV. to send him a naval force, according to the treaty of 22nd May last, but the Scottish fleet was not yet ready; it appears that

---

[1] Bergenroth, *Calendar of State Papers : England and Spain*, t. i. n° 72.
[2] Cf. *ante*, p. xii.   [3] P. 41, *note* 4.
[4] Henry VIII.'s ships protected the herring fleet on the coasts of Norfolk and Suffolk, but they were discharged on 14 Oct.
[5] R. O., *Chapter House Book* 215, pp. 202, 209.
[6] Bergenroth, n° 78.   [7] P. 46, *note* 1.

James IV. wanted money and not so many 'fair writings' (September 1512).[1]

II.—*The Naval Campaign of* 1513.

In 1512 the English had been ready long before the French; they had cruised three times in the Channel and landed in many places in Brittany, capturing the smaller ships, burning what they could not take with them. The French admiral had turned back at very first sight of them.

The tide began to turn when Prégent de Bidoux arrived in Brittany in the autumn of 1512; he had ranged along the coast of Spain and found a shelter in the ports of Emmanuel, King of Portugal, from the Spanish admiral Lezcano, to the great indignation of Ferdinand the Catholic.[2] His galleys were fitted with three basilisks, which excited Peter Martyr's admiration: 'One shot of those marvellous guns can sink any man-of-war.'[3]

Prégent, born in Gascony,[4] near Tarbes, had had a high reputation in the Mediterranean for the last fifteen years: Knight of Rhodes, he had fought against the Turks at Negropont and in the Archipelago; later, he had defended Naples against the Spaniards; in 1510 he had won a brilliant action

---

[1] Brewer, n° 3412. Letter relating the arrival of the Archdeacon of St. Andrews (Edinburgh, 6 Sept.) with credential letters of Louis XII. An undated letter of Louis XII. (n° 1407) seems to refer to that embassy: Jean Salat, who was in company of the archdeacon, was a prominent member of the Paris Parlement (High Court of Justice).
[2] Doc. 37. Cf. p. 52, *note* 4.   [3] Doc. 32.
[4] Polydore Vergil calls him Joannes, Vasco (*op. cit.* p. 635).

INTRODUCTION

against the Venetians, and had successfully guarded the Riviera from Genoa to Marseilles. He was a sound tactician, and the naval action of 1510 was still quoted as an example by Italian military writers of the middle of the sixteenth century.

Prégent had only six galleys, which were under his command independent of the admiral of the fleet. The galleys being flat-bottomed, and drawing but little water, could go where the ships could not follow them, and with their oars could move against wind or tide. In a calm one of the galleys was superior to three or four rowbarges, 'and could drown with their oars as many boats as came within the reach of them.'[1]

His arrival inspired an unusual activity in France. The galleys were supplied with convicts from the prisons of Angers (December 1512).[2] Eleven ships were equipped at Brest at the cost of the King and Queen; 15 or 16 in Normandy,[3] well provided with guns.[4] Guyon le Roy, Sr du Chillou, was appointed admiral in the place of Clermont (Blois, 25 January, 1513), and Louis XII. urged him to lose no time.[5] The Louise was victualled at Honfleur for three months (6 March).[6]

Two French ambassadors had left for Scotland in November 1512;[7] but they returned, one by the West coast, the other by the East coast, without any satisfactory result.[8]

[1] P. 155.
[2] P. 71, *note* 1.
[3] Cf. the reports of spies (Doc. 49, 57). For Upper Normandy, cf. Doc. 61.
[4] P. 73, *note* 2. [5] Doc. 52. [6] Doc. 56.
[7] Doc. 45, 46. [8] Doc. 50.

Prégent was at Brest preparing for some mysterious enterprise : 'Il y a tant grand appareil que c'est merveille' (wrote a spy), 'mais pour aller où on ne sait' (February 1513).[1] It was thought that the French would try to land at Plymouth or at Falmouth.[2]

After all, on Sunday, 13 March, Prégent left Brest with only his galleys,[3] but bad weather, lack of victual, and pestilence prevented him from crossing the Channel: 'Il y a longtemps que je n'ai escript à cause du temps contraire que j'ai eu pour passer en Angleterre, depuys le temps que je partis de Brest, qui fut le 13ᵉ jour de mars, et aussi pour les maladies et mortalités que j'ai eu aux galères.'[4]

In the meantime du Chillou left Honfleur, on board the Louise, with 15 or 16 sail, and on his way to Brest gave the islands of Guernsey and Alderney licence to carry on their trade with Normandy, under French control.[5]

It seemed that the French were not to be taken this time by surprise, like the year before, although Henry VIII. had greatly and rapidly increased his

[1] Doc. 51.
[2] 'Plesytht Your Hynes, ther ys come to Midelorght a shepp of Campfer that cam stryght owght of Brest havyn, whyche showitht me for a trewth that ther ys 35 saills of men of war with the 6 gales et all ——be redy, as he saitht, and tare bovt upon the 16 saills that are at Ou[nfleur and Di]ep whiche I thenke be ther by thys tyme. And——ther be abought an enterpryse as they say, the——in Falmought haven or Plemought. Albeit they be acustomed [to] make the breuct in one place and goo too another, this I have——doo before this time, me semeitht, under your corexshon, it were right nesesary that the west partes wer sene too and provyshon made for them' (John Wiltshire to Henry VIII., 20 March, 1513: Brit. Mus., Cott., App. L, fol. 40).
[3] Doc. 59. [4] Doc. 72. [5] Doc. 60.

naval power. Between October 1512 and February 1513 all the ships were repaired.¹ Others were built or at least begun: the Henry Grace Dieu, and three rowbarges (or galleys). Others were bought: the Catherine Forteleza, the Gabriel Royal,² the John Hopton, the Nicholas Reede (or Great Nicholas). A Genoese carrack, the Maria de Loreto, was arrested at Dartmouth. Two or three lists of ships were drawn up and revised by the King and Wolsey:³ 23 King's ships, 5 hired ships, and the victuallers.

Henry VIII. pressed Ferdinand the Catholic to send him another fleet (December 1512), but the King of Aragon, having secured the kingdom of Navarre for himself, decided to do no more, and a few months later he signed a truce with France (1 April, 1513).

The English fleet was ready by the middle of March ; it was well furnished with men and ordnance, but very badly with beer and biscuit : ' For God's sake,' says Sir Edward Howard, in his first letter, ' haste your Council to send us down our victual. . . . I pray God that He send our victual shortly, for in Christendom out of one realm was never seen such a fleet as this. I assure you, with our barkets come to us, that the first wind that come, we might be doing service.'⁴ All the pursers remained in London to hasten the victuals.

---

[1] See pp. 78 and sqq.
[2] Pilot, Darillyo, paid from 11 April only. The owner was Fernando de la Sala.
[3] Doc. 53, 54, 55.   [4] Doc. 58.

Sir Edward Howard left the Thames on 19 March, but bad weather kept him for some days in the Downs: 'I need not to write unto you what storms we had, for you know it well enough.' He wrote from Plymouth (5 April): 'God send us good tidings' of the victuallers, and he asked 'to fill their bellies full.'

Before leaving England, he commended himself to the King, to the 'Queen's noble grace,' to 'all good ladies and gentlewomen,' to his 'fellows' Sir Charles Brandon and Sir Henry Gyldeford; he besought his father for his blessing, and wrote to his wife.[1] Although he was full of enthusiasm, he felt how difficult was the enterprise of fighting against the French fleet, which would always 'resort into the chamber of Brest,'[2] where it was impossible to land; the rowbarges, in such a dangerous undertaking, ought to be manned by convicts, that 'would rather venture their lives than have a shameful death.'

Sir Edward Howard left Plymouth on Sunday, 10 April, without his victuallers, and the following day he met, near St. Matthews, 15 sail, 'which, as soon as they spied us, fled like cowards.'[3] The French were closely blockaded in Brest, however, and Prégent, who had been obliged to resort to St. Malo for refreshments, was separated from Admiral du Chillou. The opportunity was good for the English, but, 'on God's name,' let the victuallers come.

Sir Edward Howard 'came into Bertheaume Bay,

---

[1] P. 107.   [2] P. 143.   [3] P. 122.

INTRODUCTION xxxv

and there lay at anchor in sight of the French navy, which kept itself clos within the haven of Brest, without proffering to come abroad.

'The English, perceiving the manner of the Frenchmen, determined to set on them in the haven, and making forward in good order of battle, at their first entry, one of their ships, whereof Arthur Plantagenet was captain, fell on a blind rock, and burst asunder: by reason whereof, all the others stayd, and so the English captains, perceiving that the haven was dangerous to enter without an expert lodesman, they cast about and returned to their harborough at Bertheaume Bay again. The Frenchmen, perceiving that the Englishmen meant to assail them, moored their ships so near to the castle of Brest as they could, and placed bulwarks on the land on every side to shoot at the Englishmen. Also they trapped together 24 great hulks that came to the Bay for salt, and set them on a row, to the intent that if the Englishmen had come to assault them, they would have set those hulks on fire, and have let them drive with the stream amongst the English ships.'[1]

Plantagenet's[2] ship was probably the Nicholas of Hampton : 'He was in a marvellous danger, for it was marvel that the ship, being with all her sails, striking full but a rock with her stem, that she broke not on pieces at the first stroke.'[3] Plantagenet 'called upon Our Lady of Walsingham for

---
[1] Holinshed.
[2] Illegitimate son of Edward IV. Cf. *Dict. of Nat. Biog.* xlv. 399.
[3] Doc. 69.

help and comfort, and made a vow that, and it pleased God and her to deliver him out of the peril, he would never eat flesh nor fish till he had seen her.'[1] So he left the fleet, and his crew was divided among the other ships.

Sir Edward Howard had landed twice on both sides of Brest[2] 'to content somwhat the men's minds, which are hardly handled in the distributing of dayly vitalling, by reason that as yet our victualling is not come to us.'

The French 'be seen underneath the castle, and they have all the hulks afore the mouth of the haven, for because we should do them no hurt.'

Some victuallers left Queenborough, under the convoy of Edward Echyngham, 13 April; but they did not reach the Trade before the 19th.[3] 'Then I came aboard to my lord Admiral and then I trow there was never a knight more welcome to his sovereign lady than I was to my lord Admiral and to the whole army, for because I brought the victuals with me; for of ten days before there was no man in all the army that had but one meal a day and one drink.'[4] That fresh victual was soon exhausted, and when W. Sabyn arrived, on 24 April, with 9 crayers there was not sufficient for three days on board.[5] Three Spanish ships, Captains W. Gonson, J. Iseham, and Richard Barclay, had not left Queenborough on 24 April,[6] and they did not go further than Dartmouth.

The position was untenable, and Sir Edward Howard was literally compelled by want of food

[1] Doc. 69.   [2] Cf. Doc. 70.   [3] Pp. 151-153.
[4] Doc. 76.   [5] Doc. 77.   [6] Doc. 71.

INTRODUCTION xxxvii

and drink either to return to England with dishonour, or else to try to land at all risks.

He ignored the danger: 'As for the galleys, if they come any hour by day or by night, the boats and small vessels and rowgalleys shall lay them sharply aboard, and rather than they escape us, I have assigned Harper, the Thomas of Hull, my bark, Trevinian's bark, and 2 or 3 small ships not to spare to give them, and though they should run them aground for to make them sink.' Spaniards and Scots seemed to have a better appreciation of Prégent. Some Spanish victuallers in the company of Echyngham were much afraid, on 19 April, about 10 A.M., when they sighted the French galleys, for they said, 'Now is the day coming that we shall be fain to go to the hospital'! On the other hand, James IV., threatened by Nicolas West, Ambassador of England, said that he would appeal from the Pope to Prégent: 'Appellabo ad Petrum Johannem.'[1]

On Friday, 22 April, '6 galleys and 4 foists came through part of the King's navy, and they sank the ship that was master Compton's, and struck through one of the King's new barks, the which Sir Stephen Bull is captain of, in 7 places, that they that was within the ship hade much pain to hold her above the water.'[2] Prégent, having himself lost one foist, went into Whitsand Bay[3] and remained there all Saturday. Upon Sunday, 24 April, 'my lord Admiral appointed 6,000 men for to land between Whitsand bay and Conquet, and so to come unto

[1] Doc. 67.
[2] P. 146. Cf. Prégent's Narrative, Doc. 72, p. 136.
[3] Blancs Sablons. Cf. *Dict. Nat. Biog.* xxviii. 11.

the backside of the galleys, and as we were landing my lord admiral espied Sabyn coming under sail, and then that purpose was lost, for every captain had put his men into victuallers.'

Then, although Sabyn, an experienced sailor, tried to turn Howard's mind, and showed him the King's credence,[1] the Admiral, 'sore set upon by a Spaniard,' Alfonso Charran, captain of a carrack,[2] decided to go forward. The great ships returned into the Trade, 'so for to abide still before the haven of Brest, that the navy of France should not come out, whilst the small ships should run upon the galleys.'

The instructions brought by Sabyn are not preserved, neither is Howard's letter, received at the Court by Sabyn's hands on 17th April; therefore it is impossible to say if Holinshed was right or not when he wrote: 'The lord Admiral, perceiving the French navy thus lie in fear, wrote to the King to come thither in person, and to have the honour of so high an enterprise. Which writing the King's Council[3] nothing allowed, for putting the King in jeopardy upon the chance of the sea. Wherfore the King wrote to him sharply again, commanding him to accomplish that which apperteined to his duty. Which caused him to adventure things farther than wisdom would he should, to his utter undoing and casting away.' However, Sir Edward Howard decided to board Prégent's galleys. At 4 P.M. on Sunday, 25 April, 1513, he went into one of the two rowbarges, and 80 men with him; lord Ferrers

[1] P. 143.
[2] The Sancho de Gana, probably, and not the Gabriel Royal, as written by mistake p. 119.
[3] No register of the Privy Council is extant for the period 1435-1540.

was in the other rowbarge. Sherborne and Sydney went in a crayer, Wallop and Cheyne in another. 'These were they that enterprised for to win the French galleys.'

The enterprise was a mere folly : no ship could come to the galleys for want of water, and the galleys lay between rocks, defended by 'bulwarks full of ordinances, the which were so thick with guns and crossbows that the quarrels and the gunstones came together as thick as it had been hailstones.'[1]

Sir Edward Howard boarded Prégent's galley, casting his grapnel into her and fastening the rope to the capstan ; then he leaped out of his rowbarge, Charran and 16 others with him. But, for fear of the French ordnance,[2] his companions turned back and left the Admiral in Prégent's hands, with Charran : the grapnel rope had slipped or been cut ; Charran asked his boy to fetch him his hand gun, and when the boy came up the barge had drifted away. The Admiral waved with his hands and cried : 'Come aboard again ! Come aboard again !' He then took one of his whistles ('sifflet d'honneur') from his neck and 'hurled it into the sea.' He was thrust against the rails of the galley with morrice pikes and thrown overboard.

Lord Ferrers shot 200 sheaves of arrows among the French galleys ; so did Cheyne and Wallop, while Sherborne and Sydney charged Prégent's galley and broke several of her oars.[3]

[1] 'Toutes celles galées où j'estoye estoient advironnés de repères' (p. 136).
[2] On the other hand, the men in the Lizard, the Jenett Purwyn, and the Elizabeth of Newcastle 'did as well as was possible' (p. 156).
[3] See a list of killed and wounded, p. 156.

Then the English consulted and returned to the great ships in the Trade, in confusion ('comme gens confus').[1]

Three captains, Cheyne, Cornwall, and Wallop, went on shore with 'a standard of peace,' and spoke to Prégent, who answered: 'Sirs, I assure you I have no English prisoners within my galley but one, and he is a mariner, but there was one that leaped out into my galley with a gilt target on his arm, the which I cast over with morrice pikes, and the mariner that I have prisoner told me that same man was your Admiral.'

Sir Edward Howard's body was found and brought to Prégent, at Conquet, on 28th April, about midday. The body was embalmed, and Prégent sent to the Princess Claude, Louis XII.'s daughter, Howard's armour ('dépouille'), and to Queen Anne the whistle 'of command' ('celuy de quoy il commandoit').

The scene of the battle was drawn and sent to Louis XII.

The English fleet returned to Plymouth on 30th April, and was badly received by the King, who sent to the captains a very sharp letter.[2] Thomas Howard, appointed admiral on 4th May, found 'the worst ordered army and farthest out of rule' that he ever saw. The day he came there, there were more than half the army on land, robbing and stealing and doing much hurt.[3] 'At my coming to Exeter I heard of their departing, and so have sent through all the country to bring them again.' He set up a

[1] Cf. Prégent's own narrative, pp. 136, 137.
[2] Doc. 78.   [3] P. 164.

pair of gallows at the waterside, where he thought he might have to hang a dozen knaves.¹ The mariners and masters were as 'troubled' and 'discouraged' as the soldiers. 'Never man saw men in greater fear than all the masters and mariners be of the galleys, insomuch that in a maner they had as lief go into Purgatory as into the Trade.' They agreed, 'with one whole voice and all in one tale,' that if the wind had blown at S.W., or W.S.W., or W. by S., the English fleet would have run into Crozon Bay, with a great chance of being destroyed by French guns.

But the strongest excuse they gave for their 'coming from the parts of Brittany without the King's commandment' was 'they had great default of victuals.' It is always the same complaint: in his very first letter, Lord Thomas Howard says that he cannot return to the Trade before three or four days, 'considering that your army would not have their victual in before that time.' Wolsey answered that it was impossible to revictual the fleet for 6 weeks or a month at least, before it left for Brest, if the casks were broken or burnt as they were by soldiers or mariners. Whereas some ships had received, at the beginning of March, 756 pipes, they had redelivered scantly 80 foists of them.²

During a whole month Lord Thomas Howard, Richard Fox, bishop of Winchester, appointed by the King, and John Dawtrey were busy with the victualling of the fleet.³

¹ P. 164. ² Doc. 82.
³ Brewer, Nos. 4056, 4073 to 4075, 4093 to 4095, 4099, 4103, 4104, 4171; p. 157. Warrant of Sir Thomas Howard, appointing

xlii   *INTRODUCTION*

Moreover, the Spaniards, on hearing of the truce of 1st April, wished to return to their own country,[1] and practically refused to remain in the King's pay: 'As for the Spaniards here, I assure you they would fain be at home, ever since they hear of the truce.'[2]

It was thus that Thomas Howard could not long cherish the hope of avenging his brother's death, and at last he was ordered 'not to enter the water of Brest till he knew further of the King's pleasure' (4 June).[3] Then he asked the King to discharge the hired ships, if the fleet could do no good service: it would only be useful if Scots and Danes joined the French, who would never fight by themselves.

Howard's views were quite right. The Normandy ships, after remaining a few days at Concarneau,[4] returned to Honfleur, where they unloaded their ordnance,[5] while Prégent's galleys were unable to do any service for many weeks, as a great number of rowers were sick or wounded and part of the

---

W. Symons to control the victualling of the fleet (*ibid.* 5754). 'Thomas Howard, lord admyrall of Ingland and of Ffraunce, Irland, Gascone, Geane and Normandie, etc., geve and graunte unto William Symons the rome of the clarke comptrollership of the riall arme for the oversyght and destrebutyng of our vetell from hensforthe. For the whiche rome I graunte the said William for his wages 18*d*. by the day to be payd by the hands of Sir Thomas Wyndame, tresorer of this sayd ryall armey. In wittnesse wherof I have synyd this warrant wit myn awne hand and sette my seale, the 9th daye of Mai the 5th yere of the reigne of our soverayn lord Kyng Henre the viiith.

'THOMAS HOWARD.'

[1] P. 164.   [2] P. 170.   [3] P. 169.
[4] P. 169, *note* 1.   [5] P. 175, *note* 2.

convicts had been released.¹ But Louis XII. pressed once more James IV. to send his fleet: William Bruce had left Dieppe, on 20 April 1513, in John Barton's ship;² Robert Barton left Honfleur a month later in his ship, the Lion (22 May),³ while a French ambassador, La Motte, went aboard the Petite Louise at Brest, in order to reach Scotland by the west coast. However James IV. did not seem ready to declare himself against Henry VIII.; he sent him on 24 May a copy of the truce made on 1 April between France and Spain, and urged him to explain his wish to be included in it. Surely, he added, Henry VIII.'s late Admiral, 'who died to his great honour,' was a greater loss than the winning of Prégent's galleys would have been an advantage.⁴

The naval war was at an end and all the interest was in the continental struggle. Henry VIII. landed at Calais at the end of June, and made a short and successful campaign at Thérouenne and Tournai⁵ (July—Sept. 1513).

During his absence, James IV. at last pulled off the mask; he sent a fleet to Louis XII. and invaded England, where he fell at Flodden. His fleet left Leith, on 25 July, under the command of the earl of Arran, and reached Brest about six weeks later, after plundering Carrickfergus.⁶

---

[1] Doc. 79. Holinshed asserts that Prégent landed in Sussex, and 'set fire on certain poor cottages'; but 'the gentlemen that dwelt near raised the country, and came to the coast, and drove Prior John to his galleys.' The tale is not confirmed by any document.
[2] P. 125, *note* 2.   [3] P. 169, *note* 1.
[4] Brewer, n° 4112. Cf. Ferdinand's opinion, Doc. 80.
[5] Brewer, preface, l–li.   [6] P. 176, *notes* 1 and 4.

Great naval preparations were made in France; Prégent's galleys were supplied with rowers and crossbowmen (July);[1] the ships of Brittany[2] and Normandy[3] were victualled for two months (August), under the control of Philippe de la Primaudaye.[4] Louis de Rouville was appointed admiral of the Franco-Scottish fleet (17 Sept);[5] a warrant was issued for the payment of victuals and wages to Breton and Scottish ships (23 Sept.), and 400 extra mariners were levied in Normandy.

The Franco-Scottish fleet was intended to prevent Henry VIII.'s returning from Picardy to England (Oct. 1513), but it was scattered by a storm and so failed of its purpose.[6] The three largest Scottish ships remained in Louis XII.'s pay, and the remainder returned to Edinburgh at the beginning of November.[7]

During the winter 1513-1514, the English fleet was not entirely discharged,[8] and the French ships were kept at St. Malo,[9] Honfleur, and Dieppe,[10] ready to sail on the first notice, while naval preparations were steadily going on in Normandy[11] and Picardy.[12]

French privateers scoured the Channel:[13] on 12th January, 1514, a bark of Boulogne captured a boat

---

[1] Doc. 85. Cf. p. 139, n. 1, p. 143, n. 2, p. 195, n. 1.
[2] Doc. 87.   [3] Doc. 88, 89, 91.   [4] Doc. 86.
[5] Doc. 92.   [6] Doc. 96.   [7] Doc. 95.
[8] P. 185, n. 1; p. 189, n. 1.   [9] Doc. 97.
[10] Doc. 101.   [11] Doc. 98, 102.
[12] Doc. 105, 106.
[13] Doc. 109; p. 197, n. 1. On French privateering in 1513, cf. Doc. 85, p. 174, n. 1.

of Dover, 'the which was sent over for the conveyance of the budget.'[1]

The 'plain saying' was that the French King would send 20,000 men into Scotland, with the Duke of Albany, and Henry VIII. was reported to be preparing for another landing in Picardy.

But France and England wished to come to friendly terms, and a truce was agreed on in March 1514. It did not prevent Prégent leaving Dieppe about the middle of April and threatening 'to come to Calais and burn our ships in the haven.'[2] 'With his galleys and foists, charged with great basilisks and other artillery, he came on the borders of Sussex in the night season, at a poor village there called Brighthelmstone, and burnt it, taking such goods as he found. But when the people began to gather, by firing the beacons, Prior John sounded his trumpet to call his men aboard, and by that time it was day. Then certain archers that kept the watch followed Prior John to the sea, and shot so fast that they beat the galley men from the shore, and wounded many in the foist to which Prior John was constrained to wade, and was shot in the face with an arrow, so that he lost one of his eyes, and was like to have died of the hurt. And therefore he offered his image of wax before Our Lady at Boulogne, with the English arrow in the face for a miracle.

'The lord Admiral, offended with this proud part of the Frenchmen in making such attempts[3] on

---

[1] Doc. 99.   [2] P. 199.
[3] 'For the revenging of the burning of Brightenstone' (p. 206).

the English coasts, sent Sir John Wallop[1] to the sea with divers ships, which sailing to the coasts of Normandy, landed there and burnt 21 villages and towns, with divers ships in the haven of Tréport, Etaples, and otherwhere. Men marvelled greatly at the manful doings of Sir John Wallop, considering he had not past 800 men, and took land there so often'[2] [27 May].

At the beginning of June 1514, Henry VIII. commanded all the captains to 'lie still' and to make 'no attempt nor excursion out of the pale' of Calais.[3] Prégent left, two months later, for the Mediterranean, to try to save the wreck of French dominion beyond the Alps.[4] A part of the French fleet had never left St. Malo,[5] and part of the victuals stored for the navy were sold at Honfleur.[6]

Thus ended this short naval war between France and England, without any general action: the endeavour, on both sides, was to be ready first and try to blockade and burn the enemy's fleet. As M. Oppenheim has so well remarked, a navy was as yet but an accessory, and 'the army was still considered the effective weapon of offence.'[7] But two noticeable facts can be deduced from these pages: on the French side, the superiority of ordnance; on the English side, the weak part of the naval organisation, viz. the bad victualling, which prevented the fleet doing any real service, however gallant and disciplined men and captains could be.

[1] Cf. Doc. 107, p. 204. [2] Holinshed.
[3] Doc. 108. [4] Doc. 110.
[5] Doc. 111. [6] Doc. 112. [7] *Op. cit.* p. 45.

We are indebted to our friend M. Gustave Dennery for the illustrations of this volume. The two small ships are taken from Roscoff church, in Brittany. The Louise, Admiral Graville's ship, 790 tons, is taken from a MS. belonging to the late Duc d'Aumale; it is interesting for naval archæology. The Burning of the Cordelière and Regent, from the MS. Fr. 1672, in the Bibliothèque Nationale, is thus described by Jal.[1] 'The Cordelière, in the foreground of the picture and to windward of the Regent, has one sloping and two vertical masts, with round tops, above which are topmasts carrying topsails. The sails are furled, but the mainsail and the foresail are loose and are beginning to burn. The sides of the castles are fitted with a pavesade of shields, some bearing the ermine of Brittany, some white with a black cross. The streamers flying from the masts are of the same colours. The rigging of the Cordelière is correctly shown: we see distinctly the shrouds, the lifts and the stays; the artist has not forgotten to haul the bowline of the mainsail; the upper part of the ports is round, and the tops are stored with quarrels. The Regent is almost entirely hidden by the Cordelière; however we can distinguish two of her three masts, the mainsail and the mizen; the foremast ought to be seen. Castles and tops are pavesaded with shields, white with a red cross, the streamers are similar. A few men are in the shrouds: the French mariners wear red jackets and blue or black breeches.'

The documents here printed are in the Biblio-

[1] *Marie-la-Cordelière*, pp. 19, 20.

thèque Nationale (Bibl. Nat.)[1] and the Archives Nationales (Arch. Nat.) in Paris; in the Record Office (R.O.) and the British Museum (Brit. Mus.) in London. Most of the English references are given to Brewer (Calendar of State Papers, Henry VIII.); but the text has been collated with the originals. Some are only reprints: Sanuto's Diarii (published at Venice); Lettres de Louis XII. (Brussels, 1709); Le Glay, Négociations diplomatiques entre la France et l'Autriche; Desjardins, Négociations diplomatiques entre la France et la Toscane; Ellis's Original Letters; Fiddes, Life of Wolsey, etc.

[1] MS. fr.=French MS.; MS. lat.=Latin MS.

LIST OF ILLUSTRATIONS

THE BURNING OF THE CORDELIÈRE AND REGENT   *Frontispiece*

EX VOTO, FROM ROSCOFF CHURCH . . . *To face p.* 46

LA GRANDE LOUISE . . . . . . ,, 88

EX VOTO, FROM ROSCOFF CHURCH . . ,, 197

LETTERS AND PAPERS

RELATING TO THE

WAR WITH FRANCE IN 1512-13.

I.

1. *Jean le Veau, Flemish ambassador in France,
to Marguerite of Savoy.*

(Blois: 10 Feb. 1512.)

[Henry VIII. has summoned the Parliament and resolved on war against France. 15,000 men will go to Guelders, 10,000 to Normandy. Louis XII. is much afraid.]

Le Roy est adverty que le roy d'Angleterre a tenu une journée à ceste Chandeleuse avec les princes et grans seigneurs d'Angleterre, et que à icelle journée avoit conclute l'entreprinse contre France, et que desjà ledit roy d'Angleterre avoit fait toutes ses préparacions de guerre et avoit assemblé bien 25,000 hommes prestz à monter en mer, et qu'il les vouloit faire descendre à Calais, où desjà estoit descendu ung certain nombre. Et desdits 25,000 hommes, doibvent aller les 15,000 contre messire Charles de Gueldres et les 10,000 en Normandie. L'on est demy désespéré de par deçà et en aussi grand crainte que jamais l'on fust, et est le Roy depuis ces nouvelles si plain de pensement et de grande fantaisie où il demeure continuellement, que cela fait descouraiger les François.

(*Lettres de Louis XII.*, iii. 149.)

2. *The same to the same.*
(Blois : 17 Feb.)
[Naval preparations in Normandy.]

Le Roy fait venir en Normandie toutes les grosses navires qui sont tant ès ports de Gascogne que de Bretaigne et les fait armer et fournir d'artillerie.[1]

(*Ibid.*, iii. 166.)

3. *The same to the same.*
(Blois : 5 March.)
[The English seem to slacken their warlike preparations and the Duc de Longueville leaves Normandy.]

M. de Longueville, ayant entendu que les Angloys aloient assez froidement en leur affaire, est retourné icy.

(Le Glay, *Négociations diplomatiques entre la France et l'Autriche*, i. 483.)

---

[1] René de Clermont, vice-admiral of France, was sent to Rouen, and Regnaut de Moussy, vice-admiral of Guyenne, to Rochelle and Bayonne, 'pour visiter tous les navires desdits pays et les ports, faire tenir prêts navires et gens de pied le long de la coste' (Blois, 22 February, 9 March, 1512). Clermont wrote twice to the town council of Harfleur (24 Feb., 21 March) for the mending of the pier ('la gectée du Chef de Caux'); he visited Lower Normandy with Louis le Brun, s^r de Sallenelles (later captain of the Louise), and received a present of five puncheons of wine at Honfleur (5 April).

4. *Andrea di Burgo to the same.*

(Blois : 22 March.)

[Henry VIII. seems determined to keep peace.]

Le Roy a eu nouvelles de son ambassadeur[1] qui est là après le roy d'Angleterre pour sçavoir qu'il est délibéré de faire, ou d'entretenir la confédération et amytié ou de faire la guerre, et m'ont dit qu'ilz ont bon espoir qu'il s'en gardera.

(*Lettres de Louis XII.*, iii. 205.)

5. *The same to the same.*

(Blois : 7 April.)

[No more talk of war in England.]

Ex Anglia nova habuit quod illi motus armorum sunt multum refrigerati, nec amplius fit sermo de bello.[2]

(Le Glay, i. 489.)

6. *Charges of the English navy before leaving London.*

(16 April : 1512.)

Conduyte money[3] for 2,205 men, by diverse distances : 338*l.* 6*s.* 5*d.* ob.

---

[1] Pierre-Louis de Valtan, bishop of Rieux.

[2] On the contrary Clermont sent a message to Louis XII. (Honfleur, 3 April), 'pour faire savoir audit seigneur des nouvelles de l'armée des Angloys dont est bruit qu'ilz s'efforcent descendre en ce pays de Normandie.'

[3] 'Conduyte money paied as well to diverse lords, knyghts, and gentylmen sendyng men towards the Kyng's warres as to dyverse captayns and other maistairs of shipps, to every man after the rate of 6*d.* a man for every 12 myle accordyng to the distaunce of thier commyng.' The soldiers of the Mary Rose were gathered at Norfolk (100 miles from London) and other places (140 miles) ; W. Forde, of Bristol, 'lodesman,' was busy 40 days, with Myles Smyth, 'for gaderyng togyder' 28 mariners ; Thomas Spert, master

Cootes and jakettes.—Cootes, at 4s. a pece, for 1,812 men : 362l. 8s.—Also sir John Cotton, 50, and M. Broughton, 66 : nil.—Jakettes,[1] at 20d. a pece, for 1,616 men : 134l. 13s. 4d.—Men : 3,494.—Money : 497l. 16s.

The daie's wages after the musters,[2] to every man 6d., viz. to 1,523 men : 38l. 18d.

7. *Charges of the English navy for the first three months.*

(17 April—8 July 1512.)

[Without the Regent.]

Charges of the armye and navie for the first 3 monethes, begynnyng on Saturday the 17 day of Apryle the 3de yere of our soveraigne lorde kyng Henry the viij[th] and ending the 8th day of Julie the 4th yere of his reigne, as in vitayle, wages, deddeshares and toundage, as well of these 17 shippes as other vitaylers crayers.

The Marie Roose.[3]

First to syr Edward Howard, knyght, chieff capteyn and admyrall of the flete, for his wages and vitayle, at 10s. a day : 42l.

of the Mary Rose, gathered others at distances between 130 and 150 miles, etc. (*R. O.*, *Chapter House Book* 2, pp. 13-29).

[1] Including the Regent, for 300 mariners (*Ibid.*, pp. 5-11).

[2] 'The oon daye's wages payid aftyr the musters taken at Blakeheth, that ys to sey for Friday's wages, the 16 day of Apryll the 3de yere' (*Ibid.*, p. 31).

[3] Warrant directed, 29 January, 1510, to John Dawtrey for the 'new making' of the Mary Rose and Peter Pomegranate : 1°. 700l. for 'tymber, ironwerk and werkmanship of twoo new shippes to be made for us, and the oon shipp to be of the burdeyn of 400 tonnes, and the other ship to be of the burdeyn of 300 tonnes.' 2°. 316l. 13s. 4d. 'for all maner of implements and necessaries to the same twoo shippes belonging, for sailes, twyne, merling, ropes, cables, cabletts, shrowds, hawsers, boye ropes, steys, shells,

Also to syr Thomas Wyndeham, knyght, for his vitayle and wages, at 18*d*. by the day : 6*l*. 6*s*.

Also for the wages and vitayle of 2 lodesmen alias pylotts, ych of thiem at 20*s*. a mounth : 6*l*.

Also for vitayle of 411 [men], souldiours 251, maryners 120, gonners 20, and servitours 20 in the same ship, every man at 5*s*. a mounth : 308*l*. 5*s*.

Also for wages of the same 411 persons, every man at 5*s*. a mounth : 308*l*. 5*s*.

Also for 34 deddeshares ½, at 5*s*. a share 25*l*. 17*s*. 6*d*.

Also for toundage, aftyr 3*d*. a ton a weke, 500 tons : nichil, quia navis regis.

Somme : 696*l*. 13*s*. 6*d*.

The Petyr Pomegarnade.

Also to syr Wystan Browne, capteyne, payed afore aftyr a spere owte of the Kyng's cofers, here : nichil.

Also for vitaylyng of 302 [men], souldiours 162, maryners 120, gonners 20 and servitours 20 : 226*l*. 10*s*.

Also for wages of the said 302 persons: 226*l*. 10*s*.

Also for 28 deddeshares : 21*l*.

Also for toundage of 400 tons: nichil, quia navis regis. Somme : 474*l*.

boye lynes, tacks, lists, toppe armers, stremers, standerd, compasses, ronnyng glasses, tankards, bolles, disshes, lanterns, shevers of bras and poleys, vitaills and wages of men for setting up theyr mastes, shrowds and all other taclyng ' (*R. O.*, *Warrants for issues*, 1 H. VIII., n° 121)—' Pro duabus navibus de novo factis, pro maeremio, opere ferri et le workmanshyp circa easdem naves appositum, unde una earumdem erit de pondere 400 doliorum et altera erit de pondere 300 dol.' (*Ibid.*, *Augment. Off. Book* 317, fol. 40–43).

The Marie John.[1]

Also to syr Gryffyth Denne,[2] capteyn, a spere: nichil.

Also for vitaylyng of 170 [men], souldiours 100, maryners 50, gonners 10 and servitours 10: 127*l*. 10*s*.

Also for the wages of the said 170 persons: 127*l*. 10*s*.

Also for 22 deddeshares ½ : 16*l*. 17*s*. 6*d*.

Also for toundage of 240 tons: nichil, quia navis regis.   Somme: 271*l*. 17*s*. 6*d*.

The Anne of Grenewyche.[3]

Also to Thomas Lucye, capteyn, for his vytayle and wages: 6*l*. 6*s*.

Also for vitaylyng of 160 [men], souldiours 100, maryners 40, gonners 10 and servitours 10: 120*l*.

Also for the wages of the said 160 persons: 120*l*.

Also for 22 deddeshares ½ : 16*l*. 17*s*. 6*d*.

Also for toundage of 160 tons: nichil, quia navis regis.   Somme: 263*l*. 3*s*. 6*d*.

The Marie George.[4]

Also to syr Robert Morton, capteyne, a spere: nichil.

---

[1] 'Our shippys called the Mary and John and the Anne of Foy in the moneth of Aprille [1511] sent estewarde' (Brewer, i. 5720).

[2] Called Griffendon (Brewer, i. 3427) by Marguerite of Savoy in a complaint for an act of piracy committed against Jacques Berenghier in Lent 1512 (Antwerp, 15 Sept. 1512).

[3] The Anne of Greenwich was also called the Anne of London, the Anne of Fowey or Foy (Brewer, i. 5720; *R. O., Chapter House Book* 215, p. 143).

[4] Built in 1510 (Ellis, 2nd Series, i. 218). The expenses for 'our shipp called the Mary George' begin on 14 Feb. 1512

IN 1512-13

Also for vitaylyng of 201 [men], souldiours 121, maryners 54, gonners 10 and servitours 6 : 150*l*. 15*s*.
Also for the wages of the said 201 persons : 150*l*. 15*s*.
Also for 22 deddeshares ½ : 16*l*. 17*s*. 6*d*.
Also for toundage of 300 tons : nichil, quia navis regis.   Somme : 318*l*. 7*s*. 6*d*.

The John Baptyst Hopton.[1]

Also to John Hopton, capteyn : 6*l*. 6*s*.
Also for lyke wages and vitayle of syr William Pyrton, whuch brought mylorde of Oxenford men : 6*l*. 6*s*.
Also for vitaylyng of 294 [men], souldiours 184, maryners 90, gonners 10 and servitours 10 : 220*l*. 10*s*.
Also for wages of the said 294 persons : 220*l*. 10*s*.
Also for 23 deddeshares ½ : 17*l*. 12*s*. 6*d*.
Also for toundage of 400 tons : 60*l*.
                Somme : 531*l*. 4*s*. 6*d*.

The Nicholas Reede.

Also to William Gonnson, capteyn : 6*l*. 6*s*.
Also for vitaylyng of 286 [men], souldiours 177, maryners 90, gonners 10 and servitours 10 : 215*l*. 5*s*.
Also for wages of the said 287 persons : 215*l*. 5*s*.
Also for 23 deddeshares ½ : 17*l*. 12*s*. 6*d*.
Also for toundage of 400 tons : 60*l*.
                Somme : 514*l*. 8*s*. 6*d*.

(Brewer, i. 5720); the Mary George was previously called the Mary Howard, and bought of admiral Howard (Oppenheim, *Administration of the Royal Navy*, p. 49). Yet we find a Mary Howard, 240 t., capt. W. Gonson, hired by the King in April 1514 (Brewer, i. 5112).

[1] Built in 1512 (Ellis, 2nd Series, i. 218).

The George of Falmouth.

Also to syr William Trevanyon, capteyn: 6*l.* 6*s.*
Also for vitaylyng of 144 [men], souldiours 84, maryners 50, gonners 5 and servitours 5 : 108*l.*
Also for wages of the said 144 persons : 108*l.*
Also for 22 deddeshares ½ : 16*l.* 17*s.* 6*d.*
Also for toundage of 140 tons : 21*l.*
Somme : 260*l.* 3*s.* 6*d.*

The Petre of Fowey.

Also to John Power, capteyn : 6*l.* 6*s.*
Also for vitaylyng of 120 [men], souldiours 70, maryners 40, gonners 5 and servitours 5 : 90*l.*
Also for wages of the said 120 persons : 90*l.*
Also for 22 deddeshares ½ : 16*l.* 17*s.* 6*d.*
Also for toundage of 120 tons : 18*l.*
Somme : 221*l.* 3*s.* 6*d.*

The Lyon of Grenewych.[1]

Also to syr John Burdett, capteyn, a spere : nichil.
Also for vitaylyng of 130 [men], souldiours 80, maryners 40, gonners 5 and servitours 5 : 97*l.* 10*s.*
Also for wages of the said 130 persons : 97*l.* 10*s.*
Also for 22 deddeshares ½ : 16*l.* 17*s.* 6*d.*
Also for toundage of 120 tons : nichil, quia navis regis.   Somme : 211*l.* 17*s.* 6*d.*

The Cristofer Davye.

Also to John Iseham, capteyn : 6*l.* 6*s.*
Also for vitaylyng of 130 [men], souldiours 59, maryners 61, gonners 5 and servitours 5 : 97*l.* 10*s.*

---

[1] Taken from Andrew Barton in 1511 ; the expenses for 'our shipp called the Lyon' begin on 9 Dec. 1511 (Brewer, i. 5720).

Also for wages of the said 130 persons : 97*l.* 10*s.*
Also for 22 deddeshares : 16*l.* 10*s.*
Also for toundage of 160 tons : 24*l.*
       Somme : 241*l.* 16*s.*

The Sabyen.

Also to William Sabyen, capteyn : 6*l.* 6*s.*
Also for vitaylyng of 100 [men], souldiours 60, maryners 34, gonners 4 and servitours 2 : 75*l.*
Also for wages of the said 100 persons : 75*l.*
Also for 22 deddeshares : 16*l.* 10*s.*
Also for toundage of 120 tons : 18*l.*
       Somme : 190*l.* 16*s.*

The Barbara of Grenewyche.[1]

Also to syr Edward Cobham, capteyn, spere : nichil.
Also for vitaylyng of 130 [men], souldiours 85, maryners 35, gonners 5 and servitours 5 : 97*l.* 10*s.*
Also for wages of the said 130 persons : 97*l.* 10*s.*
Also for 22 deddeshares ½ : 16*l.* 17*s.* 6*d.*
Also for toundage of 140 tons : nichil, quia navis regis.   Somme : 211*l.* 17*s.* 6*d.*

The Dragon of Grenewiche.[2]

Also to syr William Sydney, capteyn, spere : nichil.
Also for vitaylyng of 103 [men], souldiours 63, maryners 30, gonners 5 and servitours 5 : 77*l.* 5*s.*
Also for wages of the said 103 persons : 77*l.* 5*s.*
Also for 22 deddeshares ½ : 16*l.* 17*s.* 6*d.*

---

[1] The expenses for 'our shipp called the Barbara' begin on 23 Jan. 1512 (*ibid.*).
[2] The expenses for 'our shipp called the Dragon' begin on 22 Jan. 1512 (*ibid.*).

Also for toundage of 100 tons: nichil, quia navis regis.   Somme: 171*l.* 7*s.* 6*d.*

The Jenett of Pyrwyn.[1]

Also to Thomas Gurney, capteyn : 6*l.* 6*s.*
Also for vitaylyng of 65 [men], souldiours 20, maryners 40, gonners 3, and servitours 2 : 48*l.* 15*s.*
Also for wages of the said 65 persons : 48*l.* 15*s.*
Also for 22 deddeshares ½ : 16*l.* 17*s.* 6*d.*
Also for toundage of 70 tons: 10*l.* 10*s.*
     Somme : 131*l.* 3*s.* 6*d.*

The Martynet.

Also to syr Henry Sherbourne, capteyn, spere: nichil.
Also for vitaylyng of 126 [men], souldiours 73, maryners 40, gonners 10 and servitours 5 : 94*l.* 10*s.*
Also for wages of the said 126 persons : 94*l.* 10*s.*
Also for 22 deddeshares ½ : 16*l.* 17*s.* 6*d.*
Also for toundage of 180 tons: 27*l.*
     Somme : 232*l.* 17*s.* 6*d.*

The Nicholas of Hampton.

Also to John Flemyng, capteyn : 6*l.* 6*s.*
Also for vitaylyng of 163 [men], souldiours 90, maryners 60, gonners 10 and servitours 3 : 122*l.* 5*s.*
Also for wages of the said 163 persons : 122*l.* 5*s.*
Also for 22 deddeshares ½ : 16*l.* 17*s.* 6*d.*
Also for toundage of 200 tons : 30*l.*
     Somme : 297*l.* 13*s.* 6*d.*

The vitaylyng crayer called the John of Goston.

Also to John of Goston, maister, and to 12 maryners and 1 boy, every man takyng for his

---

[1] Taken from Andrew Barton (1511).

vitayle 5s. and the boy 5s. by the mounth: 10l. 10s.

Also for wages of the said maister and 12 maryners and the boy, every man takyng 5s. by the mounth and the boy 2s. 6d.: 10l. 2s. 6d.

Also for 3 deddeshares: 45s.

Also for toundage of 65 tons: 9l. 15s.

Somme: 32l. 12s. 6d.

The vitaylyng crayer called the Marie Alynson.

Also to William Alynson, maister, and to 10 maryners and 1 boy: 9l.

Also for the wages of the said maister, 10 maryners and the boy: 8l. 12s. 6d.

Also for 3 deddeshares: 45s.

Also for toundage of 55 tons: 8l. 5s.

Somme: 28l. 2s. 6d.

The roobarge called the Roose Henry.[1]

Also to Robert Yelverton, capteyn: 6l. 6s.

Also for vitayle for [ ] Goodard, maister, and 49 other persons: 37l. 10s.

Also for wages of the said 50 persons: 37l. 10s.

Also for 10 deddeshares: 7l. 10s.

Also for toundage of [ ] tons: nichil, quia navis regis.   Somme: 88l. 16s.

The roobarge called the Kateryn Pomegarnade.

Also to [ ] Cooke, capteyn: 6l. 6s.

Also for vitayle of 50 persons: 37l. 10s.

Also for wages of the said 50 persons: 37l. 10s.

Also for 10 deddeshares: 7l. 10s.

Also for toundage of [ ] tons: nichil, quia navis regis.   Somme: 88l. 16s.

---

[1] 300l. for the two 'newe rowe barges,' 1 May, 1512 (Brewer, i. 3422 (2)).

The Margret of Topsham.
(14 May—8 July.)

Also to James Knyvett, capteyn, by 2 the last mounthes, of the said 3 mounthes: 4*l*. 4*s*.

Also for vitaylyng of 100 souldiours, maryners, gonners and servitours: 50*l*.

Also for wages of the said 100 persons: 50*l*.

Also for 22 deddeshares: 11*l*.

Also for toundage of 140 tons: 14*l*.

Somme: 129*l*. 4*s*.

Somme totall of the charges of the 22 shippes aforesaid, as in vitayle, wages, deddeshares and toundage for the said first 3 mounthes: 5608*l*. 2*s*.[1]

Syr Edward Howard, the admyrall's, dyetts: 42*l*.

Capteyns, as speres, 7 men: nichil.

Vitayle and wages of 14 captens: 86*l*. 2*s*.

Vitayle and wages of 2 lodesmen: 6*l*.

Vitayle of 3,262 souldiours, maryners, gonners and servitours: 2,421*l*. 10*s*.

Wages of the same 3,262 persons (except 2 boyes): 2,420*l*. 15*s*.

Deddeshares, 449: 331*l*. 5*s*.

Toundage, after 3*d*. a ton a weke, of 12 shippes, for 2,050 tons: 300*l*. 10*s*.

---

[1] Extract of admiral Howard's brief account: 'The first 3 mounthes charges:—

Capteyns, as speres paied aforehande, 7 men: nichil	
Men besides: 3,279 men	
Deddeshares: 449 shares	5,608*l*. 2*s*.'
Toundage of hired shippes: 2,050 tons	
Toundage of the Kyng's shippes: nichil	

IN 1512–13

Toundage of the Kyng's 8 shippes, 1960 tons: nichil.

Also roobarges, 2 barges, cont. 100 tons: nichil.

(*R. O., Chapter House Book* 2, pp. 33–46.)

8. *The book of the victualling of the Regent.*[1]

(May–July, 1512.)

The first vitayling of the Kyng's riall shippe called the Regent, that is to saye from the 4 day of May unto the 14 day of May, for 300 maryners, for 10 dayes.

In biscute: 3,000 lb., price the 100, 3s. 4d. 100s.

Bere: 30 pipes, price the pipe with the foyste, 8s. 4d.: 12l. 10s.

Beffe: 4½ pipes, price the pipe, 51s.: 11l. 9s. 6d.

Fisshe: 200, after 106 to the 100, price the 100, 36s. 6d.: 73s.

The vitaylyng of the Regent foresaide from the 14 day of Maye unto the 9 day of July for 2 monythes for 700 men.

In biscute: 43,201 quarters, at 3s. 6d. the 100: 75l. 12s. 10d. ob.—For the freyght of 31,000 of the same from Hampton to Portismouthe: 20s.—In bere: 392 pipes, price the pipe, with the foyste, 8s. 4d.: 163l. 6s. 8d.—For the lyghterage of 33

[1] 'To Henry Haywarde, master of the Regiaunte, for his wages and for keping of the same shippe by the space of 32 moneths, at 13s. 3d. the monethe: 21l. 6s. 8d.' [18 April, 1512] (*R. O., Chapter House Book* 215, p. 178).

'To H. Tuthill, master of the John of London, for conveyaunce of certen ordenaunce from the Tower of London to Portsmouth to the Regient: 10l.' [9 May] (*ibid.*, p. 184).

tons, 3 hogsheds : 8s. 6d.—For freyght of 86 tons, 1 hh. from Hampton to Portismouthe, at 12d. per ton : 4l. 6s. 3d. And the rest by the Regent's boote and the Soveraigne's boote from Hampton and at Portismouthe, freyght : nichil.

In beffe : 56 pipes, price the pipe, 51s. : 162l. 16s.

In rewarde to the crane of Hampton for the cranage of the saide beffe and bere : 28s.

In western fisshe : 2,400, after 105 to the 100, price the 100, 41s. 8d. : 50l.

In drye fisshe : 100, price 60s., after 124 to the 100, 60s.

In stokefisshe : 1 quarter, the price : 6s. 8d.

In dryehake : 100, after 124 to the 100 : 17s. 6d.

To the Regent's vitayler, in fysshe, 1 burden : 8s. 4d.

In candell : 30 dozens, 6 lb. : 30s. 6d.

In wode : 6,700 : 44s. 8d.

In lanterns : 2 dozens, 1 great lantern : 17s. 4d.

In drynkyng boles and cups : 17 dozens, and 2 great boles : 9s. 4d.

In platers : 13 dozens : 14s. 6d.

Tancards : 9 of 4 galons, price 10s. 6d. ; 7 of 3 gal., price 5s. 10d. ; 5 of 2 gal., 3s. 4d. ; 9 of one galon, 4s. 6d. ; 6 of a potill, 2s. : 26s. 2d.

Bascatts : 2 doz. 3 peny basketts, 6s. 8d. ; 4 greate maundys, price 16d. : 8s.

Stepping fattys for the shippe : 2 greate fattys to water fisshe in : 2s. 8d.

Scoppys and shovillys for the shipp's store : scoppis 6, price 2s. ; 2 doz. shovillys, ½ shoyde, the rest unshoyde, price 6s. : 8s.

White salt : one bushel : 8d.

Greate salt : 3½ quarters : 14s.

Musterde sede : one pekke : 10d.

Delyverde aborde the Regent in the Downes by syr Stevyn Bull and Richard Phellipps, by the commaundement of syr Edward Howard, lord admyrall of Ynglonde.

In bredde : 90 doz., price 4*l*. 10*s*.
For the carkassys of 7 oxen, price the carkasse, 13*s*. 3*d*. : 4*l*. 14*s*. 4*d*.
For the carkassys of 4 oxyn, at 12*s*. the carkasse : 48*s*.
In bere : 4 bunys of dobill bere, price the pece, 3*s*. : 12*s*.
More in bere : 9 tons : 8*l*.

The revytaylyng of the Regent for 3 monythes begynnynge the 10th day of July for 700 men.

In biscute : 44,200 at 3*s*. 8*d*. le 100 : 81*l*. 8*d*.
In bere : 198 tons hh. : 169*l*. 9*d*.
In beffe : 70 pipes, 1 hh. : 174*l*. 10*s*. 6*d*.
In fisshe : 1,110 score, and 10 to the 100, price every 100, 77*s*. 8*d*. : 42*l*. 14*s*. 4*d*.
More in fysshe : 510 score, and 10 to the 100, price the 100, 4*l*. 2*s*. 2*d*. : 20*l*. 10*s*. 10*d*.
Item in dryelinges : 500 delyverd abord the Regent in the Downes by mylord Admyrall, for the whiche His Lordshippe reseyvide of me, Richard Palshid, for every 100 60*s*., summe : 15*l*. And more in coddes delyverd by His Lordshippe : 300½, price 55*s* : 20*l*. 5*s*.
More delyverd aborde the Regent in the Downes by Thomas Vaughan, of Dover : 1,000 of mudfysshe, price 11*l*., whiche mylorde admyrall sir Edward Howarde, then lord admyrall (whom God perdon !) commandid me to pay for it : 11*l*.
Item paide to the porters of Hampton in rewarde for carying of bere and fysshe : 15*s*.

Item alowide to the crane of Hampton for the strikynge of the seide bere, in rewarde : 40s.

Item paide for the freyght of the seid biscute, bere and fysshe from Hampton to Portismouthe and lyghterage : 9*l*. 9s. 3*d*.

Item in salt for the ship's store : 4 bushels : 2s.

In whit salt : 1 pekke : 3*d*.

In woode : 4,900, price the 1,000, 6s. 8*d*. : 32s. 8*d*.

In candels : 22 doz., 6 lb. in 2 barellys, price, with the barrellys : 23s. 8*d*.

In tancards greate and small : 2 doz. : 13s. 8*d*.

In lanterns : one doz. : 7s. 10*d*. ob.

In dishes to drinke in : 4 doz. : 4s.

In platers : 13 : 7*d*.

In baskettys : a doz. : 3s.

For 13 pipes of beffe with all maner charges, price every pipe 39s. 11*d*., whiche were not delyvered, but remayn : 25*l*. 17s. 10*d*.—Whiche 13 pipes of beffe was lost and cast away, by the Kyng's commaundement, by the oversyght and viewing of Elderton, among other vytaill remaining in Mr. Dawtrey's keeping.

Item paid to Thomas Meynerde for the rente of a slawterhouse and a powdering house by the space of half a yere : 20s.

Item to William Clarke for a selar and a biscute lofte to lay in the biscute, for the same space, and a selar for the fisshe : 20s.

(Brewer, i. 5747.)

9. *Lorenzo Pasqualigo, Venetian consul in London, to Aloixe and Francesco, his brothers.*

(London : 6 May, 1512.)

[Florentine and Genoese traders seized as allied to France and enemies of the Holy See.]

Laqual armada e nave del Re par habi prexo 10 barche Bretone e 4 Spagnole su le qual erano robe di merchadanti Fiorentini e Zenoesi e hanno fato bon butino, et dicti merchadanti è venuti a doler si dil Re. Soa Maestà à terminato siano ben tolti, perchè li ditti, tenendo con Franza, sono excomunichati et maledeti per esser contra la Chiexia.

(Sanuto, *Diarii*, xiv. 249.)

10. *Alain de Chantrezac, lieutenant of the Duc de la Trémoille, to M. d'Aumont.*[1]

(Caen : 20 May [1512].)

[King Henry VIII. is preparing to invade Picardy (Calais), Normandy, and Guyenne (Fontarabia). He knows of the victory of Louis XII. in Italy, and fears a breach with Scotland ; his Council is divided about the advisability of war. However, the English Admiral chases the fishing boats ; he has captured a bark of Dieppe.]

Despuis que sommes en ce pays, a esté tousjours gros bruyt de la descente des Angloys. Monsieur[2] a parlé à ung homme qui est venu d'Angleterre puis dix jours, qui dit que leur armée est toute preste, mès que leurs navires ne le peuvent estre que vers la fin de ce moys, et que si tost que le seront, ilz s'embarqueront pour aller faire leur descente, le Roy à Calays, partie de son armée en ce pays et l'autre partie à Fontarabie, et dit que n'oseroient faillir de descendre, pour la despence qu'ilz ont faicte, et de peur que ceulx du pays luy courussent sus. Ilz n'ont encores que de 120 à 140 navires, qu'on dit estre peu pour mener une si grosse armée.

[1] Lieutenant of La Trémoille in Burgundy.
[2] La Trémoille, Lieutenant-General of Normandy by letters patent (Blois, 12 April), reached Rouen on the 18th at 2 P.M., and visited Dieppe, Harfleur, Honfleur, Pont-Audemer, accompanied by René de Clermont. He appointed (28 April) Jehannequin de

Et dit qu'ilz se sont ung peu refroidys,[1] quant ilz ont sceu la victoire que le Roy a eu delà les Monts [2] et aussi qui doubte que le roy d'Escosse [3] leur fasse la guerre. Les vieux serviteurs du feu roy Henry, roy d'Engleterre, ne luy conseillent pas la descente, mais les jeunes qui gouvernent leur Roy la conseillent.

Il y a 15 ou 16 navires angloys qui se sont monstrez et ont prins une barque de Dieppe et quelques pescheurs de maquereauls et des poissonniers, et a baillé l'amyral d'Engleterre sauf conduyt ausdiz poissonniers de aller quérir leur renson : qui est signe de guerre.[4]

(Bib. Nat., MSS. fr. 3925, fol. 113.)

11. *Lorenzo Pasqualigo to his brothers.*

(London : 27 May, 1512.)

[30 English men-of-war are chasing the French fishing-boats. The French men-of-war do not dare to leave the coast. Genoese and Florentine goods expected to be plundered by Englishmen.]

. . . Ne li Canali se atrova 30 nave grosse armade de Englexi, le qual non lasa ussir una

---

Thieuville, s' de la Houssaye, to inquire into the disposable victualling in the 'pays d'Auge' ('sildres, chairs, grains et autres victuailles').

[1] M. de Montmorency wrote, from Blois, to M. d'Aumont (23 May) : 'L'on vous a fait savoir les nouvelles . . . touchant les Angloys, lesquelz ne bougent encores' (Bib. Nat., MSS. fr. 3925, fol. 68).

[2] Battle of Ravenna, 12 April.

[3] Peter Martyr mentions (Burgos, 20 May) that Louis XII. sent to James IV. five ships, and that they were destroyed or captured by the English : 'Quinque navium classiculam in Caledoniam, dico Scotiam, rex Gallus cum pecuniis ad stipendia Scotis praebenda mittebat. Classiculam adorti Britanni partim tormentorum vi submerserunt, partim ceperunt. Evasisse nullam dicitur' (Ep. n° 486).

[4] Guns were sent from Harfleur to the Chef de Caux to

barcha de peschadori de' Franzesi che non la prendino.

Se dice che n' è armate alcune franzese, ma che non osano ussir fora.

Se aspeta alcune nave de Syo e Candia con robe de Zenoesi e de Fiorentini : che se le troverano, le meterano a sacho. . . .   (Sanuto, xiv. 388.)

12. *Letters of marque and reprisal against the English delivered by the French Privy Council to some merchants of Rouen.*

(Blois : 8 June, 1512.)

Sur la requeste présentée au Conseil par Nicolas de la Chesnaye[1] et ses consors, marchans demourans en la ville de Rouen, demandans et requérans l'entérinement de ladite requeste, et en ce faisant que les patentes leur soient octroyées par lesquelles ilz puissent user de marque et représailles sur les marchans, biens et marchandises des subgectz du roy d'Angleterre, soit par mer, terre, eaue doulce, et quelque part qu'ilz pourront, recouvrer des subgectz dudit roy d'Angleterre les biens et marchandises qui leur ont, jusques à la valeur et estimation de 22000 livres tournois,[2] esté raviz et déprédez par Mathiew Cradot[3] et ses complices, marchans angloys et subgectz du roy d'Angleterre.

Veue par le Conseil ladite requeste, lettres de charte partie datées du 10ᵉ jour de décembre 1511, une sentence donnée en Angleterre le 3ᵉ jour de mars le 3ᵉ an du regne de Henry, 8ᵉ de ce nom,

prevent the landing of the English (Bib. Nat., MSS. fr. 26,112, n° 1155).

[1] Previous to the issuing of those official letters, two English trading ships had been arrested at Bordeaux, at La Chesnaye's request, and the Duc de Longueville had delivered a safe-conduct to the crew, Bayonne, 6 June, 1512 (*Arch. Poitiers*).

[2] In French papers *livre tournois*, or *l. t.*,=franc.

[3] Matthew Cradock : cf. p. 78, note 9.

roy d'Angleterre, informacions et tout ce que par ledit de la Chesnaye et ses consors a esté mis et produit par devers ledit Conseil, et tout considéré,

Dit a esté que, pour certaines bonnes et grandes causes et raisons à ce mouvans ledit Conseil, que ledit Nicolas de la Chesnaye et sesdits consors pourront, à leur requeste et pour la seureté de leur deu, faire arrester jusques à la valeur et estimation de 20000 l.t. des biens qu'ilz trouveront appartenans aux subgectz du roy d'Angleterre et iceulx biens ainsi arrestez faire inventorier et mectre en seure garde jusques à ce que par ledit Conseil autrement en soit ordonné. Et pour ce faire a ledit Conseil octroyé et octroye audit de la Chesnaye et à sesdits consors commission adressans aux baillyz et séneschaulx de Rouen, Boulongne, Montreuil sur la mer, Honnefleur, Bourdeaulx, et à tous autres justiciers et officiers et à chacun d'eulx sur ce premier requis.

(Arch. Nat., V^s 1044.)

13. *Alain de Chantrezac to M. d'Aumont.*

(Rouen : 10 June [1512].)

[20 English men-of-war seen before Fécamp are said to be bound to Fontarabia. Henry VIII. is preparing to land at Calais with 20,000 men; he has lent 60,000 crowns to Maximilian and will meet him at St. Omer.]

Il s'est monstré devant Fescamp 20 navires, et dit l'on qu'ilz s'en vont à Fontarabie pour se joindre au roy d'Espaigne. Le roy d'Angleterre s'en va à Calais avec 20000 hommes, et a presté 60000 angelos au roy des Romains. Ledit roy des Romains s'en vient à Saint Omer, et se doibvent voir le roy d'Angleterre et luy là, et c'est pour nous faire le pis qu'ilz pourront.

(Bib. Nat., MSS. fr. 3925, fol. 111.

14. *La Trémoille*[1] *to M. d'Aumont.*

(Rouen : 10 June [1512].)

[It is reported that the English will land in force at Fontarabia, Calais, and Rouen ; they must wait for the harvest so that they may get provisions. Louis XII. is advised to prepare a powerful fleet ; if he does, he will be master of the sea.]

Les Angloys font tousjours grosse assemblée, et dict on qu'ilz veullent faire trois descentes, assavoir Fontarabye, Callaix et yci, et croy que de leurs gros navires ne sont encores prestz, et aussi actendent que les fruictz et blés soient venuz, car ilz ne trouveroient à vivre comme ilz feront.

Je suys encores yci, et croys que je n'y demoureré plus guières, si le Roy ne faict quelque armée sur mer, où je me suys offert aller, comme l'un de ses Admiraulx. Et si la faict telle que on luy a devisée, elle luy fera ung merveilleux proffit, et si donnera à penser au roy d'Angleterre, et sans point de doubte, si veult il sera maistre de la mer.[2]

(Bib. Nat., MSS. fr. 3925, fol. 56.)

15. *Philippe de Montauban, Chancellor of Brittany, to the local officers at Guingamp.*

(Dinan : 10 June [1512].)

[Establishment of a post between Dinan and Brest for the news of enemies' landing.]

Messieurs, pour ce qu'il est requis mettre et asseoir postes en lieux propres et nécessaires de 7 en

---

[1] The Duc de la Trémoille preserves in his archives the original account of a ship built by Louis II. de la Trémoille in 1509–1510, in the river Charente, at a cost of 18,000 francs.

[2] Mathurin du Pont, paymaster of the troops in garrison in

7 lieues sur le chemin de cette ville de Dinan, tirant à Brest, pour savoir et apprendre les choses que les Anglois et ennemis de ce pays veulent et entendent faire, affin qu'il y soit pourveu plus promptement, à ceste cause vous prie et commande faire dilligence, chacun en droit soy, sur peine d'estre punis comme rebelles et désobéissans au Roy, de mettre et asseoir poste au lieu qui vous sera envoyé par brevet ci dedans enclos, en contraignant les receveurs de vostre juridiction de bailler et payer auxdites postes le prix qu'aurez appointé avec lesdites postes pour leur salaire. Et gardez qu'il n'y ait faulte.

De Dinan, ce 10ᵉ jour de juin.
Le bien vostre
PHILIPPE DE MONTAUBAN.
(Dom Morice, *Mém. de Bretagne*, iii. 903.)

16. *W. Knight to Wolsey.*

(La Renteria : 14 June, 1512.)

[Sir Edward Howard in Brittany.]

Aftyr oure departing from the ile of Wighte, which was the 3ᵈ of June, we enterid the seas, folowing syr Edward Howard, which guydyd us tyll we cam against the coasts of the Trade,[1] and ther he departid, full mynded, as yt was aftyr spokyn, to espie in what place of that countrie he mighte damage the Frenshemen.

(Brewer, i. 3243.)

Normandy, says (Rouen, 19 April) that the Frenchmen are decided to shake the English well, if they come ('bien secouer les Angloiz, se viengnent').

[1] About that geographical term, cf. *State Papers relating to the defeat of the Spanish Armada, anno* 1588 (N.R.S., 2 vol.) i. 196, 215, 246, 324 ; ii. 348.

17. *Letters patent of Louis XII. ordering warlike preparations.*

(Blois: 15 June, 1512.)

[The enemies of France have decided on invading and destroying the kingdom. Henry VIII. has sent an army towards Guyenne and is preparing to land at Calais. In order, with God's help, to resist this, Louis XII. will raise a numerous army and equip a powerful fleet.]

Loys, par la grace de Dieu, roy de France . . . Comme chacun puisse clèrement congnoistre et entendre la grant desloyaulté dont usent envers nous aucuns princes, noz confédérez et alliez, lesquelz, sans aucune cause, querelle, raison ou occasion, et en contrevenant à leur foy et promesse, et aux amitiez, confédéracions et alliances estans entre nous et eulx, et noz royaumes, pays, seigneuries et subjectz, solempnellement par eulx jurées et promises, se sont joincts avec noz ennemys et fait une ligue et conspiracion ensemble, délibérez de nous courir sus et faire la guerre par tous endroiz et principallement en nostre royaume qu'ilz entendent ruyner, destruire, butiner et despartir entre eulx. Et qu'il soit vray le roy d'Angleterre, ancien ennemy de nostredict royaume, a jà fait descente en icelluy nostre royaume par deux endroiz et s'efforce entrer en nostre pais de Guienne, et prépare encores une autre descente du costé de Picardie.[1]

Ausquelles machinacions, conspiracions et dampnées entreprinses, à l'aide de Dieu, nostre Créateur, qui congnoist nostre bon droit et le grant tort que lesdicts princes ont de ainsi contrevenir à leur foy

---

[1] 'Il est bruyt que les Angloys sont enbarquez, et veullent aller une partie en Espaigne et l'autre partie à Calles' (Blois, 7 June, Bib. Nat., MSS. fr. 3925, folio 131).

et promesse, et aussi par le moyen de noz bons et loyaulx subjectz, espérons résister.

Et pour ce faire avons mis de nouveau 1,200 lances d'ordonnance,[1] grant nombre de gens de pié, tant de nostre royaume que estrangiers,[2] artillerie[3] et autres choses nécessaires, et davantaige fait dresser une grosse et puissante armée de mer.

Donné à Bloys, le 15ᵉ jour de juing l'an de grace 1512, et de nostre règne le 15ᵉ.

Par le Roy, en son Conseil : auquel Messeigneurs les ducz de Valoys et de Bourbon,[4] les contes de Vendosme et de Guyse, l'évesque de Paris, les seigneurs du Bouchaige et de Bucy, les trésoriers de France et généraulx des finances, et autres estoient.

GEDOYN.[5]

(Bib. Nat., MSS. fr. 25,719, n° 172.)

18. *Letters patent of Louis XII. appointing Pierre Gautier to control the victualling of the French fleet in Normandy.*[6]

(Blois : 20 June, 1512.)

Loys, par la grace de Dieu, roy de France . . . Comme nous ayons présentement ordonné mectre

[1] Each 'lance d'ordonnance' included six horsemen, one man-at-arms, two bowmen and three valets.

[2] 24,000 French and 12 or 16,000 lansquenets ('landsknechte') recruited principally in Guelders.

[3] Charles de la Chastre, sʳ de Parey, 'commissaire ordinaire de l'artillerie,' is occupied six months in the year 1512, supplying with guns and powder men-of-war and towns in Normandy : 'pour donner ordre aux affaires deppendans du fait de nostre artillerie, tant pour l'armement des navires, barques et autres vaisseaulx que y avons fait équipper . . que pour faire munyr et garnir de nostre artillerie, boullets, pouldres et aultres municions de guerre noz villes, places fortes et chasteaulx estans assis le long de la coste de la mer' (Bib. Nat., MSS. fr. 25,719, n° 216).

[4] According to Lasagni, Genoese agent, the Duc de Bourbon was sent into Brittany with 300 horsemen (Blois, 13 June).

[5] Secretary of State for Finance.

[6] Cf. Doc. 35 and 85 for the wages of the controller.

sus et équipper certain nombre de navires pour faire dresser une bonne et puissante armée sur mer du costé de noz pays et duché de Normandie pour résister aux entreprinses et invasions que les Anglois, anciens ennemys de France, se sont puis naguères efforcez et pourroient encores efforcer faire et entreprendre : lesquelz navires et armée il est très nécessaire advitailler et fournir de toutes choses qui y seront requises et nécessaires. Pour quoy faire et aussi pour contreroller lesdicts advitaillemens et fournitures, ensemble les payemens qu'il en conviendra faire, soit besoing y commectre et ordonner de par nous quelque bon et féal personnaige à ce bien entendu et expérimenté et en qui ayons toute fiance. Savoir faisons que, pour la bonne, grande et entière confiance que nous avons de la personne de nostre cher et bien amé Pierre Gautier, receveur de noz tailles[1] en la viconté[2] d'Argentan, et de ses sens, souffisance, loyauté, expérience et bonne dilligence, icelluy pour ces causes et autres à ce nous mouvans avons commis et ordonné, commectons et ordonnons par ces présentes à soy prendre garde, contreroller et avoir l'ueil à tous et chacuns les paiemens des fraiz, mises et despences qu'on fera et conviendra faire pour l'advitaillement et fourniture de nostredicte armée de mer et de bailler et passer toutes et chacunes les quictances et acquitz nécessaires et ainsi qu'il appartiendra . . .

Donné à Bloys, le 20e jour de juing l'an de grace 1512, et de nostre règne le 15e.

Par le Roy
GEDOYN.

[Endorsed.] Commission du Roy pour le fait de l'advitaillement des navires.

(Bib. Nat., MSS. fr. 25,719, n° 173.)

[1] Land-tax.
[2] The financial districts were called 'vicomtés' (Normandy),

19. [*Wolsey ?*] to [*Cardinal Bainbridge*].

(London : 1 July, 1512.)

[Admiral Howard lately landed in Brittany, where he remained four days, burning towns and boroughs over a space of thirty miles. With his 5,000 men he offered battle to 15,000 French and Bretons, who refused it, declaring they did not fight of their own free will against the Pope. Admiral Howard has since returned to Southampton, where he had an interview with the King. He has captured many ships sent by Louis XII. to Guelders. The English ambassadors, who have returned from Scotland, say that James IV. wishes to keep the peace, but that the people are against it. A French envoy is at Edinburgh.]

Classis regia, cujus generalis præfectus est dominus Hovarde, strenuissime his diebus se gessit et multa præclara facinora edidit, nam et multas hostium naves cœpit et illorum terras invasit. Quatuor continue diebus, invitis hostibus, in Britannia permansit, et in pluribus commissis prœliis victoriam reportavit ; magnus numerus hostium occisus est ; multi capti domini equites aurati et alii nobiles viri ; 30 milliariorum spatio oppida et pagos combussit. Dominus Hovarde cum parvo suo exercitu 5,000 hominum provocavit ad pugnam 15 milia Gallorum et Britannorum. Illi recusarunt, dicentes se non sua sponte, licet coactos, defendere Gallorum regem contra Sanctissimum Dominum Nostrum,[1] ita ut nostri illinc victores recesserunt.

Ab illo tempore, dominus Hovarde fuit cum Maiestate Regia apud Hamptonam, ubi dicitur

'élections' (Picardy, Vermandois, Ile-de-France, Champagne, Poitou, etc.), or 'diocèses' (Brittany, Languedoc).

[1] The Pope Julius II.

moratus in colloquio. Retinuit classem et multas naves cœpit [cum] vario genere divitiarum et tormentis bellicis missis a rege Gallorum ad ducem Gueldriæ ut invadat Flandriam.

Oratores regii ex Scotia redierunt et nuntiant Regem ipsum pacem velle, sed populum contra tendere. Est illic orator Gallus, qui tanquam Terentianus Dacos intertenebat.[1]

(Sanuto, xv. 95.)

20. *Letters patent of Louis XII. appointing René de Clermont, vice-admiral of France, chief captain of the French fleet in Normandy, Brittany and Guyenne.*

(Blois: 2 July, 1512.)

[A powerful fleet is fitted out in Normandy, Brittany, and Guyenne; René de Clermont is appointed admiral, with power:

(1) to harass and assail the enemies of the Crown;

[1] After a preliminary draft (6 March 1512), a treaty of close friendship had been signed between France and Scotland (Blois, 22 May), and notified to James IV. by Charles de Tocques, s^r de la Mothe (20 June). A week later, James Ogilvy brought a letter of Louis XII. dated Blois, 7 June (Exchequer Rolls of Scotland, xiii. p. lxviii.; Bib. Nat., MSS. fr. 2930, fol. 36, 39, 41) and James IV. sent a message to Henry VIII., Edinburgh, 26 July (Brewer, i. 3339, 3346, 3347, 3372). War was practically declared between English and Scots. La Mothe and Ogilvy left Edinburgh on 11 July, and were attacked by the English: 'le s^r de la Mothe et nostre familier clerk et serviteur James Ogilvuy, eulx retournans par devers nous avecques toutes les charges que leur avions baillies, ont esté par un coup de canonne sur le bord de la navire contraintz lascher jusques en Dannemarck' (James IV. to Louis XII., Edinburgh, 17 Aug. 1512). The two ambassadors were in company of Robert Brownhill, Robert Barton and David Faulconer; the latter was slain, and Henry VIII. gave a reward of 100*l*. 'to the company of the navy beyng northward at the takyng of David Faulconer' (*R. O., Chapter House Book* 215, p. 198). That company was under the conduct of Sir Edward Echyngham, John Lewes, John Loveday and others (Holinshed).

(2) to buy victuals and necessary ammunition in any harbour;
(3) to lay siege and give battle;
(4) to muster soldiers and mariners;
(5) to order small payments;
(6) to keep good order;
(7) to summon the captains for council;
(8) to land in any island belonging to the enemies;
(9) to send cruisers against enemies;
(10) to forbid any cruise against friends;
(11) to receive oaths of captains, owners and masters of ships;
(12) to require help from friends;
(13) to deliver safe-conducts and receive pledges;
(14) to grant the King's protection to any one claiming it;
(15) to take measures for victualling of the fleet.]

Loys, par la grace de Dieu, roy de France . . .

Comme pour résister aux mauvaises et dampnables vollentez, entreprinses, descent[es et invasions] que les Anglois, anciens ennemys de la couronne de France, et autres leurs adhérans se parforcent de faire à grant force et puissance de gens de guerre qu'ilz ont mis et mectent sus et font préparer, tant par mer que par terre, pour nous [cuider] invahir, destruyre, faire tout effort de ruiner, s'ilz peuvent, noz royaume, païz, terres, seigneuries et subgectz, nous ayons, oultre noz armées que avons par terre, fait et faisons dresser, armer, avitailler et équipper une grosse et puissante armée par mer, où il y a et aura grant nombre de naux, barches et autres vaisseaulx, tant de noz païs et duchié de Normandie, Bretaigne, Guyenne que autres, et sur iceux bonne multitude de gens de guerre et grosse bande d'artillerie, et autres municions et provisions requises au fait de ladite armée. Pour la conduicte, gouvernement et exploitacion de laquelle soit besoing commectre et depputer personnaige notable, vertueux, prudent et expérimenté en telle charge, duquel nous ayons toute seurté et confidence.

Savoir faisons que nous, ce consideré, et la bonne, grande, parfaicte et entière fidélité que par vraye et longue expérience nous avons de la personne de nostre amé et féal conseiller et visadmiral de France, le sire de Clermont, chevalier, et de ses sens, prudence, loyauté, vaillance et delligence, icelluy, par ces causes et autres ad ce nous mouvans, avons fait, constitué, ordonné et establi, faisons, constituons, ordonnons et établissons par ces présentes nostre lieutenant général, chef et conducteur de nostre armée de mer que, comme dit est, avons fait, faisons et pourrons encores faire dresser et mectre sus en nosdits pays de Normandie, Guyenne et Bretaigne, pour le bien, seurté, tuicion et deffence de nosdicts royaume, pays, seigneuries, et luy avons donné et donnons plain pouvoir et auctorité :

(1°) De icelle armée et armées de mer mener, conduyre, exploicter et faire mener, conduyre et exploicter par gens congnoissans en fait de guerre maritime, et icelle exploicter à l'encontre de nosdicts ennemys et adversaires par tous les bons et meilleurs moyens et expédiens, lieux, passaiges et endroictz que besoing sera, et comme il verra et congnoistra bon estre, et par la force, puissance et vertu d'icelle leur courir sus, grever, fouller et endommager, obvier et resister en leur descentes, courses, invasions et surprinses qu'ilz s'efforcent de faire sur nosdicts royaume, pays, seigneuries et subgectz, villes, portz et havres d'iceux ;

(2°) De aller asseoir, appleiger, séjourner et

reposer nostredite armée en telz lieux, portz et havres qu'il verra estre à faire, et les rafreschir et pourvoir de vivres et autres municions nécessaires, en les faisant payer raisonnablement à ceux de nosdits subgectz desquelz ilz les prendront ;

(3°) De mectre, asseoir, apposer sièges, livrer batailles et assaulx, et faire tous autres actes de guerre pour grever et endommaiger nosdicts ennemys le plus que faire se pourra ;

(4°) De faire et faire faire les monstres et reveues de tous les mariniers, et gens de guerre de ladicte armée de mer, leur faire bailler leurs paiemens aux feurs et prix que leur ont esté ou seront ordonnez ;

(5°) De ordonner des menus fretz nécessaires en ladicte armée et les faire payer par celuy ou ceulx qui ad ce seront par nous commis et ordonnez ;

(6°) De faire vivre en bonne ordre et pollice tous ceux de ladicte armée, faire faire justice, pugnicion et correction de tous cas et crimes commis et perpétrez en ladicte armée par quelques personnes que ce soient, ou les remectre, quicter et pardonner, s'il voyt que faire se doye ;

(7°) De mander et faire venir devers luy tous les cappitaines, patrons, et autres chefs et conducteurs particulliers desdits navires, carracques, barches, gallères, gallions et brigandins, toutes et quantes foys que bon luy semblera, pour tenir conseil, et avoir leurs advis, oppinions du fait, conduicte et exploitacion de ladite armée, et des moyens par lesquelz on pourra mieux grever nosdits ennemys, ou pour à iceulx cappitaines, patrons et gens de guerre et autres, et à chacun d'eux commander, enjoindre et donner loy et statut des choses qu'ilz auront à faire et comme ilz auront à eux conduyre et gouverner, ainsi qu'il trouvera par conseil et qu'il congnoistra estre nécessaire, soit de combatre, aborder et investir l'armée ou les armées de nosdits ennemys, s'ilz les peuvent trouver et rencontrer en mer et en lieu opportun, ou deffendre à le faire, s'il voit et trouve que faire ne se doye par l'indisposicion du temps, lieu et heure ;

(8°) De faire toutes et telles descentes ès isles et terres de nosdits ennemys et en icelles faire courses, prinses et autres exploictz de guerre au dommaige de nosdicts ennemys ;

(9°) D'envoyer en cours sur nosdicts ennemys et leurs alliez et partisans déclarez, noz adversaires deument congneuz, et non sur aultres, telles desdictes naux, carraques, barches et autres vaisseaux de ladite armée qu'il advisera et verra bon pour les grever et endommaiger par tous les moyens que possible sera ;

(10°) De garder et deffendre que aucuns de ladite armée ne courent sus à aucuns qui soient noz amys, confédérez, alliez, ou soubz nostre protection, seureté, et sauvegarde, et s'ilz faisoient le contraire, le faire réparer, et au surplus faire pugnicion des malfaicteurs et délinquans telle que ce soit exemple à tous autres ;

(11°) De prendre et recevoir de tous les cappitaines, patrons et maistres des navires, les sermens de bien et loyaument nous servir durant qu'ilz seront en nostredit service en ce présent affaire et de luy estre, comme à nostre lieutenant général, bons et obéyssans, comme il appartient et faire se doibt ;

(12°) De demander, en cedit affaire, l'aide, secours, renffort et assistance de tous princes et autres noz amys, allyez et bienveillans, et en telle manière que besoing sera, envoyer et délléguer ambassades et autres messagiers pour lesdicts affaires ;

(13°) De bailler et octroyer seuretez, saufz conduicts à toux ceulx qu'il verra estre affaire, recevoir toutes manières d'ostaiges ;

(14°) De prendre et recevoir en nostre grace et

mercy, party et obayssance tous ceulx que libérallement se y vouldroient rendre cappables d'en estre ;

(15°) De commectre et depputer gens à tous les actes nécessaires à la provision des vivres de ladite armée.

Et sur toutes et chacunes les choses dessusdites bailler et décerner ses lettres patentes, mandemens, commissions et autres choses nécessaires, et telles que besoing sera. Lesquelles nous voullons et auctorizons valloir par ces présentes et estre d'un tel effect, vertu et valleur comme s'ilz estoient faiz par noz lettres.

Et générallement de faire exploicter, poursuyr et besongner touchant ledit fait et conduicte de nostredite armée tout ce qu'il verra et congnoistra estre au bien, profficit et honneur de nous et de nostredit royaume, pays, seigneuries et subgectz, et à la plus grant foulle, perte, honte, confusion et dommaige de nosdits ennemys et adversaires que faire ce pourra, et tout autant que nous mesmes ferions, si nous y estions en personne, et comme à lieutenant général et chef d'armée appartient, jaçoit ce que par aventure il y eust chose qui requist mandement plus espécial.

Si donnons en mandement par ces mesmes présentes à tous noz cappitaines, chefz et conducteurs particulliers desdites navires, carraques, barques, gallères et autres vaisseaulx, et aussi aux cappitaines desdits gens de guerre, et à tous noz autres gens, justiciers et officiers, que à nostredit lieutenant général, le sire de Clermont, ès choses dessusdites et chacune d'icelles en leurs deppendences, ilz obayssent et facent obayr dilligement.

Prions et requérons à tous nosdicts autres amys et alliez que à luy et ses commis et depputez, et à toute nostredite armée et suppostz d'icelle, ilz donnent passaige, assistance, faveur et ayde, tant de victuailles que autres choses nécessaires, y faisans pour nous ainsi qu'ilz vouldroient que fissions pour eulx et les leurs en cas semblables. Et d'abondant voullons que le vidimus de ces présentes fait soubz scel royal ou auctentique et les ordonnances et acquict de nostredit lieutenant général touchant lesditz menuz fraiz par vertu de ce servent à l'acquict de celuy ou ceux que avons commis ou commectons à faire les payemens d'iceulx menuz fraiz. Car tel est nostre plaisir.

En tesmoing de ce, nous avons signé cesdites présentes de nostre main et à icelles faict mectre nostre scel.

Donné à Bloys, le 2e jour de juillet, l'an de grace 1512, et de nostre règne le 15e.

     Loys. Par le Roy,
              Robertet.

[Endorsed.] Povoir de lieutenant général par la mer baillé à M. de Clermont, vis admiral de France. (Bib. Nat., Pièces originales 785, dossier *Clermont*, pièce 49.)

21. *Estimation of charges of the English navy for the second three months.*[1]

(9 July—30 Sept. 1512.)

[Including the Regent.]

A rate for wages, vitayle, toundage, deddeshares and other charges of the Kyng's navie of 17 shippes

---

[1] Sir Edward Howard received, on 22 May, of John Dawtry, by the hands of Wistan Brown, captain of the Peter Pomegranate, 2,500*l*. 'for revitaylyng of the seid armye and navye for three mounthes begynnyng the 9 day of July'; and, later, another 3,500*l*. This estimate can be dated end of June, as the first three months are said to be 'almost past' (cf. p. 35), but a larger sum was spent (*R.O., Chapter House Book* 2, pp. 47–60).

and the army of 3,000 men in thiem, apon the see, for 3 mounthes:—

Vytayle and charges.

Vytayle for 3 mounthes for 2,983[1] soldiours, maryners and gonners, after 5s. a man a mounth: 2,237*l*. 5s.

Wages of the saide nombre for the seyd 3 mounthes after the same rate: 2,237*l*. 5s.

Wages and vitayle of sir Edward Howard, at 10s. a day for 3 mounthes: 42*l*.

Wages and vytayle of 9[2] other captayns, at 18*d*. a man a day, by the sayd 3 mounthes: 56*l*. 14s.

Toundage.

Toundage, after 12*d*. a ton, a mounth, for 9[3] shippes tyght 1,780 ton,[4] amountyng for 3 mounthes to: 268*l*. 10s.

Deddeshares.

Deddeshares, at 5s. a man a mounth in the 17 shippes: 400 shares,[5] or amountyng for 3 mounthes to: 300*l*. 7s. 6*d*.

The 2 crayers for vytallyng.

Vytayle, wages, toundage and deddeshares of the 2 crayers vitelers for 3 mounthes amounteth, for

---

[1] 3391 men (*R. O., Chapter House Book* 2).
[2] 15 captains (*ibid.*).
[3] 8 King's ships, the 2 rowbarges, and 13 hired ships. Cf. the list of the first 3 months: the Lion of Greenwich is replaced by the Henry Katherine of Hampton, 120 tons; the rowbarge Katherine Pomegranate leaves Portsmouth with the Sovereign at the beginning of August; the Magdalene is paid only from the 6th August (*ibid.*).
[4] 2,150 tons (*ibid.*). [5] 471 (*ibid.*).

IN 1512-13

24 men, 2 boyes, 6 deddeshares, toundage of 120 tons tyght: 60*l*. 15*s*. Somme: 5,201*l*. 16*s*. 6*d*.[1]

The Regent's charges for 3 mounthes.

Vytayle for 700 souldiours, maryners and gonners: 525*l*.
Wages for the same nombre: 525*l*.
Deddeshares, 50 shares: 37*l*. 10*s*.
Pylotts at 20*s*. a man a mounthe, 4 pylotts: 12*l*.
Somme: 1,099*l*. 10*s*.

Ovyrcharges and excesses for Sir Edward Howard, as well hereafore payed as hereafter to be remembred for warrants for them to be sued.

For 3 mounthes wages and vytayle of 27 men in the navie in diverse shippes, by appointing of the breve abstracts by Mr. Awmener[2] drawen oute of the musters, and ovyr the nombre of 3,000 men first apoynted, the said 3 mounthes to be ended the 8 day of Julie: 40*l*. 10*s*.

Also for lyke 3 mounthes wages and vytayle to begyn the 9 day of Julie next commyng: 40*l*. 10*s*.

Also for lyke wages and vytayle, as well for the 3 mounthes almost past as for the said 3 mounthes to begyn the 9 day of Julie for 52 maryners in the

---

[1] Cf. admiral Howard's brief account: 'The secounde 3 mounthes charges in vitayle, wages, deddeshares, and toundage of 23 shippes:

Capteyns as speres paied aforehande, 7 men:
  nichil
Men beside: 3,409 men
Deddeshares: 471 shares   5,821*l*. 18*s*.'
Toundage of 13 hired shippes: 2,150 tons
Toundage of the Kyng's shippes: 1,960 tons:
  nichil

[2] Wolsey.

2 landyng barges : a newe charge to the Admyrall besyde his indenture : 156*l*.

Also for 20 shares to the said 2 barges for the sayd 6 mounthes : 30*l*.

Also for extraordinarie charges of syr Edward Howard, as purser of the sayd 2 barges and other causes accidentalls as well for the 3 mounthes past as for 3 mounthes next to comme, by estymacion : 200*l*.

Also for ovyrwages of sir John Carewe, knyght, captayn of the Regent, at 5*s*. a day for 3 mounthes to begyn the 9 day of Julie next ensuyng, by apoyntment of the kyng's Councell and wrytyngs in that behalf of late made and to M. Daunce and other directed : 21*l*.

Also for lyke ovyrcharge and wages of Stevyn Bull, at 18*d*. by day for the said 3 mounthes : 6*l*. 6*s*.

Also for the overcharge and excesse of wages and vytayle of 31 men charged and being on Sir Howard's ship, the Mary Rose, over his first muster, with 16 of Thomas Wyndam's servaunts not recovered in his muster, with 5 trumpetts and sertayne maryners and gonners, forasmoch as he ys allowed for 400 men and hath 431, so in excesse for 3 monethes past : 46*l*. 10*s*., and 3 mounthes next to come : 46*l*. 10*s*.=93*l*.   Somme : 587*l*. 6*s*.

The totall of this roll : 6,889*l*. 6*s*. 6*d*.

(Brit. Mus., MSS. Harleian 309, fol. 41, 39, 37.[1])

22. *Lorenzo Pasqualigo to his brothers.*

[The English landed twice in Brittany, burnt many castles and villages and captured 40 ships. Moreover they met in the Channel 26 Flemish hulks well fitted with ordnance and on their way to Brittany to fetch salt. Afterwards they returned to

---

[1] The folios of the MS. are badly placed.

the Downs where the King sent them refreshments. They left one night since for an unknown destination. Louis XII. is preparing a powerful fleet, but it will fear to leave the harbour, because Henry VIII. is expecting 30 Spanish ships from Biscay. In sight of Cape Finistère a French privateer has seized a Portuguese ship laden with pepper. In the Mediterranean, near Cartagena, another privateer has taken two Spanish barks.]

(London: 14 July, 1512.)

Tornando, l' armada de Ingaltera messe in terra in Bertagna in do lochi e brusò molti castelli e ville di quelli lochi, e prese molte nave e navilii trovono per quelli porti, e menole via, sachizando el tutto. E poi, intrando ne li Chanali, si scontrò in urche[1] 26 che havea suso artellaria assai, e andava a la baia in Bertagna per sali. Li preseno, e tutti insieme andò a Le Dunes,[2] dove la maestà de sto Re messe zente assai su dita armata, e armò ditte urche e nave prexe in Bertagna. E una note se levono, che fo nave 60, et urche 26, e le nave prexe ne li porti de Bertagna, che era da 40, et non si sa dove siano andate. Ma si judica habino qualche intelligentia con qualche locho de Franza dove serano andate.

Assi per certo a la Corte come in Franza se arma e fanno grossa armada, ma credo non oseranno ussir fora, perchè, oltra la armada che à al presente

---

[1] 'En la grant mer Occéane,' says Antoine de Conflans in his naval treatise (1517-8), 'aux parties froides, tenans aux Basses Allemaignes, ou Germanies, comme Roussie, Norvaigue, Dampnemarc, venant en Frise, en la Hanse Teutonicque, Holande, Zélande et Breban, y a gros nombre de *hourques*, qui vont par flotes au Brouage ou en Bretaigne ou à Saint-Tunal, en Portingal, quérir du sel. Et sont gros navires de 200, 300, 400, 500 et jusques à 600 tonneaux, et quelc'unes plus grandes' (*Annales Maritimes*, 1842, iii. 37).

[2] The Downs.

sto Re, aspeta etiam nave 30 armate a sue spexe in Bischaia,[1] le qual hora mai dovrebeno comparer ; che si sa za zorni ch' erano per partir ; che costoro desidera che diti Francesi eschi ; che non ussirà per certo ; che non à modo nè lochi di far la mità di l' armada che averà costoro senza l'armata di Spagna, che è assai.

. . . Sopra Cao Finistere una nave Francese [2] à preso una nave Portogese, veniva qui con bale 60 piper, con dir che l' è de' Spagnoli.

Item si ha che in mar de Lion sopra Chartagenia uno corsaro Provenzal [2] con 3 nave e una galia à preso do barche Spagnole.

(Sanuto, xiv. 580.)

23. *Freighting of a man-of-war belonging to René de Clermont.*

(Honfleur : 19 July, 1512.)

[For two months beginning the 17th July : 150 francs per month.]

Nous, René de Clermont, chevalier, seigneur dudit lieu, lieutenant général de l'armée de mer que le Roy nostre sire fait présentement mectre suz en son royaulme, vis admiral de France et maistre après Dieu d'une nef nommée la Marie de Clermont à nous appartenant, du port de 140 tonneaux ou environ, dont est cappitaine G^{me} Carmerien, confessons avoir eu et receu de sire Jehan Lalemant, conseiller du Roy nostredict seigneur, receveur général de ses finances ès païs et duché de Normandie, et par luy commis à tenir le compte et faire

---

[1] About the preparing of the Spanish fleet, cf. Peter Martyr, Ep. n° 479 ; F. Duro, *Armada Española*, i. (documents dated 16 March, 18 June 1512) ; Zurita, *Anales de la corona de Aragon*, vi. folio 290.

[2] Cf. Doc. 26.

le paiement des fraiz extraordinaires de ses guerres et armée de mer [1] que ledit seigneur fait présentement mectre suz au port et havre de ceste ville de Honnefleu audict païs de Normandie, la somme de 300 *l. t.* à nous ordonnée pour le noliaige et frect d'icelle navire de deux mois entiers commançans le 17ᵉ jour de ce présent mois de juillet, qui est au feur de 150 *l. t.* par chacun mois. Laquelle nef a esté prinse pour servir à ladicte armée de mer, qui est partie dudit havre de Honnefleu pour ledit service ledit 17ᵉ de ce présent mois. De laquelle somme de 300 *l. t.* nous tenons content et bien paié et en quictons ledit receveur général, commis susdit, et tous autres.

En temoing de ce, nous avons signé ceste présente de nostre main et scellée de nostre scel, audict lieu de Honnefleu, le 19ᵉ jour de juillet, l'an 1512.

RENÉ DE CLERMONT.

(Bib. Nat., Pièces orig. 784, dossier *Clermont*, pièce 203.)

24. *Victualling of a French man-of-war.*

(Villerville : 28 July, 1512.

[One day extra over two months.]

Je, Raoulin Guérin, cappitaine de la nef Sibille, à moy appartenant, confesse avoir eu et receu de sire Jehan Lalement, conseiller du Roy nostre seigneur, receveur général de ses finances ès pays et duché de Normandie, et par luy commis à tenir

[1] There was no regular treasurer of the French navy before the appointment of Jean Robineau (1517), at the time of the building of Havre de Grace. Jean Lalemant, general receiver of Normandy, in 1512 and 1513, and Astremoine Faure, in 1514 (Doc. 98), were only temporary commissioners for the navy of Normandy; also Jean Corbeil was temporary commissioner for the navy of Brittany (Bib. Nat., MSS. fr. 5,501, fol. 106).

le compte et faire le paiement des fraiz extraordinaires de ses guerres et armée de mer audit pays, les victuailles cy après déclairées, à moy ordonnées pour manière de renforcement de vivres, et ce oultre l'ordinaire des autres victuailles que ledit receveur général m'a cy devant fait délivrer pour la nourriture de deux moys entiers [1] de 90 hommes ordonnez pour l'équipage d'icelle nef, servant seullement ce qui s'ensuit pour la despense du jour duy, date de ce présent roolle.

Pain fraiz : 90 pains.

Bière : $\frac{1}{2}$ pippe.

Cher fresche : $\frac{1}{2}$ bœuf et la moictié de $\frac{1}{2}$ quartier de bœuf.

Sel : demy boissel.

Desquelles victuailles je me tiens content et en quicte ledit receveur général, commis susdit, et tous autres.

Tesmoing mon seing manuel cy mis.

A Villerville, mercredi 28 jour de juillet, l'an 1512.

RAULLIN GUÉRIN.

(Bib. Nat., MSS. fr. 26,113, n° 1116.)

25. *Lorenzo Pasqualigo to his brothers.*

(London : 3 August, 1512.)

[Henry VIII. is fitting out all the ships of his kingdom, even the small ones of 80 tons. The largest is the Sovereign. He will have 60 ships besides the first fleet, not including 30 Spanish ships daily expected. 20,000 men are ready to go on board, and to land in Normandy or in Brittany. Two French privateers are in the Mediterranean, and another on the north coast of Spain.]

---

[1] The French ships seem to be generally victualled for two months, the English for three.

IN 1512-13

Qui la maestà de sto Re arma quante nave pol aver fina a le picole,[1] ch' è di toneli 80, e la mazor serà la Soprana,[2] ch' è di botte[3] 2500 : che credo sarano da nave 60 oltra la prima armada, e oltra nave 30 armade per suo conto in Biscaia, che se aspeta de hora in hora.[4] E poi meterà suso questi altri combatenti, che è presto da homeni 20,000, e se dize meterà in Normandia[5] over Bertagna[6] a l' improvista. Che Dio li dia victoria! . . . Sapiate che in mar de Lion ce sono do corsari Provenzali, uno con barche 3 e una galia, l' altro con barza una e uno galion e do galie, e da prexo 3 o 4 barze, che veniva a Ponente : si chè non si trova asegurar su le barze de Candia a 10 per 100.

[1] Andrea Badoer, Venetian ambassador, wrote (London : 26 July) : 'Qual magnanimo Re haver preparato una hoste maritima tanto in ordine e ben a ponto de nave 70 grande' (Sanuto, xv. 596).
[2] The Sovereign, 1,000 tons, sailed from Portsmouth with the fleet the 5th or 6th August, having for victuallers the Trinity of Wight (80 t.) and the James of London (80 t.), (Brewer, i. 4475) and the Katherine Pomegranate with her.
[3] *Botta*=½ ton.
[4] The Spanish fleet left Guipuzcoa about the 15th August (W. Knight to Wolsey, San Sebastian, 5 August ; J. Style to Henry VIII., San Sebastian, 4 October : Brewer, i. 3355 ; Ellis, 2nd series, i. 202), and reached Southampton on 8 Sept., under the command of Joan de Lezcano : 'Don Zuanne de Lascorno, con 15 grosse nave et 8 caravelle et pinazie con 5000 homeni, capitano dil Re Catholico, arivò in Ingaltera nel porto di Antona a dì 8 septembrio, et con l' armata d' Ingaltera, che sarà nave 50 et homeni 4000 de avantaggio et più de l' altra volta, partirano con il primo tempo per andar contra li inimici, in quelli lochi dove più existimarano dannificharli' (Sanuto, xv. 227). Lezcano received a reward : 'To the Admyrall of the Spanysshe navye that comme to the Kyng : 6*l.* 13*s.* 4*d.*' [12 Sept.] (*R.O., Chapter House Book* 215, p. 202).
[5] The French fleet was moored at Honfleur and guarded by four large men-of-war (Brewer, i. 3357).
[6] There was still much uncertainty about the military designs of the English : P. Martyr twice reports Henry VIII.'s landing at Calais (Ep. Nos. 495, 497).

Etiam in mar di Spagna z' è uno Francese con barche do, ch' à preso una nave Portogexe con bale 60 piper, che andava in Fiandra.

(Sanuto, xiv. 596.)

26. *John Style to Henry VIII.*

(San Sebastian : 5 August, 1512.)

[Fray Bernardin, of Rhodes, knight, and Hervé de Porzmoguer on the coasts of Spain.]

On the coast of Portyngale and of Galysya there be diverse Frenshe men of warre, oon capytayn Bernaldyng,[1] knyght of the Rodys, and Perysmogher,[2] the whiche, of late and thys weke passyd, have taken 9 or 10 schyppys bound towardys the Andalosya and oon towardys Lysbonne wythe grete ankers for the kyng of Portyngal.

(Brewer, i. 3355.)[3]

---

[1] Nephew or son of Prégent de Bidoux, captured two Biscayan barks laden with Genoese goods (Arch. of Genoa : 21 Aug. 1512). Cf. Doc. 22.

[2] Hervé de Porzmoguer (La Nicollière-Teijeiro, *La Marine bretonne aux xve et xvie siècles*, p. 103). Cf. Doc. 22.

[3] In the same time a Malouin, Philippe Roussel, scoured the coasts of Ireland and Scotland : ' Pierre May, bourgeois et marchant demeurant en la ville de St. Mallo, aagé de 50 ans ou environ . . . . ., dit que, dès le commancement des guerres qui ont eu cours en ce païs et duché, il vit Phelippes Rouxel, qui pour lors estoit maistre d'une barque nommée la Pourrie, du port d'environ 50 tonneaulx, la faire razer et baisser l'enchatelleure d'icelle pour myeulx servir à la guerre, et l'esquipper et acoutrer pour servir et aller à la guerre. Et de fait yssit hors du havre de St. Mallo avec ladite barque, bien esquipée de gens et artillerie, et allèrent à leurs aventures. Et après ce fut chose toute commune et notoire au païs de St. Mallo que ledit Phelippes avoit prins environ 11 ou 12 navires de grande valleur à la couste d'Irlande sur les Angloys et Yroys, et qu'il avoyt mené lesdites prinses en Escosse et illec les avoit venduz et proffitez en partie, et autre partie avoit amené audit St. Mallo, comme draps, cuirs et merluz paré et sallé, et laynes d'Escosse à la valleur de plus de 3000 livres. Et dit

27. *Letters patent of Louis XII. forbidding commercial intercourse with Aragon, Castille, Portugal and England.*
(Blois : 6 Aug. 1512.)

Loys, par la grace de Dieu, roy de France, à tous ceulx qui ces présentes lettres verront, salut. Nous avons receue l'umble supplicacion de noz chers et bien amez les marchans, maistres de navires et mariniers de nostre royaume, duché de Bretaigne et autres noz subgectz de noz pays, terres et s^{ries} de nostre obéissance, exposant que, combien qu'il ait esté tolléré à tous estrangiers quelxconques, de quelque pays ou contrée, de hanter et fréquenter marchandamment, aller et venir seurement et paisiblement, tant par terre que par mer, en nostredict royaume, duché de Bretaigne, et autres noz pays et s^{ries}, et y apporter et rapporter avec les navires or et argent et autres manières et espèces de marchandises, sans aucune contradiction ne empeschement, mais ont esté tousjours lesdicts marchans estrangiers bien favorablement et humainement traictez et entretenuz en bonne amour et justice autant ou mieulx que les nostres propres jusques à l'eure présente.

Ce néantmoins aucuns roys et princes circumvoisins de nostredict royaume, pays et s^{ries}, et signantement les roys de Castille, d'Aragon, d'Angleterre, Portingal et autres ont fait en leurs pays et obéissance certains statutz et édictz, par lesquelz est estroictement prohibé et deffendu à leurs subgectz,

le savoir, pour tant qu'il vit lesdits biens et marchandises et qu'il en acheta partie dudit merluz de partie de compaignons de ladite barque' (*R. O., Chapter House Book* 83, p. 76). Cf. *ibid.* pp. 9 and 16 : 'A faict plusieurs prinses de navires sur les Angloys, Yroys [Irish] et Espaignolz, et entre autres une nef d'Espaigne qu'ils avoient prins devant Kercomby [Kirkcudbright], ès parties d'Escosse.'

savoir est desdicts roys de Castille, Aragon et Portingal de non fréter aucuns navires estrangiers pour tirer ne apporter nulles ne aucunes marchandises quelxconques hors desdicts pays, et pareillement aux estrangiers, mesmement à nosdictz subgectz, de non charger, prandre, rapporter ne recuillir biens ne marchandises desdicts pays en leurs propres vaisseaulx et navires, aussi de apporter ne rapporter audict royaume d'Angleterre vins, malvesies, or ne monnoye, aluns, vrède ne pastel, sans le congié du Roy dudict pays, le tout sur peine de confiscacion desdictes navires, biens et marchandises.

Au moyen desquelz édictz et deffences plusieurs autres par iceulx roys et princes faitz et ordonnez en leursdictz pays et obéissance, nosdictz subgectz sont à présent réduictz à très grande pauvreté indigence et nécessité pour tant que par icelles deffences et injonctions ilz sont totalement privez et frustrez de tous les gaings, advantaiges, prouffitz et utilitez qu'ilz souloient avoir et prendre soubz le fait et excercice de navigaige.

Pourquoy chose impossible leur seroit en l'advenir ainsi vivre, avoir ne entretenir bons navires comme ilz avoient acoustumé, ne continuer ledict fait et traffique de marchandise, ains sont et seront neccessairement contrainctz de la délaisser, cesser et habandonner à leur grant desplaisir, désolation et interestz, et au très grant grief, préjudice et dommaige de nous et de la chose publique de nosdictz royaume, duché, pays et s^{ries} et obéissance dessusdictz, et encores plus grant inconvénient leur pourroit cy après ensuivir si par nous n'estoit promptement sur ce donné ordre et provision. Ce que nosdictz subjectz nous ont très humblement supplié et requis.

Pourquoy nous, considérans ce que dessus, et que soubz icelluy train de navigaige et fait de marchandise, tant par mer que par terre, conciste une grande partye de la richesse et oppulence de nosdictz pays, désirans de tout nostre cueur icelluy navigaige et fait de marchandise entretenir, continuer et faire augmenter et multiplier en nostredict pays, et ausdictz marchans, maistres de navires et mariniers et autres noz subgectz supplians subvenir et aider, à ce que au temps advenir ilz se puissent mieulx que jamais équipper et accoustrer en mer, tant pour la force et seurté de nosdictz pays que pour mieulx prouffiter, augmenter, enrichir. Et pour toutes autres causes à ce nous mouvans.

Avons aujourdhuy, de noz auctorité, grace espécial et plaine puissance et auctorité royale, par l'adviz et délibéracion des princes et seigneurs de nostre sang, gens de nostre Grant Conseil et de plusieurs autres bons, gens et notables personnaiges estans à l'entour de nostre personne, statué et ordonné, statuons et ordonnons et voulons et nous plaist par ces présentes, par édict et ordonnance irrévocable,

Que doresnavant il ne soit permis et loyssible à aucuns noz subgectz de nostre royaulme, duché de Bretaigne, et autres nosdictz pays, terres, s^{ries} et obéissance, fréter ne charger aucuns navires estrangiers ne par iceulx tirer ou emporter ne souffrir estre tiré ne transporté hors iceulx nosdictz pays et obéissances ne aucunes marchandises ne biens quelxconques. Ne pareillement aux estrangiers, marchans, maistres de navires et mariniers de n'en prandre, recevoir, charger, recueillir ne emporter en leurs vaisseaulx et navires ne en autres que ceulx de nosdictz pays et s^{ries} nulles ne aucunes marchandises ne biens, sous peine de perdicion et confiscation d'iceulx navires, biens et marchandises.

Et que en ce et en toutes autres choses les estrangiers soient traictez en nosdictz pays de la forme et manière que nosdictz subgectz sont ou seront traictez èsdicts royaumes de Castille, Aragon, Angleterre, Portingal et autres pays respectivement.

Donné à Bloys, le 6ᵉ jour d'aost, l'an de grace 1512, et de nostre règne le 15ᵉ.

Par le Roy : l'évesque de Paris, les seigneurs du Bouschaige, de Morvilliers, bailly d'Amiens, et autres présens.

ROBERTET.[1]

(Arch. Gironde, B 30, fol. 8 v°.)

28. *Th. Spinelly to Henry VIII.*[2]

(Brussels : 17 Aug. 1512.)

[The fleet of Brittany at Brest on the 2nd August, 1512 : three large men-of-war and four smaller ones. They are in fear of another landing. A ship of Normandy has captured a Portuguese ship.]

Ung chappellain de la duchesse de Coymbre de Portingal [est] venu vers Madame et luy a apporté

---

[1] By way of compensation, Louis XII. granted licence to the King of Denmark to send 40 hulks to Rochelle for salt (Blois, 5 Sept. 1512), and to John Morley, James IV.'s secretary, to buy at Dieppe 100 sacks of flour (Bib. Nat., MSS. fr. 5501, fol. 315). The tax-gatherers complained, and their contracts were reduced by the Privy Council (750 l. at Lisieux, 184 l. at St. Valery en Caux), 'à raison des guerres et divisions qui lors survinrent entre le Roy, les roys d'Espaigne et d'Angleterre.' The English bought no more Anjou wine : 'Au moyen de l'esmocion et ouverture de guerre d'entre nous et les Angloys, lesdits Angloys ne aultres estrangiers n'ont tiré ne emmené aucuns vins ' (*ibid.*, MSS. fr. 5,501, fol. 73).

[2] Cf. W. Knight's letter to Wolsey (San Sebastian : 4 Oct. 1512) : 'The flete of France is grete. There went in August owte of the havyn of Breste 47 shippis to the borders of the west contre of Inglond, and 15 to Irelond, item 15 into Galice, and 10 remaynyd to kepe the costs of Britaigne. The 47 be returned to Breste, the rest be abrode ' (Ellis, 2nd series, i. 202).

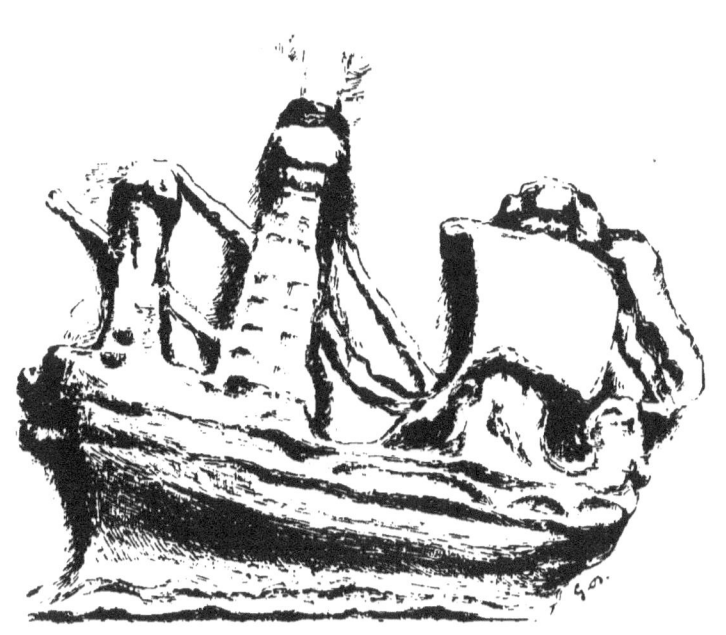

SHIP OF THE XVIth CENTURY.
(Roscoff Church.)

ung beau présent de diverses senteurs et aultres choses de Ghinea et de Calcout. Lequel me dit que hier fut 15 jours qu'il estoit à Brest en Bretaigne,[1] où il y avoit ung grand navire de 700 tonneaulx,

[1] Although Anne, daughter of Duke François II. (who died in 1488), married Charles VIII., king of France (1492), and later Louis XII. (1498), Brittany kept its national independence; it only became a French province in 1532. Therefore the Queen had her private fleet, consisting of four men-of-war: nef de Brest, nef de Morlaix, nef de la Rochelle, nef de Bordeaux. One of them was on the coasts of Galice, on 2nd August, under the command of Hervé de Porzmoguer.—Whether the famous Cordelière was the nef de Brest or the nef de Morlaix is doubtful. On the one hand, she is always styled Caraque de Brest in English and Italian documents. On the other hand, we are told that a celebrated privateer, Nicolas Coetanlem, 'fist construire et édiffier la carracque appellée la Cordelière au havre et cay de Morlaix' (*Bulletin de la Soc. Archéol. du Finistère*, viii. 170); and the chronicler, Alain Bouchart, writes: 'Une grande nef nommée la Cordellière, laquelle nef la royne de France avoit fait faire en la ville de Mourlaix.' The nef de Brest and the nef de Morlaix were, however, contemporaries: the first was fitted out, on 22 Dec. 1499 (*Arch. Loire Inférieure*, E 203); the second was built, from 7 May, 1496, to 30 June, 1498, at a cost of 22,512*l*. 9*s*. 2*d*. *t*. ('Bordereau de la mise faicte pour le parachèvement de la grant nef de Mourlays, appellée la Mareschalle,' *ibid.*, E 208). The Cordelière spent some years in the Mediterranean (1501-4), and returned to Brittany, after the loss of Naples; she was equipped a second time in 1508 (29 March), at an expense of 4,244*l*. 14*s*. 8*d*. *t*. (*Chroniques de Jean d'Auton*, *passim*; *Arch. Loire Inférieure*, reg. xvii. of Chancery, fol. 32; Bib. Nat., MSS. fr. 25,720, n° 62).—The nef de la Rochelle, begun by Charles VIII., was finished by Queen Anne in Oct. 1500, when G. Geuffroy went to Tonnay-Charente 'veoir le corps d'une carracque piéça encommancée et non parachevée' (*Arch. Loire Inférieure*, E 19). There was another ship belonging to the town of Rochelle called Saint-Sauveur (Amos Barbot, *Histoire de la Rochelle*, i. 474-5).—The Queen's nef de Bordeaux must not be confused with a King's ship bearing the same name.—For other ships of Brittany, in the year 1503, cf. La Nicollière-Teijeiro, *op. cit.*, p. 102: grand nef de la Bouvardière (300 men); grand nef de St. Malo (150); nef de Guemadeuc (60); nef de Tréguier (70); l'Espaigneul, of Quimper (70); grand nef of G. Finamour (100); nef Jean Frolai (80); nef de Vannes (120); Michelle, of Croisic (140); Sénéchal and Chapon (300).

ung de 400 venu de Bordeaulx, ung de 300 de la Rocelle, et 4 autres de 150 jusques à 200 tonneaulx, et que l'on avoit fait une assemblée de gens pour mectre dedans lesdits navires, mais que par faulte d'argent la plus grand partie s'en estoyent allez, desrobant et pillant par le pays.

Dit encores qu'ilz sont en grand craincte de vostre armée, et luy semble, se l'on mectoit à terre une bonne puissance de gens, qu'ilz pourront brusler lesdits navires. Aussy m'a dit que ung navire de guerre de Normandie de 120 tonneaulx avoit prins ung navire Portingalois chargé de draps sortant de vostre royaulme et que les maistres dudit navire et 6 hommes avec luy furent tuez.

(Brewer, i. 3,377.)

29. *Roberto Acciajuoli, Florentine ambassador in France, to the Council of Florence.*

(Blois: 18 Aug. 1512.)

[80 English ships came in sight of the coast of Brittany and fought eight hours with 40 French sails, which at last retired into Brest harbour. The Cordelière and the Regent are both lost, with three smaller English ships.[1]]

Di Bretagna tre giorni sono ci furono nuove che l' armata Inghilese era venuta vicina al porto di Brest per trovare l' armata di questa Maestà che si era messa in ordine in que' mari in grosso numero, et erano insieme circa 40 nave Francese che le terre di Normandia[2] et Bretagna havevano armate, et li

---

[1] 'To the man that brought tethings from sir Edward Howard, King's lord Admyrall, of the drownyng of the caryke of Brest, in reward: 10*l.*' [20 Aug. 1512] (*R. O., Chapter House Book* 215, p. 199).

[2] We know the names of 14 men-of-war of Normandy: nef de Rouen, nef d'Orléans, 453 tons (Capt. Louis de Bigars, s^r

IN 1512-13

Inghilesi erano più de 80 vele. Essendo venuta ad trovare la Franzese, furono insieme alle mani per più 8 hore senza pendere la victoria più di quà che di là, perche li Franzesi, come inferiori di numero, si retirorono in porto con perdita della principal nave che gli havessino, che si chiama la Cordelliera. La quale incatenatasi colla principale Inghilese, decta la Regenta, ambedua perirono di fuocho, et le nave et le persone. Oltra la quale costoro dicono esserne perite 3 altre Inghilese. Di che mi rapporto ad chi ne havessi più vera notitia, non potendo scriver di quà senon quello si intende per altri.

(*Firenze, Archivio di Stato, Reformazioni, Dieci di Balia, Responsive*, filza 110.)

30. *Wolsey to the Bishop of Worcester.*

(Farnham : 26 August [1512].)

[The burning of the Cordelière and Regent.]

And to ascerteyne yow of the lamentabyll and sorowfull tydyngs and chance wych hath fortunyd by the see, owr folks, on Tuysday was fortnygth, met with 21 gret shyppys of Frawnce, the best with sayle and furnyshyd with artylllery and men that evyr was seyn. And after innumerabyll shotyng of gunnys and long chasyng one another, at the last the Regent most valyently bordyd the gret caryke of Brest, wherin wer 4 lords, 300 gentylmen, 800 solgers and maryners, 400[2] crossbowemen, 100[3] guners,

---

de la Londe), nef de Bordeaux (Capt. Cristophe de Chanoy), nef de Dieppe (Capt. Rigault de Berquetot), Rose, Béthune, barque Moricet (Capt. Antoine de Conflans), Petite Louise, 173 tons (Capt. Adenet Legendre), Romaine (Capt. Etienne des Roux), barque Jean Denis (Capt. Alonce de Bellesonce), Sibille (Capt. Jean Robin), Foy (Capt. Jacques d'Etimauville), Marie de Clermont (Capt. Guill. Kermerien), Grand Louise, 790 tons (Capt. René de Clermont, admiral).

[2] 100 (Doc. 33).   [3] 50 (*ibid.*)

200 tonnes of wyne, 100 pypys of befe, 60 barells of gonepowder and 15 gret brasyn cortawds with so marvelose nombyr of schot and other gunys of every sorte. Owr men so valyently acquyt themsylfe that within one ower fygth they had utterly vanquyshyd with schot of gonnys and arows the said caryke, and slayne moste parte of the men within the same. And sodenly as they war yelding themsylf, the caryke was one a flamyng fyre, and lyke wyse the Regent within the turnyng of one hand. She was so ankyrryd and fastyd to the caryke that by no meanys possybyll she mygth for hyr salfgarde depart from the same and so bothe in fyght within three owrys war burnt, and moste parte of the men in them. Sir Thomas Knyvet, which most valyently acquit hymsylf that day, was slayne with one gonne. Sir John Carewe,[1] with dyverse others whos namys be not yet knowne, be lycke wyse slayne. . .

The resydue of the Frenche flete, after longe chasyng, was by owr folks put to flyght and drevyn of into Brest havyn. There were 6 as gret shyppes of the sayd flet as the Regent or Soverayn,[2] howbeyt as cowards they flede. Sir Edward hath made hys vowe to God that he wyl nevyr se the Kyng in the face tyl he hath revengyd the deth of the nobyll and valyant knygth sir Th. Knyvet.[3]

(Fiddes, *Life of Wolsey*, Collections, p. 18.)

---

[1] 'Sir John Carowe, to do the Kyng servyce of warre apon the see in the Regient as capitain of the same: 100*l.*' [9 May, 1512] (*R. O., Chapter House Book* 215, p. 184).

[2] The largest French man-of-war was the Louise, 790 tons.

[3] Commissions of array were sent, Oxford, 28 Aug., to the justices of peace and sheriffs for defence of the coasts against the French, and another one to Edward Ponynges, lord of the Cinque Ports (Brewer, i. 3393-4).

31. *Certificate of a French captain.*

(Brest: 1st Sept. 1512.)

[The victuals sent to the fleet are bad.][1]

Je, Anthoine de Conflans, varlet de chambre du Roy nostre sire, cappitaine de la nef la Rose et de la barque Béthune, certiffie que les victuailles qui m'avoient esté ordonnées pour renforcement de vivres de deux jours sont deppéries, perdues et gastées sur la mer ès allèges où elles avoient esté chargées à Honnefleu, de sorte que on ne sçauroit boyre ne manger d'icelle, fors 3 poinssons de bière que nous avons prins et receu sur icelluy renforcement de vivres.

En tesmoing de ce, j'ay signé ces présentes de ma main.

A Brest, le 1ᵉʳ jour de septembre, l'an 1512.

DE CONFLANS

(Bib. Nat., Pièces originales 837, dossier *Conflans*, pièce 14.)

32. *Letter of Peter Martyr.*

(Logroño: 3 Sept. 1512.)

[Prégent de Bidoux has left the Mediterranean with four galleys, fitted with three Venetian basilisks; one shot of those guns can strike through any ship.]

Perijoannes,[2] Galli regis præfectus maritimus,

[1] For the bad victualling of the English fleet, cf. Doc. 58, 62, 66, 69, 71, 76.

[2] Prégent de Bidoux had been called to Blois by Louis XII. in July 1512, and sent back to Marseilles for the relief of Genoa, threatened by the combined fleets of the Holy League. Lasagni, the Genoese agent, wrote (Blois, 13 July) that Prégent complained of bad weather and was obliged to mend the masts of his galleys. M. de Crussol was at Nice on 14 July, and did not

cum magnis quatuor armatis triremibus[1] ad Oceanum tendit.[2] Insunt triremibus basilisci tres, in strage Venetorum[3] habiti, machinæ genus, quod uno ictu potis est navim unam, quocumque illa sit, perterebrare atque discerpere.[4]

(Ep. n° 498.)

33. *Antonio Bavarin to Francesco Pesaro.*

(London : 5 Sept. 1512.)

[50 English ships have left Southampton ; 27 French men-of-war proceeded three miles out of Brest harbour, but turned back as soon as they spied the enemies. The carrack of Brest remained behind, and was boarded by the Regent and another small vessel. After $2\frac{1}{2}$ hours' battle, the French were defeated, but they set their ship on fire ; the carrack and the Regent were both destroyed. Thomas Knyvet, captain of the Regent, perished, and 120 English escaped out of 800 ; 20 Frenchmen have been taken prisoners out of 1,500. Another French man-of-war was shot at and pursued. The English fleet

expect Prégent's galleys before a week ; Marco de Martinengo applied then to the Parliament of Provence (Bib. Nat., MSS. Dupuy 261, fol. 120). Prégent was expected at Genoa since a fortnight: the Doge Campofregoso thought (1 July) 'quod dicuntur venire galee magnifici Peringiani, et jam sunt in Ripparia,' and the Venetian ambassador at Rome wrote (7 Aug. 1512) : 'Si ha nova a Zenoa si armava 6 galioni, 2 nave, e 2 barze, perche Zenoesi intendevano veniva armada di alcune galie di Franza ch' è in Provenza per socorer il castello di Lanterna' (Sanuto, xiv. 594). But really Prégent was preparing to join the French fleet in Brittany.

[1] 'Galères *bastardes.*'
[2] It was rumoured at Rome (6 Sept.) that Prégent had been captured by the Spaniards before Malaga (Sanuto, xv. 61).
[3] On the battlefield of Agnadel (May 1509).
[4] 'They have brought, as it is saide, as gay artilliarie owte of Italie as there was none in all Fraunce' (W. Knight to Wolsey, San Sebastian, 4 Oct. 1512 : Ellis, 2nd Series, i. 202).

returned then, part to Dartmouth, part to Southampton, after having burnt 24 small ships on the coast of Brittany. On September 5, a French ship was captured. On board the carrack were: 300 gentlemen; 800 soldiers and mariners; 50 gunners; 100 crossbowmen; 400 pipes of biscuit; 100 of salt meat; 16 brass guns with their carriages; 160 barrels of gunpowder. All these details are given by the prisoners. Moreover many golden chains and a large sum of money were taken.]

Come, hessendo per avanti ussito d' Antona velle 50 di quel Re, andono sopra la costa di Bertagna, dove inteseno in porto del Brest erano 27[1] nave grosse armade per ussir fuora. Et cussi la dita armata di Franza ussite fora, e sortì tre mia lontano dil porto, la qual, auto vista di la englese, lassono l' anchore per ochio e tornono in porto predito; ma restò fuora do nave le più grosse, tra le qual la granda charachia de Brest de portada de tonelli 1500,[2] in ordine. El vento era grande e grosso mar, tamen, maistro Thomaso Chanivet, capitano di la nave dita Regente, qual non era a tonelli 500 a quella di Franza, e una altra naveta Englese, andono adosso a questa grossa Francesse e la sfondrono. La Regente se andò a bordar, e gitato el ganzo, se inchadenono insieme. Fo combatuto assai; durò la bataglia hore 2½, morti de una parte e l' altra assai, tandem Englesi restò vincitori. Visto cussì Francesi, per non venir in man de Englesi, gitò il focho per brusar Englesi, e l' una e l' altra nave se destruse. Lauda molto el capitano Chanivet, et dize scampono vivi de Englesi da 120, di 800 ch' erano su dita Rezente. Di Francesi scapoladi

---

[1] 21 only according to Wolsey (Doc. 30).
[2] False report: 'La neff de la Royne, qui fut appellée la Cordelière, estoit navire de 6 à 700 tonneaulx' (*Bulletin Soc. Archéol. du Finistère*, viii. 170).

20, di 1500 ch' erano, e fati presoni. Et una altra di tonelli 1000 Francese,[1] che non potè intrar in porto, fo bombardata assai, la qual si levò e andò in mar, e una nave Englese ben in hordine la seguitoe. Poi l' armata Englese andò in Artamura[2] per conzarsi, e qualchuna è ritornata in Antona. Poi riconzate le navi tornerano fuora.

Manda la nota di quelli era sopra la nave Francese sopradita, e dice l' armata Englese brusò in assai lochi su la Bertagna da nave 24 de Francesi.

Item, quel zorno, a di 5, hanno preso una nave de Francesi,[3] sopra la qual era capitano Drepa, e più che hanno de altre nave armade butade a fondi.

Qui serano notadi i homeni e ordinanza et altro, erano sopra la grande charachia de Brest del re di Franza . . ., barza de portata tonelli 1400 in 1500.

Monsignor di Chiaramonte,[4] grande armirajo di Franza.

Monsignor Primoia,[5] capitanio di la nave.

---

[1] The nef de Dieppe, Captain Rigault de Berquetot, 336 tons.

[2] Dartmouth.

[3] Perhaps 'the pinnace that was taken,' Bristol, 16 Jan. 1513 (Brewer, i. 3663).

[4] Clermont : the report is false.

[5] Porzmoguer. A contemporary French report gives a list of some of the Frenchmen killed in the battle. 'Il en mourut de Bretons environ 500. Entre lesquelz mourut capitaine Porzmoguer, Prigent Coatmenech, expectant de Coatjunval, Morice Kerasquer, expectant de Quillimadec, François le Baillif, seigneur de Coatjunval, Tangu Kerleroux, Martin le Nault, maistre de la caraque, Jehan le Saint, Cristofle de l'Isle, Gabriel Brezal, Ollivier et Yvon Nez, Yvon Kerdren, Jehan Bouteville, Mandez Quiniou, Jehan Tanguy, N. Dolou, Yvon le Digouris, Guillaume Marrec, Jehan Kermelec et plusieurs autres gentilshommes, mariniers et autres. Ceux cy estoient cousins germains ou alliés bien prez. Et le seigneur de Coatjunval y fut brulé qui avoit nom Hervé. Le capitaine Porzmoguer estoit marié à la veuve de l'Estang qui estoit fille

Monsignor Enores de Claricha.
Monsignor Simon de Loy.
Monsignor Vangel.
300 cavalieri zentilhomeni.
800 tra marinari e soldati.
50 bombardieri.
100 balestrieri.
400 pipe de biscoto.
100 pipe di carne salata.
16 bombarde grossissime di bronzo sopra charete, et altre bombarde, schiopeti e archibusi senza numero.
160[1] meze bote di polvere di bombarda.
2 . . ., di portata di 40 bote, l' uno di bronzo.
Questo se ha dal nochiero e altri presi vivi.
Oltra questo, cadene d' oro de cavalieri e danari contadi per valuta grandissima.

(Sanuto, xv. 209.)[2]

34. *Wages of a French captain.*[3]

(15 Sept. 1512.)

Nous, Loys de Bigars, chevalier, seigneur de la Londe, cappitaine de la nef nommée la Françoise d'Orléans, appartenant au Roy nostre sire, du port de 453 tonneaulx, confessons avoir eu et receu comptant de sire Jehan Lalemant, conseiller dudit seigneur et receveur général de ses finances ès pays et duché de Normandie, la somme de 396*l*. 7*s*. 10*d.t.*, à nous ordonnée par le Roy nostredit sire pour l'adob, garde, entretenement et repparacion dudit navire, et ce pour demie année commancée le 1ᵉʳ jour de janvier dernier passé et finie le dernier jour de juing ensuivant

---

de Coatjunval' (*Bulletin Soc. Archéol. du Finistère*, viii. 164).

[1] 60 barrels (Doc. 30).

[2] Cf. another letter, London, 9 Sept. (Sanuto, xv. 192).

[3] Cf. a signed bill, dated Blois, 21 Feb. 1511, for the wages of Adenet Legendre, captain of the Petite Louise (Bib. Nat., Pièces orig. 1307, dossier *Legendre*, pièce 9).

aussi dernier passé, qui est au feur de 35s.t.[1] pour chacun tonneau. De laquelle somme de 396l. 7s. 10d. t. nous tenons content et bien paié et en quictons ledit receveur général et tous autres.

En tesmoing de ce nous avons signé ceste présente de nostre main et scellé du scel de noz armes, le 15ᵉ jour de septembre, l'an 1512.

Loys de Bigars.

(Bib. Nat., MSS. fr. 26,113, n° 1121.)

35. *Wages of the controller of the French navy.*

(Blois : 22 Sept. 1512.)

Loys, par la grace de Dieu, roy de France . . .

Nous voulons et vous mandons que par nostre amé et féal conseiller et receveur général de nosdictes finances ès pays et généralité de Normandie, Jehan Lalemant l'aisné, vous faictes paier et bailler à nostre cher et bien amé Pierre Gautier, receveur d'Argentan, la somme de 120 l.t. Auquel nous l'avons tauxé et ordonné, tauxons et ordonnons par ces présentes pour avoir, par nostre ordonnance et commission, contrerollé et passé les quictances des paiemens et despence qui a esté faicte à Honnefleu pour le fait de l'advitaillement de l'armée de mer naguères mise sus et dressée audit lieu pour nous servir au fait de la guerre. En quoy il a vacqué, ainsi que avons esté certifiez par vous, luy 2ᵉ et deux chevaulx l'espace de deux moys,[2] qui sont 60 jours, compris son retour dudit Honnefleu en ceste ville. Qui est, au feur de 40 s.t. par jour, ladicte somme de 120 l.t.

Donné à Bloys, le 22ᵉ jour de septembre l'an de grace 1512, et de nostre règne le 15ᵉ.

Loys.   Par le Roy,
Gedoyn.

(*Ibid.*, MSS. fr. 25,719, no. 180.)

[1] 35 s.t.=1 golden crown (*écu d'or*).
[2] 20 June to 20 August, 1512 (cf. Doc. 18).

36. [*Wolsey ?*] *to Cardinal Bainbridge.*

(London: 27 Sept. 1512.

[The Regent was under the command of Thomas Knyvet and John Carew and had 600 men on board. The carrack of Brest had 800 men and six captains; 450 guns; 200 pipes of biscuit; 100 of salt meat; 60 barrels of gunpowder. The carrack was about to surrender, when a Frenchman set the powder on fire, and both ships, grappled together, were burnt. Sixty English escaped and a few Frenchmen are prisoners. Another French man-of-war has been run down. Louis XII. boasted that he would destroy the whole of the English fleet with one of his ships; the contrary has happened.]

Conflictus inter Regentem nostram, navem regiam, et maximam Gallorum navem, caracham Brestensem, ita se habet. In Regente nostra duo erant valentissimi duces equites aurati, dominus Thomas Knivet et dominus Joannes Carew, cum 600 militibus optime et armis et tormentis bellicis instructis. Illi in quadam regione maris Britannici inciderunt in caracham supradictam, quæ sex habuit duces in Gallia primarios dominos, quorum nomina subsequuntur: dominus admiraldus, monsignor de Claramont, monsignor Premongier, monsignor Gabriel de Chathei, monsignor Alons Claristanc, monsignor Schiamon de Ley, cum quodam alio cujus nomen non recordor, equites aurati. Erant in illa excellentes milites 800, bombardæ 50, scorpiones 400; in commeatu 200 vegetes panis biscaini, 100 carnis bovinæ salatæ; magnæ bombardæ confectæ 320, ultra alias bombardas minores; item 60 vegetes pulveris. Inter istos Gallos et nostros fuit aliquandiu atrox prœlium; ad ultimum gallica navis penitus devicta succubuit et nostris se dedidit.

Quod cum videret quidam Gallus qui maluit hæreticus quam christianus mori, omnem pulverem navis suæ incendit, cujus inextinguibili flamma utraque navis combusta fuit, una cum militibus et ducibus, exceptis 60 ex nostris, quos natantes duæ naves nostræ, cum maximo periculo suo, exceperunt; nam Regens nostra ita erat cathenis alligata, ut alterius incendium nullo modo fugere potuerit. Perpauci Galli evaserunt, qui omnes a nostris capti illico ad majestatem Regiam ducti sunt. Præterea classis regia aliam quamdam fugientem navem, nomine Admiraldam,[1] subruerunt. Rex Gallorum jactabat se una navi sua omnem classem Regis nostri deleturum; sed favente Deo et justitia causæ nostræ, aliter accidit, nam una navis nostra omnes fere vires ejus maritimas delevit.

Data ex Londino, die 27 Septembris 1512.

(Sanuto, xv. 281.)[2]

37. *Letter of Peter Martyr.*

(Logroño: 28 Sept. 1512.)

[Emmanuel, king of Portugal, son-in-law of Ferdinand the Catholic, allowed Prégent de Bidoux to refit his galleys and take in provisions in his realm. Thus Prégent escaped from Don Juan de Lezcano, the Spanish admiral, and has gone to sea to cruise against Spanish ships.]

Portugalliæ regem Emmanuelem, nostri Regis generum, inquiunt non modo non deturbasse a suis littoribus Perijoannem, Gallorum præfectum maritimum, jam in Oceanum cum triremibus delapsum per fretum Herculeum, sed quassatas naves ei refecisse, fulsisse etiam commeatibus.

[1] The nef de Dieppe.
[2] Cf. a letter of Nicolo di Favri, London, 16 Dec. 1512 (Sanuto, xv. 576).

IN 1512—13

Liscanus, nostræ classis cujusdam præfectus, Perijoannem insequebatur, ut deprehensum in mari nostro aut sterneret aut ipse vinceretur ab eo, inclusum intra portus Portugallicos pertransivit, neque uspiam ultra sese repererunt.¹ Evasit ergo Perijoannes, pyraticam in Oceano contra classes hyspanas exercitaturus.

(Ep. n° 500.)

38. *Message sent by René de Clermont to Louis XII.; payments ordered.*

(Sept. 1512.)

Loys, par la grace de Dieu, roy de France . . . Nous voullons et vous mandons que par nostre amé et féal aussi conseiller et receveur général de nosdites finances en noz païs et duchié de Normandie, Jehan Lalemant, . . . vous faictes payer, bailler et délivrer comptant à Loys le Brun, escuier, seigneur de Sallenelles,² la somme de 100 l.t. Auquel nous l'avons donnée et ordonnée, donnons et ordonnons par ces présentes, pour ung voyaige par lui fait en dilligence et par chevaulx de poste, luy 2ᵉ, de Brest en Bretaigne devers nous en nostre ville et chastel de Bloys, au moys de septembre dernier passé, par l'ordonnance et commandement de nostre amé et féal conseiller, le seigneur de Clermont, visadmiral et nostre lieutenant général au fait de nostre armée de mer, pour nous advertir de l'exécucion que avoit faicte nostredite armée à l'encontre de noz ennemys.

[1] 'Sythins [August] there be 6 galeys from Italye, whiche laye about Galice well 6 wekes and were never countred withall' (W. Knight to Wolsey, San Sebastian, 4 Oct. 1512). However, the chronicler Passero mentions that a fight between 'Pietro Joanne' (Prégent) and 'Lo Scanno' (Lezcano) was reported at Naples (17 Oct. 1512).
[2] Captain of the Louise.

Donné à Bloys, le 4ᵉ jour d'octobre l'an de grace 1512 et de nostre règne le 15ᵉ.
Loys.   Par le Roy : GEDOYN.
(Bib. Nat., MSS. fr. 20,616, pièce 54.)

39. *Piero Lando, Venetian agent to the cardinal of Gurk, to the Council of Venice.*

(Verona : 12 Oct. 1512.)[1]

[Admiral Howard left Portsmouth with 50 ships and 10,000 men ; 10 sails remained along the coast of England. On the 10th of August, about 11 A.M., the French fleet was spied at a distance of two leagues, in the entrance of Brest harbour. The Mary Rose and the Mary James, Captain Ant. Ughtred, fell on the enemies ; the French Admiral's ship was much damaged and fled with her mainmast broken to pieces and 300 men wounded. The Mary James cannonaded the Cordelière and had nearly sunk her, when the Regent fell foul of her. 400 English had boarded the Cordelière, when the gunpowder was fired and both ships were burnt. 180 English escaped, and 6 French. The Mary James fled with 30 men. During two days Admiral Howard remained in sight of Brest harbour ; 27 small French ships were burnt, and 5 captured out of 54 ; 800 enemies taken prisoners ; 600 men perished in the Regent. In the Cordelière, 800 soldiers and sailors, 60 gunners, 400 crossbowmen, and 300 knights and gentlemen, of whom many, with their wives, had gone on board, on St. Laurence's day, on a visit, and had remained.]

Come, a dì 9 dil mexe di Avosto, parti lo admiragio d' Ingalterra dil porto di Portus[2] con nave 50 et

---

[1] Cf. a first letter of P. Lando, Trent, 12 Sept. (Sanuto, xv. 78).

[2] Portsmouth.

homeni 10,000, senza li marinari, facendo suo corso longo la costa d' Ingaltera fin a la intrata dil mare hispano, per veder se alcuni de li inimici se trovavano in quelle parte. Et vedendo il paese neto, lassate nave 10 in certi porti, con el restante, al nome del signor Dio et de Monsignor Sancto Zorzi, prese suo corso verso Britania per zerchar scontrare et combatere li dicti inimici, in tal maniera che, la vigilia di Sancto Laurentio, sul tardi, have vista de la terra di Britania, et cossì con poche velle la costezorno tutta note. Et venuto il dì sequente, zerca 11 hore da matina, sopra Breste, la guardia di la galia dil ditto Admirajo discopri zerca due lege di lontano in bocha dil colfo di Breste molte nave, quale era l' armata Francese. Et andando con summa letitia a la lor volta, la nave de dicto Admiraio, di tonele 500,[1] e una altra, di 400, de la qual era capitano uno valente cavalier chiamato missier Antonio Utrect,[2] lassando uno quarto di lega le altre

[1] The Mary Rose.
[2] The Mary James, also called James of Hull, built in 1509 (Ellis, 2nd series, i. 218), bought from Richard Benlowe on 11th July, 1512 (260*l*.), Captain Ant. Ughtred. She was severely hurt, and needed repair in Sept. 1512:

'Payd, by M. Amner's letter, to Antony Ughtrede, late capitayne of the Mary James off Grenewyche, for condute mony of 60 men, which wer so sore hurte that they be not able to [go] ageyn to see, from Portsmouth to Yorke within mylis 240, after 6*d*. for 12 miles: 30*l*. Also paid, by way of the King's gracious reward, forasmuche as they be soo hurt for his sak and in his servys: 20*l*. And more paid for divers things for [the] seid Mary Jamys for the new mending of her: 4*l*. 3*s*. 5*d*.

'Item paid to Antonye Ughtrede, late capitayne of the Mary Jamys of Grenewyche, for the costes and expense of 136 sowdiers lying on lande by the space of 9 days, for lakk of vytayle in ther shipp, after 6*d*. every man a day: 30*l*. 12*s*. Item more to hym for condute mony of 14 sowdiers from Portsmouth to York within mylis 240, after 6*d*. for every 12 myle: 7*l*.

'Item payd to Raffe Ellerkar, capitayne of the Mary Jamys of Grenewyche, for the wages of 60 sowdiers for 19 days ending the last day of September, the yere aforesaid, over and above 9 days

nave, da dreto, a fin li Francesi che erano a l' anchora et tanto vicini di terra non si fuzisseno, come tutta volta fesseno. Niente di manco el dito Admirajo, tirando infinito numero di bombarde alla nave del admirajo de Françia, nè li dando agio de sapar le anchore, ma costrengendolo a lassarle corere in mare, et de un colpo de una grossa bombarda rompendoli l' arboro, havendoli morto et feriti più di 300 homeni, se salvò in tra gli scogli. Nel qual tempo, la nave de toneli 400 si messe sotto la caracha di Breste chiamata la Reina, dove erano homeni 400, et essa di portata di tonelli 400, senza pertanto incatenarsi, et bombardandola da 6 grossi cortos raso di l' aqua, in un momento li feze una brescha si grande, che era a li Francesi impossibile poter più sostenir sopra l' aqua la dita caracha, et che non andasse in fondo. Sopravvenendo il restante de le nave d' Ingaltera, la nave Rezente, di tonelli 800, andò abordar ed investir la dicta characha, et in essa entrando nel primo afronto circha 400 Inglesi, la ditta characha si rese. Tamen subitamente si apizò el fuogo ne la polvere, dove ne era barili 300 per servir a la armata francese, et fo el fuoco tanto impetuoso et grande, che si atachò in la Regente, et brusarno tutte due insieme con la Regente, benchè de la Regente si salvasse homeni 180 butandosi in mare, et essendo ajutati et presi da le barche de le nave d' Ingaltera. De li Francesi solo sei, qual furono presoni. La nave di missier Antonio Utrech con homeni 30 se tirò.

Per dui giorni restò tutta l' armata d' Ingaltera a la dita bocha di Breste a ricogliere et sarpar tutte la

rebatid for land wages to them paid after 5*s*. a man a monyth : 10*l*. 5*s*. And for 94 maryners and gunners for ther wagis for one monythe ending the said last day of Sept. at 5*s*. a man a monyth : 23*l*. 10*s*. Item for his wages for one monythe ending the said last day of Sept., at 18*d*. a day : 42*s*. And more for 24 dedsharys for the seid monythe, at 5*s*. every share a monythe: 6*l*.'

(Brewer, i. 4475.)

nave, de 54 francese che lì erano. Il terzo giorno in ditto locho, disceseno in terra e abrusorono di le ditte Francese nave 27, et cinque ne preseno,[1] et asai presoni fino al numero di 800 in diversi luoghi, et havendo facto molti incendii in terra per gli fortunosi tempi regnavano, se ne ritornorono in Ingaltera.

Inglesi perirono in la nave Rezente.

Missier Thomas Kenivet, cavalier et grande scudier d'Ingaltera et capitanio.
Missier Zovane Caro, cavalier.
Item, soldati et marinari, numero 600.[2]

Francesi periti.

El signor di Promagrer, capitanio.
El signor Cabriel de Chacho.
El signor Symon de la Hay.
El signor Cornaugel.
Lo siniscalcho di Morles.
Cavalieri et gentilhomeni 300, dei quali une parte erano andati el dì de Sancto Laurentio sopra la dita characha a far bona ciera con li loro parenti, et menato alcuni di loro so mogliere.
Soldati et marinari, numero 800.
Bombardieri 60.
Balestrieri 400.

(Sanuto, xv. 227.)

[1] Cf. a letter of Lorenzo Pasqualigo, London, 9 Nov. (Sanuto, xv. 462).
[2] 'For the wages of three gunners remaynyng on lyve of them that were brent and afterward servyd in the Soveraigne: 42s. 6d.' (Brewer, i. 4475)—'To John Westall, in reward towards his lechecrafte, late beyng in the Regient: 8l. 10s. 10d.' [5 Dec. 1512] (R. O., Chapter House Book 215, p. 215).

40. *The English fleet in October* 1512.[1]

(1–14 October 1512.)[2]

The 7th mounth's charges, in vitayle, wages, deddeshares and toundage of 18 shippes:

Capteyns, as speres paied afore-hand, 6 men : nil
Men besides : 3,062 men
Dedeshares : 410½
Toundage of 9 shippes[3] : 1,750 tons
Toundage of the Kyng's shippes 9 : 2,060 tons : nil
} 1,413*l*. 6*s*. 6*d*.

41. *Declaration of the account of Admiral Howard*.

(April–Oct. 1512.)

Money as first receyved of John Heron, John Daunce and John Dawtrie, at diverse tymes, as apperith : 14,111*l*. 10*s*. 10*d*.

Conduyte money : 338*l*. 6*s*. 5*d*. ob.

Cootes and jakettes : 497*l*. 16*d*.

---

[1] Cf. *R. O., Chapter House Book* 2, pp. 61–71 : 'Victualling ... for the King's arme apone the see in whafting of the heryng flete apon the coste of Norfolk and Suffolk wher dyvers of the Frenche ships of war laye' (Brewer, i. 3445).

[2] The Sabyn, the Jenett Purwyn and the Margaret of Topsham (215 men in all) were paid for the whole month (1–28 Oct.) 'bycause they were forth at see aborde in the Cambre or the kyng's letter comme.'

[3] Other payments made by John Dawtrey, at Portsmouth— 1° Ragusa's ship, 40 foreign mariners for one month, and one victualler (50 t.) for two months ending the 1st Oct. 2° Charity, Capt. Maurice Berkeley, 280 t., 121 soldiers and 80 mariners or gunners, for 14 days ending the 1 Oct., and the Mary Bird (50 t.) victualler ; 3° Nicholas Neville, also called Nicholas Draper, Capt. Robert Draper, 180 t., 138 men for 24 days ending 7 Sept. ; 4° Gabriel of Topsham, 140 t., 61 men for 3 weeks and one day ending 30 Sept. (Brewer, i. 4475).

The daie's wages after the musters : 38*l.* 18*d*.¹
The first 3 mounthes charges : 5608*l.* 2*s*.²
The secounde 3 mounthes charges : 5821*l.* 18*s*.³
The 7th mounth's charges : 1413*l.* 6*s.* 6*d*.⁴
Empcion of certeyn stuff and necessaries : 20*l*. 7*s*.⁵
Necessarie and foreyn charges and payments : 124*l*. 11*s*.⁶
Money prested to diverse persons : 186*l.* 14*s*.⁷
Somme of the deduccions, charges, and payments aforesaid : 14,903*l*. 9*s.* 9*d.* ob.
And yet remainith in the syr Edward Howard's hands : 208*l.* 12*d*. ob.

42. *Reward to admiral Howard.*⁸

(10 Oct. 1512.)

To sir Edward Howarde, lorde admyrall, for his goode attendaunce and goode service don upon the see : 66*l.* 13*s.* 4*d*.

(*R. O., Chapter House Book* 215, p. 208.)

43. *The charge of Rigault de Berquetot, captain of the nef de Dieppe, against René de Clermont, vice-admiral of France.*

(Blois : 29 Dec. 1512.)

[On St. Laurence's day the French fleet was attacked, near Brest, by the English, and Hervé de Porzmoguer was boarded by the Regent; Rigault de Berquetot, captain of the nef de Dieppe, could not

---

¹ For that article and the two before, cf. Doc. 6.
² Cf. Doc. 7.   ³ Cf. Doc. 21.
⁴ Cf. Doc. 40.
⁵ *R. O., Chapter House Book* 2, p. 73 : 'Great and small hawser and newe cabull' for the Dragon.
⁶ *Ibid.* pp. 75-76.   ⁷ *Ibid.* p. 77.
⁸ Reversion of the office of Admiral of England, 15 Aug. 1512 (Brewer, i. 3373).

help Porzmoguer, as he had to fight seven hours with five English ships; he lost 32 men, and was rescued by some Guérandais. If René de Clermont had not turned back so cowardly, the French would have beaten the English.]

Je, Rigault de Berquetot, chevallier, seigneur dudict lieu, me inscrips ès registres du Roy, sur les peines accoustumées, maintenir et prouver les parolles dictes de par moy, mises en avant, qui sont telles, c'est assavoir pour ce que, tant en présence du Roy nostre sire que par son roy d'armes Clèrevoye, le seigneur de Clermont, visadmiral de France, a fait sommacion à moy, Rigault de Berquetot, chevalier, seigneur dudict lieu, de déclarer mon intencion sur le contenu en sa lettre escripte en papier et signée de son seing, datée le 20ᵉ jour du moys de décembre.

Je ditz que, le jour Sainct Laurans dernier, moy estant au service du Roy en sa nef de Dyepe en l'armée de mer que ledict seigneur avoit près Brest, où estoit ledict visadmiral, l'armée de mer d'Angleterre se trouva celle part et assaillit l'armée dudict seigneur ; que ce voyant, le feu cappitaine Pozmoger, comme vaillant et vertueulx, estant en la nef de la Royne, donna parmy ladicte armée d'Angleterre et fut abordé par la Régente, du party des Anglois.

Et comme vouloye luy donner ayde et secours, cinq navires dedicts Anglois assaillirent ladicte nef de Dyepe où j'estoye, et avec eulx combaty environ sept heures, dont fut tué en mon bort 32 des gens y estans et plusieurs blecez. Et par les Guérandays qui vindrent environ ungne heure de nuyt fuz secouru de sorte que ladicte nef fut saulvée, et à l'eure s'enfouyrent lesdictz navires angloys qui combatirent ladicte nef de Diepe. Pourquoy est à présumer que, si ledict de Clermont se feust tenu avecques nous, eussions eu victoire sur les ennemys, considéré que tous lesdicts Anglois ne seurent prendre ladicte nef de Diepe. Mais par ledict de Clermont ne fut donné secours ausdictes nefz, ains s'enfuyt, comme il est comung et notoire en celles parties.

De quoy j'offre faire prouver, tant par ceulx qui estoient en ladicte armée que sur la coste, et, si mestier est, par les adversaires et ennemys qui y estoient. Dont supplie le Roy à ceste fin ordonner commissaires, et, combien que de raison ne se doit trouver combat[1] de chose qui se peult aultrement prouver, toutesfois, en deffault de preuve, j'entans soutenir mon dire par combat, au bon plaisir dudict seigneur.

Et pour ce j'ay signé ces présentes, le 29ᵉ jour de décembre, l'an 1512.

(autog.) RIGAULT DE BERQUETOT.

(Arch. Nat., V⁵ 1044.)

---

[1] The 'duel judiciaire' had long fallen into disuse, and an inquiry was held, the result of which discredited the vice-admiral (29 May, 1514); all the captains of the fleet of 1512 had joined with Berquetot.

II.

44. *Piero Lando to Venice.*

(12 Oct. 1512.,

[Four ships, each of 800 t., are to be built in England before next Easter. Armour bought abroad. Peace still kept with Scotland.]

La sacra regia Maiestà ha facto far nave 4 de tonelli 800 l' una, le quale li maistri se sono obligati haver presto compite a Pasqua proxima 1513.[1]

Item, sua Maiestà ha comprato da alcuni stranieri armature 12,000, zoè corzete, cellate et brazalleti.[2]

Et Scoci con sua Maiestà ancora non hanno che bona paze.

(Sanuto, xv. 227.)

45. *Indenture between Adenet Legendre, captain of the Petite Louise, and Thomas Bohier, 'général des finances,' for the passage of French ambassadors, Martin Péguineau and the s^r de la Mothe, to Scotland.*

(Rouen : 1 Nov. 1512.)

L'an de grace 1512, le 1er jour de novembre, par devant Adrien de Bessin, et Guillaume Viart, tabellions en la viconté de Rouen, fut présent Adenet

---

[1] John Fleming, Hervy Hayward, master of the Regent, Thomas Spert, master of the Mary Rose, and John Cloge, master of the Peter Pomegranate, received 100s. 'for their costs, with horse-hire for them all, by the space of 7 days, comyng to the kyng's Grace, by his commaundement, from Southampton to Eltham and so from Eltham to Southampton ayene, in the monythe of October . . ., for thier mynde in bestowyng the Kyng's shipps this wynter.'—For the keeping and repairing of the ships from 28 Oct. 1512 to 11 Feb. 1513, cf. p. 79, note 6, pp. 80-83 (notes).

[2] Cf. Doc. 52, *in fine*. Escrevisses=corzete ; servellières=cellate ; garde-bras=brazalleti (cuirasses, helmets and armlets).

Legendre, cappitaine de la nef nommée la petite Louise, a fait marché, en ceste ville de Rouen, avec M^r. messire Thomas Bohier, chevalier, conseiller du Roy nostre sire et général de ses finances, de passer en Escosse en ladite nef Charles de Tocques, seigneur de la Mothe, Martin Péguineau, varlet de chambre ordinaire du Roy nostredit seigneur, et Jehan Piéfort, canonnier ordinaire en l'artillerie dudit seigneur, et leurs serviteurs, lesquelz le Roy nostredit seigneur envoie par devers le roy d'Escosse pour aucuns ses secretz affaires, avec 100 ou 120 poinçons de vin que le Roy nostredit seigneur luy envoie, et iceulx seigneur de la Mothe, Péguineau, Piéfort et leurs serviteurs rapasser, après ce qu'ilz seront dépeschez dudit roy d'Escosse, pour leur retour. Et sera tenu ledit Adenet de les nourrir et fournir de victuailles et de toutes municions qui leur feront besoing jusques à trois mois prochains venans, à commencer du jour qu'ilz partiront du lieu de Honnefleu, si tant ilz mectent à faire le voiaige. Et sera tenu de leur bailler gens de marine et de guerre à ses despens pour les conduire et reconduire pour leur seureté jusques au nombre de 100 hommes, sans ce que lesdits seigneurs de la Mothe, Péguineau et Piéfort soient tenuz de fournir d'aucune chose oultre l'artillerie qui jà a esté livrée audit Legendre. Et a promis et promect ledit Legendre d'estre prest à partir dedans le 12e jour de ce présent mois, et à ce s'est obligé et oblige comme pour les propres affaires du Roy nostredit seigneur, moiennant le pris et somme de 1510 l.t. que mondit seigneur le général lui a fait bailler et délivrer comptant par sire Jehan Lalemant, receveur général de Normandie.[1]

(Bib. Nat., MSS. fr. 20,977, fol. 206.)

---

[1] The ambassadors reached Scotland on 29 Nov. 1512 (*Exchequer Rolls of Scotland*, xiii. p. lxviii.)

46. *Warrant for the passage of the said French ambassadors to Scotland with* 108 *puncheons of wine,* 800 *iron shot, and* 15,000 *lbs. of powder.*

(Blois : 8 Dec. 1512.)

Loys, par la grace de Dieu, roy de France . . .

Nous voulons et mandons que la somme de 3147*l.* 16*s.* 6*d.*, laquelle nostre amé et féal conseiller et receveur général de nos finances en noz païs et duché de Normandie, Jehan Lalement, a payée, baillée et délivrée comptant, . . . c'est assavoir:

la somme de 1510 l.t. à Adenet Legendre, cappitaine de la nef nommée la Petite Loyse, le 1er jour du moys de novembre dernier passé pour le passaige en Escosse de Charles de Tocques, escuier, seigneur de la Mothe, de maistre Martin Péguineau, nostre varlet de chambre ordinaire, et Jehan Piéfort, canonnier ordinaire en nostre artillerie, selon et en ensuivant le marché pour ce fait avecques ledit Adenet par nostre amé et féal conseiller Thomas Bohier, chevalier, général de nosdites finances. Lesquelz de la Mothe, Péguineau et Piéfort nous y avons envoiez par devers nostre très cher et amé cousin et allyé, le roy d'Escosse, pour aucuns noz secretz affaires, avecques 100 poinçons de vin nouveau, tant de Beaune, d'Orléans que d'ailleurs, dont luy faisons présent, ensemble de 800 boulletz de fer et de 15 milliers de pouldre à canon—

la somme de 1552*l.* 15*s.* à plusieurs marchans qui ont vendu et livré lesdits cent poinçons de vin et huit autres poinçons qu'il a convenu avoir pour les aoutillaiges et remplisaiges d'iceulx cent poinçons [1]—

---

[1] Receipt of the 108 puncheons of wine : (Honfleur, 10 novembre, 1512).

'36 poinçons de vin de Beaulne cléret.
51 poinçons de vin cléret d'Orléans.
8 poinçons de vin blanc de Bloys.
12 poinçons de vin blanc du cru de Bagneux, près Paris.'

et la somme de 85*l.* 1*s.* 6*d.* à Jacques le Fèvre pour les fraiz qui ont esté faiz et paiez pour le port et conduicte desdits vins, boulletz et pouldres, depuis nostre ville de Rouen jusques au havre de Honnefleu, où ils ont esté délivrez ausdits de la Mothe et Péguineau.

Vous permectez, souffrez et consentez estre allouée en la despense des comptes dudit Lalemant . . .

Donné à Bloys, le 8ᵉ jour de décembre, l'an de grace 1512, et de nostre règne le 15ᵉ.

 Loys.   Par le Roy.
      Robertet.
 (Bib. Nat., MSS. fr. 20,616, fol. 56.)

47. *Antonio Bavarin, Venetian consul, to Venice.*
      (London : 18 Dec. 1512.)

[Henry VIII. intends to cross the Channel next spring. He will ask for some Venetian galleys because Prégent de Bidoux is in Brittany. Louis XII. has ordered galleys to be built at Rouen.]

Come è stà terminato nel Parlamento e cussi la maiestà dil Re ha terminato a tempo nuovo di passar il mar in persona contra Franza con grandissima possanza. Se dice manderà a Venetia per galie bastarde, perche Prejan,[1] capitano dil re di

---

[1] Jean d'Alencé was directed by Louis XII. to send rowers out of the prisons of Angers to ' Mʳᵉ Prégent, cappitaine des gallées de France ès parties de la mer de Bretaigne' (22 Dec. 1512 : C. Port, *Inventaire des archives d'Angers*, p. 359). The town council of Angers sold also ordnance for the galleys.—Cf. *Arch. Loire Inférieure*, reg. xxi. of Chancery, fol. 26 (Vannes, 22 Jan. 1513): 'Ayons faict descendre et venir à la coste de cestuy nostre pays et duché de Bretaigne plusieurs navires et gallères, lesquelles gallères ne sont pourveues et garnyes de gens, quelque soit, en tel nombre qu'il est requis.'

Franza, è venuto in Bertagna za più zorni con 6 galie, do bastarde et 4 sotil, et ha passato per Spagna, Galizia e Biscaja.

Et a Roano il Roy ha fato venir marangoni per far galie.

(Sanuto, xv. 533.)

48. *Lorenzo Pasqualigo to his brothers.*

(London: 18 Dec. 1512.)

[A ship of 2,000 t., the largest ever seen, is to be built; she will have 2,000 men and 200 guns. All English ships above 150 t. are hired. Twelve men-of-war are cruising in the Channel.]

Sapiate che il Re fa far una nave over characha di botte[1] 4,000, con tre coverte. El nome è la Rezente,[2] come nomeva l' altra che si brusò con quella di Franza: la qual averà homeni 2,000 et 200 boche da fuogo, che sarà la mazor nave che fosse mai in mar e la più forte. Le nave Englexe tutte sono a suo soldo da botte 300 in su, e parte, ch' è 12, sono intro li Canali in armada a guarda de li ditti, e parte si conza e mete in hordine; sichè non sperate di nave Inglexe. (Sanuto, xv. 530.)

49. *Th. Spinelly to Henry VIII.*

(Malines: 26 January [1513].)

[The towns of Normandy fortified and victualled. The largest ships are at Brest; only 10 or 12 of 120 tons. Two Scottish ships brought fish. 150 ships with 25,000 men will leave Brest. Two barks of Dieppe sent on the coast of England.]

---

[1] The Italian *botta*=½ ton.
[2] The report was false, and the ship was called Henry Grace-Dieu (M. Oppenheim, *op. cit.* pp. 372-381). The account of her building begins on 3 Oct. 1512 (*R. O., Chapter House Book* 5).

Sire, il est retourné de Normandie ung petit compaignon que y avois envoyé. Lequel m'a rapporté que les François font réparer et fortiffier toutes leurs villes dudit quartier, assavoir principallement Amflour, Arflour,[1] Cain, Rouain, et les ont pourveues d'artillerie [2] et certain nombre de mortespayes [3] pour le présent ; item, ordonné que tous les vivres du plat pays soient mis ès bonnes villes ; item faict aucuns cappitaines ausquelz est assigné les lieux et places, et en l'espace de 3 jours ilz se sont obligez entrer en garnison avec certain nombre de gens du pays.

Sire, ledit compaignon venu de Normandie a rapporté encores que en tous les havres dudit quartier où il a esté n'avoit veu grande provision de navires pour aller en la guerre, qu'il luy sembloit n'estre de grand extime, attendu que tous les grosses sont à Brest. Toutesfoiz il dit avoir oy que, tant de Hamflour, Arflour et Dieppe, en doit sortir 10 ou 12, et que les plus grandes soient de 120 tonneaulx, et yront audit Brest eulx joindre avec les autres.

Item, qu'il y avoit deux navires d'Ecoche qui avoient porté du poisson.

Item qu'il a entendu que de Brest sortira 150 navires avec 25000 hommes le plus tost quilz pourront.

Item que ceulx de Dieppe avoient ordonné deux

---

[1] Louis XII. granted 1000 frs. and 1000 beech-trees (hêtres) 'pour faire plusieurs tranchées et jetées neuves' at Harfleur (1st May, 1513).

[2] Warrant, dated Blois, 30 Jan. 1513 : 12,000*l*. for 'deux grosses bendes d'artillerie, façons de pouldres, boulletz, et autres municions ... que avons puis naguère ordonnées estre faictes en nostre bonne ville et cité de Rouen' (Bib. Nat., MSS. fr. 25,719, n° 186). Another warrant, dated Blois, 18 March : 3983*l*. partly 'pour armer noz navires estans en la coste de Normandie, dont a la charge le s^r du Chillou' (*Ibid*. n° 193).

[3] Mortespayes (dead-pays) : soldiers in garrison in the towns, with 5 francs a month (small pay) instead of 7½ (large pay) given to the soldiers (archers) on active service.

barques pour aller sur la coste de vostre royaulme et prendre les petits bateaux et prisonniers pour sçavoir nouvelles des préparacions et apprests qui se font de vostre cousté.

(Brit. Mus., MSS. Galba B iii, fol. 116 v°.)

50. *Return of the French ambassadors from Scotland.*

(Jan.—Feb. 1513.)

[Martin Péguineau reaches Brest on 15th January [1] in the Rochelaise, Capt. Philippe Roussel, and the Sr de la Mothe leaves Scotland on 14th Feb.[2] for Honfleur, in the Petite Louise.]

Jean de Cantepye, dit Mercerot, de la parroisse de St. Léonart de Honfleur, pilote de la nef nommée la Petite Louise . . ., dit que, au temps qu'il eust premier congnoissance à Rouxel, iceluy Rouxel estoit au pays d'Escosse en la ville de Lidebourg,[3] où ledit Rouxel vendoit des vins . . . Lors y avoit audit pays d'Escosse des ambassadeurs de France qui cerchoient passage pour eulx s'en retourner en France, et entre aultres y estoient maistre Martin Péguineau et le s^r de la Mothe . . . Ledit maistre Martin, que l'on disoit estre chamberlain du Roy, vouloit passer la mer, et ne pouvoit trouver aucun pour le passer, pour la crainte des Anglois qui estoient sur la mer à grosse puissance, et fut choisi et esleu ledit Rouxel pour passer ledit maistre Martin, et vit ce tesmoing le roy d'Escosse en parler audit Rouxel pour faire ledit passage. Lequel en print la charge, et vit ledit maistre Martin partir de ladite ville pour monter sur la mer . . . Et depuis ce tesmoing a ouy dire et confesser audit maistre

---

[1] *R. O., Chapter House Book* 83, p. 48.
[2] *Exchequer Rolls of Scotland*, xiii. p. lxviii.   [3] Edinburgh.

Martin à Honfleur, lequel se louoit du service dudit Rouxel . . . Il qui parle en cedit temps estoit pillote de la Petite Louyse, et en icelle avoit conduit et mené le s^r de la Mote audit royaulme d'Escosse. . . . Et depuis reconduysit et mena ledit s^r de la Mote audit Honfleur.

(*R. O., Chapter House Book* 83, p. 36.)

51. *News of the French court sent by Spinelly to Henry VIII.*

(Blois: 10-25 Feb. 1513.)

[Louis XII. sent to Scotland six ships laden with wine, and James IV. assured him that he would invade England and help him with a fleet. Prégent de Bidoux at Brest; preparations in Normandy. Ordnance at Rouen.]

Le roy de France a envoyé au roy d'Ecosse 6 navires chargés de vin,[1] et a envoyé ledit roy d'Ecosse ung gentilhomme vers le Roy par lequel il luy a mandé qu'il ne se doubte en rien du roy d'Angleterre, car se il passe la mer, il entrera en si grant puissance en Angleterre et leur baillera tant d'affaire que ilz seront tout ayse de retorner, et doibt ledit roy d'Ecosse envoyer au Roy les navires que il avoit fait apprester pour faire son voyage.

D'autre part Préjan, chevalier de Rodes, est à Bret en Bretaigne,[2] auquel lieu il fait radouber toutes les navires de France, et a esté mandé sur paine de confiscation de corps et de biens de non partir nulz navires de leurs havres, et assemble l'on tous les

---

[1] John Barton and Unicorn King at arms reached Scotland from France on 20 March with corn, cannon balls, and powder (Brewer, i. 3814, 3838).

[2] Eight ships are equipped for the King in Brittany, 18 Feb. 1513 (*Arch. Loire Inférieure*, reg. xxi. of Chancery, fol. 41), besides the three of Queen Anne.

navires à Dieppe et à Honefleur, et y a tant grant appareil de gens que c'est merveilles, mais pour aller où on ne scet.

Le Roy a fait mener de Bloix tout plain de grosse artillerie à Rouan.[1]

(Brewer, i. 3752.)

52. *Thomas Bohier, 'général des finances' of Normandy, to Louis de Brézé, high seneschal.*

(Blois: 19 Feb. [1513].)

[Brézé and du Chillou are preparing the fleet. Ordnance and armour.]

Mgr., je me recommande tousjours humblement à vostre bonne grace.

Mgr., j'ay receu les lettres qu'il vous a pleu m'escripre des 12 et 15ᵉ de ce moys et présenté au Roy celles que luy escripvez et ce que luy avez envoyé. De quoy il a esté bien content et très aize de ce que vous et M. du Chillou[2] dilligentez le fait de la marine, car il désire très fort que son armée puisse partir au temps que M. du Chillou luy a escript, et pour ceste cause il a ordonné des gens d'armes qui voisent en son armée de mer, ainsi que pourrez veoir par ses lettres qu'il m'a chargé vous envoier. Mgr., comme vous avez peu sçavoir, le Roy a baillé la charge de la nef de Dieppe[3] à celluy qui fut cappitaine de la nef de Bordeaux, et au regard de la nef d'Orléans il a acordé à M. de la Londe[4] de y envoier Lespargne, s'il n'y peult aller.

Et touchant le contenu en vosdites lettres, prians

---

[1] 27 Feb. 1513: 'To Mr. Aumener, for a man that brought tithings out of France, 10s.'

[2] Guyon le Roy, sʳ du Chillou, appointed Admiral (Blois, 25 Jan. 1513: Brewer, i. 3830).

[3] Cristofle de Chanoy, Captain of the nef de Dieppe since 20 Feb. 1513.

[4] Commissioner for the victualling of the fleet (p. 93, note 1).

bailler des harnoys qui sont au chasteau de Rouen jusques à quelque nombre pour armer partie des compagnons qui seront dedans les gros navires, le Roy l'a acordé à M. du Chillou devant qu'il partist, et veult expressément qu'il ait 500 escrevisses et autant de servellières et de garde-bras, et qu'on pregne seureté des cappitaines à qui ilz seront délivrez pour les rendre, le voiaige fait. . . .

Mgr., je prie Dieu vous donner très bonne et longue vie.

Escript à Bloys, le 19ᵉ jour de février.

Vostre humble serviteur,
Thomas Bohier.

[Endorsed.] A Mgr. le conte de Maulevrier, lieutenant général du Roy et grant séneschal de Normandie.

(Bib. Nat., MSS. fr. 3081, fol. 95.)

53. *List of ships appointed to the sea.*[1]

(February or March 1513.)

Ships	Captains	Masters
Imperyall [Gret] carrik[2]	Lord Feres . . [Edward Howard, Robert Morton]	J. Toborowgh
Trynyte [Souverain] .	Courtney, Cornwall .	J. Clerc
Gabryell Royall[3] [carrik of Gene or of Savona][4]	W. Trevenyan . .	J. Rutt
Katereyn Fortaleza [lesse carek][5]	Flemmyng [Burdet] .	Freman
Mare Rose . . .	Edw. Howard . .	Th. Spert
Petur	Weston Brown . .	J. Clog

[1] Additions (*) and corrections ([ ]) in the King's own hand.
[2] Henry Grace Dieu.
[3] Bought from Fernando de la Sala for 6,000 ducats (1,350*l.* sterling), 13 March 1513 (*R. O., Chapter House Book* 215, p. 236); built in 1509 (Ellis, 2nd Series, i. 218).
[4] Carrack of Gene or of Savona: Maria de Loreto: cf. p. 86, note 3.
[5] 'To Domyngo Alos for a caryke bought of hym by the Kyng for 4,600 ducats at 4*s.* 8*d.* the pece: 1035*l.*,' 1st Nov. 1512 (*R. O., Chapter House Book* 215, p. 211). Cf. Doc. 80.

LIST OF SHIPS APPOINTED TO SEA—*continued.*

Ships	Captains	Masters
John Hopton[1]	Th. Wyndham .	—
Nicholas Reede[2]	W. Pirton	—
Mare Georg .	Barclay [Sidney, Shurborne] .	Spodell
Mare James .	Eldorkar .	—
Crist[3]	Candisshe	Mychell
Great Bark	Sydney, Shurborne [Th. Lucy]	Browne
Mare and John	John Hopton [Barkeley]	Edm. Cony
Lesse Bark[4]	Stephen Bull	Spert
Nycolas of Hampton [Trenyte of Bristowe]	Master Arture [A servant of my lord Chamberlain]	—
A scyppe off Brystowe[5] [Anne of Fowey][6]	Poynes .	Fuller
Lezard .	Rygynall .	—
Germyn	Ichengham	—
Sabyne .	Sabyne	—
Jenet	Gornay	Freman
Swalowe [Roose Henry][7]	Keby	Godart
Swepstaak [Kateryn Pomegranat][8]	Cooke	—
Christopher Davy *	Wyseman	—
Mathue Cradok *[9]	A servant of my lord Chamberlain	

[1] Bought from John Hopton, Jan. 1513 (Oppenheim, *op. cit.*, p. 49, note 9).
[2] Bought from W. Gonson and others (*ibid.*, note 10).
[3] *Ibid.*, note 13.
[4] 'To Robert Porte, for costs to be done upon the King's newe barke to be prepared and sent to the see as shortly as it may be: 40s.' (23 May, 1512)—Indenture between W. Bonde and Robert Brigandine (28 July, 1512); cf. Brewer, i. 4475.
[5] The Trinity, belonging to Compton.
[6] 60*l.* 5*s.* 7½*d.* spent by John Hopton for the Anne of Fowey, 28 Oct. 1512—11 Feb. 1513; 26*l.* 16*s.* 8*d.* 21 Feb.—5 March at Ratcliff. She is then called Anne Gallaund.
[7] Rose Henry, or Swallow, rowbarge: 32*l.* 2*s.* 11*d.* 'in bryngyng into Temys from Land's End to Sancte Cateryne, 5–14 Feb. 1513.'
[8] Catherine Pomegranate, or Sweepstake, rowbarge.
[9] Indenture between Matthew Cradok and John Daunce (27

Victuallers

[Walter Champion]—Nicholas Draper.[1]
Barbara of Grenwyche—Henry of Hampton.
Elisabeth of Newcastell—[Cristofer Davy].
Dragon—Lyon—George of Falmouth.
Petour of Fowey—Margret of Topsam.
Baptist of Cales—Thomas of Hull.
Barbara Isham—Baptist of Harwich.

Sum: 24 ships, 8030 tuns, 25 capt., 3390 soldiers, 2740 mariners, 22 masters, 13 victuallers. (Brewer, i. 3591.)

54. *List of ships appointed to sea* (Feb. or March 1513).

The namys of the shippes, capitayns and maisters with the nowmbre, aswell off souldiors as maryners and tonnes, which be appoynted to be in the Kyng's army roiall by the see this yere.[2]

The Henry Imperiall,[3] Portage 1,000
[Lord Ferrers] Sir William Trevenyan,
  of his awne retynewe . 400 ⎫
John Toborow, maister   ⎬ Sum 701[4]
Maryners . . . 300 ⎭
                  Wherof 20 [gunners][5]

The Trynyte,[6] Portage 1,000
[Courteney and Cornewall] Lorde ⎫
  Ferys, capitayns of ther awne 200 ⎪
Of mylord of Deven . . 200 ⎬ Sum 701
John Clerke, maister   ⎪
Maryners . . . . 300 ⎭
                  Wherof 40 [gunners]

Jan. 1513: Brewer, i. 5720):—Rigging, 7-28 Feb.; wages of soldiers and mariners, 1-28 March (*ibid.*, 5721).

[1] Of London: called Nicholas Neville, p. 64, note 3.
[2] The corrections [ ] and number of gunners added by Wolsey.
[3] Henry Grace Dieu.
[4] The master is always counted for one.
[5] For ordnance cf. Brit. Mus., MSS. Stowe 146, *passim*.
[6] 310*l*. 10*s*. 7*d*. spent by John Hopton for the Sovereign, at

The Gabriell Royall,[1] Portage 800

[Sir William Trevenyan] Cortney and Cornewale,
capitayn of his awne	100
The buysshop of Excetor	100
Mylord of Arundell	100
The lord Sturton	50
John Rutte, maister	
Maryners	250

Sum 601

Wherof 20 gunners

The Kateryn Fortileza,[2] Portage 700

Gunston ⎱ capitayns of his awne
Flemyng ⎰ retynewe . . 50
Mylord of Arundell	100
Of the lorde off Ormonde	50
Sir William Scotte	50
Henry Wodale	25
Sir Amys Pollet	25
Freman, maister	
Maryners	250

Sum 551

Wherof 40 gunners

The Mary Rose,[3] Portage 600

Sir Edward Howard, capitayn
  of his awne retynew . . . 200
Thomas Spert, maister
Maryners . . . 200

Sum 401

Wherof 40 gunners

Erith, 25 Nov. 1512—11 Feb. 1513 (*R. O., Chapter House Book* 12).

[1] 88*s.* 6*d.* spent for the Gabryell Royall, at Portsmouth.
[2] 8*l.* 5*s.* 6*d.* spent by John Hopton 'at the fyrste comyng of her into the Tamys byfore Wollewyche,' partly 'for making of stremers that were belonging to the Mary and John.'
[3] 132*l.* 4*s.* 3½*d.* spent by John Hopton, at Blackwall, 28

IN 1512-13

The Petir,[1] Portage 450

Sir Weston Browne, capitayn of
  his awne 150
John Clogge, maister . . .   } Sum 301
Maryners 150
                    Wherof 40 gunners

The Nicholas Reede, Portage 400

Sir William Pirton, capitayn of
  his owne 100
Of mylord of Oxford . . . 150 } Sum 401
Maister, [   ] . . .
Maryners 150
                    Wherof 15 gunners

John Hopton,[2] Portage 400

Sir Thomas Wyndam, capitayn of
  his owne retynew . . . 100
Mylord of Oxford . . . 50 } Sum 301
Maister, [   ] . . .
Maryners 150
                        Gunners 15

The Mary George,[3] Portage 300

Barkley, capitayn of his owne . 100
Of Sir Roger Lewknor . . 25
[Throgmorton] . . . .
Sir John Devennyshe . . . 25 } Sum 251
Maister, Spodell . . . .
Maryners 100
                    Wherof gunners 12

Oct. 1512–11 Feb. 1513: 'unto John Browne, paynter, of London, for flaggs wit St. Georg's crosse at 3*s.* the pece, for 14 of them.'

[1] 125*l.* 4½*d.* spent by John Hopton,'at Blackwall, 28 Oct. 1512–11 Feb. 1513. Cf. Brewer, i. 5751 (Woolwich, 17 Jan.–7 March, 1513).

[2] 106*l.* 8*s.* 5*d.* spent by John Hopton, 28 Oct. 1512–11 Feb. 1513.

[3] 86*l.* 13*s.* 10*d.* spent by John Hopton, 28 Oct. 1512–11 Feb. 1513.

The Mary Jamys,[1] Portage 300

Eldicar, capitayn of his own retynew	100
Of Milis Busshe	25
Of Milis Ascewe	25
Maister, [ ]	
Maryners	100

Sum 251

Wherof 15 gunners

The Criste,[2] Portage 300

Candisshe, capitayn of his owne retynew	150
Maister, Mychell	
Maryners	100

Sum 251

The Grete Bark,[3] Portage 400

Shurborne and Sidney, capitayns of their owne retynew	50
Sir John Cutte	25
Sir Robert Southwell	25
Sir Ric. Lewis	25
Sir William Walgrove	25
Browne, maister	
Maryners	100

Sum 251

Wherof 12 gunners

---

[1] 101*l*. 12*s*. 9*d*. spent by John Hopton, at Ratcliffe, 28 Oct. 1512–11 Feb. 1513.

[2] 123*l*. 2*s*. 8*d*. spent by John Hopton for the Cryste of 'Lynne,' in the Thames, 28 Oct. 1512–11 Feb. 1513.

[3] 109*l*. 6*s*. 2*d*. spent by John Hopton, in the Thames, 2 Nov. 1512–11 Feb. 1513: 'For the payntyng of 100 pavassys,' 16*s*.; 'For lyterage of certain gons, which war had and conveyd from the Henry Cateryn.'

IN 1512–13

The Mary and John,[1] Portage 240

John Hopton, capitayn of his
 owne retynew 100
Edmunde Cony, maister . . } Sum 201
Maryners 100

The Lesse Bark,[2] Portage 240

Sir Stephyn Bull and Thomas
 Cherry, of his own retynew . 25
Sir Robert Throgmorton . . 50 } Sum 201
Sir George Taylboys . . . 25
Sperte, maister . . . .
Maryners 100
 Wherof 12 gunners

The Nicholas of Hampton, Portage 200

Mr. Arthur, capitayn of his own
 retynew 55
Sir William Mewis . . . 25 } Sum 161
Maister, [   ] . . .
Maryners 80
 Wherof gunners 8

A shippe of Bristowe,[3] Portage 160

Anthony Poyntes, capitayn of his
 own retynew 100
Maister, Fuller . . . . } Sum 161
Maryners 60

---

[1] 508*l.* 17*s.* spent by John Hopton for the new building of the Mary and John, 'whan she was bornte, as of the havyng forthe of her ordynance and cuttyng downe of decks and klenche worke' (28 Oct. 1512–16 July, 1513). She was in the Downs on 5 June.

[2] 85*l.* 17*s.* 5½*d.* spent by John Hopton, 28 Oct. 1512–11 Feb. 1513.

[3] The Trinity.

G 2

The Lezarde,[1] Portage 120

Rygynall, capitayn of his owne
   retynew . . . . . 60 ⎫
Maister, [   ] . . . ⎬ Sum 101
Maryners . . . . . 40 ⎭

Wherof 8 gunners

The Germyne, Portage 100

Ichyngham, capitayn of his own
   retynewe . . . . . 10 ⎫
Sir Robert Lovell . . . 10 ⎪
Sir Thomas Lovell . . . 40 ⎬ Sum 101
Maister, [   ] . . . ⎪
Maryners . . . . . 40 ⎭

The Sabyne, Portage 120

Sabyne, capitayn of his own
   retynew . . . . . 60 ⎫
Maister, [   ] . . . ⎬ Sum 101
Maryners . . . . . 40 ⎭

Wherof gunners 6

The Jenet, Portage 70

Gournay, capitayne of sir Edward
   Howard's retynew . . [30] 10 ⎫
Freman, maister . . . ⎬ Sum 61
Maryners . . . . [30] 50 ⎭

The Swalowe, Portage 80

Capitayn Coke of his own re-
   tynew . . . 20 solgers ⎫
[Thomas   ] . . . ⎪
[Sir Robert Clere . . . 20] ⎬ Sum 71
Maister, Godart . . . ⎪
Maryners . . . . . 50 ⎭

Wherof 4 gunners

---

[1] At Woolwich in Feb. 1513.

IN 1512-13

The Swipestake, Portage 80

[Coke, capitayne] Tooley
[Sir Edmund Lucy . . . 20]
[Sir James Hobard . . . 20] } Sum 71
Maister, [ ] . . .
Maryners . . . . [30] 70

The Cristofer Davy, Portage 160

Wiseman, capitayn of his own
  retynew 80
Maister, [ ] . . . } Sum 160
Maryners 80
                    Wherof gunners 7

Mathew Cradoke's, Portage 240

Hymself, capitayn of my lord
  Chamberlayn's retynew . 100
Maister, [ ] . . . } Sum 201
Maryners 100

Sum wherof

Shippes 24
Portage 8460
Capitayns 26
Souldiors 3550
Maisters 24
Maryners 2880

Sum total of the capitayns, souldiors,
  maisters and maryners . . . 6480

Vittelers for the said Army

Shippes	Portage	Maryners	Captain
Nicholas Draper, vittelar to the Trinitie Soverayn	140	40	hymself
The Barbara of Grenewich,[1] vittelar to the [Gabriel Roiall] Kateryn	140	40	Loveday
The Henry of Hampton, vitellar to the [Mary John] Soverayn	140	40	—
Elizabeth of New Castell, vittelar to the Kateryn Forteleza	120	40	[hymself] Loyes
The Dragon, vitelar to the Petur	100	30	Loveday
The Lion, vitellar to the Baptist Hopton	120	40	—
The George of Famouth, vitteler to Nicholas Reede	140	40	—
The Petir of Foway, vitteler to the Grete Barke and Germyn	120	30	Lyonell Lo . . .
The Margaret of Topsam, vittelar to Mary George and Jenett	120	30	Jamys . . . [?]
The Baptist of Calice, vitellar to the Crist and the Lesse Bark	120	40	Clyfford
The Thomas of Hull, vitteler to Mary Jamys and the Lezard	100	30	—
The Barbara Isham, vitteler to Nicholas of Hampton and Swalow	100	30	Isham
The Baptist of Harwich, vitteler to the [Sabyne and Swepestake] Mary Rose	80	30	—
[2]The Jamys of Dertmowth, vitellar to the Carake of Savona[3]	100	30	—
The Mary of Bryxam	120	40	Calthorp
The Mary of Walsyngham	120	—	Yelderton
The Erasymus	140	—	Frogmerton
Mathu Cradockes Bark, vitteller to his own schyp	100	40	—
3 Spanyards { Sanchyo de Garra	300	—	Wallop
Erassimus shype	240	—	Montford
Antony de Montrygo	240	—	Dalabre
The Spanyshe barke with orys	—	—	George [of the Fellet]
The Julyan of Dertmowth	—	—	Robt. Leygtton
Margaret of Bonaventure, vitteler to the Henry Imperial	—	—	—

(Brewer, i. 3977.)

[1] 69*l*. 6*s*. 10*d*. spent by John Hopton, at Greenwich, 28 Oct. 1512–11 Feb. 1513.
[2] From here in Wolsey's hand.
[3] Maria de Loreto: Genoese carrack belonging to Andrew

55. Another list of admiral Edward Howard's ships.

(Feb. or March 1513.)

King's Ships.

—	Tons	—	Men
Trynyte Soveraigne	1,000	lord Ferrers	747
Gabryell	1,000	W. Trevellian	602
Maria de Loreto	800	Courteney and Cornewall	604
Katryn Fortileza	700	Flemyng	500
Mary Rose	600	Edward Howard	402
Petur Pomegarnet	450	Wistan Browne	302
John Hopton	400	Thomas Wyndham	302
Nicholas Rede	400	W. Pyrton	302
Grette Barke	400	Sherburne and Sydney	253
Mary George	300	Barkeley	252
Mary James	300	Eldircar	152
Cryste	300	Thomas Cheyney	152
Lesse Barke	240	Stephen Bull	122
Lezarde	120	Coo	102
Jenett Piryn	70	Gurney	62
Barbara of Grenwich	160	Yeldirton	162
Anne Galant	140	Loveday	132
Henry of Hampton	120	West	75
Swepstake	80	Toley	72
Swalowe	80	Cooke	72
Barke for the Soverayn	80	—	68
Bark for the Mary Rose	80	—	68
Bark for the Katryn Fortileza [1]	80	—	108

Ships hired by the kyng's Grace.

—	Tons	—	Men
A ship of Bristowe	160	Antony Pones	162
Nicholas of Hampton	160	Arthur	162
Cristofer Davy	160	Wyseman	162
Nicholas Draper	160	Draper	162
Elisabeth of Newecastell	120	Lewes [Southern]	132

Scarella, taken by the English at Dartmouth (12 Jan. 1513), and valued at 25,996 ducats (Brewer, i. 3445, 3678, 3836, 3973, 4665; *R. O., Chapter House Book* 215, p. 229; Brit. Mus., MSS. Stowe 146, pp. 36-38, 107).

[1] 'The iij new galeys, whereof one is the Rose, another Henry, and the iiij^{de} the Katerine,' built at Woolwich (Brewer, i. 3831). One of them was lost at the beginning of April 1513 (Doc. 62, *in fine*).

SHIPS HIRED BY THE KYNG'S GRACE—*continued*.

	Tons		Men
Erasmus of London	160	Richard Mercer	142
Mathewe Cradock	240	Mariswell	222
Jermayne	100	John Fitzwilliam	92
Sabyn	120	Sabyn	102
Margaret of Toppisham	140	James Knyvett	104
Baptist of Calis	120	Charles Clifford	102
Mary of Walsingham	120	Barnarde	102
Mary of Bryxham	120	Calthorp	101
Gybb's shippe	120	Gybbis	122
Julyan of Dartmouth	—	George Witewombe	104
James of Dartmouth	120	Goldenshan	107
Margaret Bonaventure	120	Richard Bardysley	102
Cristofer of Dartmouth	120	Vowell	102
Thomas of Hull	—	W. Eldecar	76
Baptyste of Harwiche	70	Harper	62
Leonard Frescobald	300	Alexander	252
Sanchio de Gara	320	Wallop	297
Erasmus Sebastian	250	Fr. Pygott	197
Antony Montrigo	[250]	James de la Bere	201
Sta. Maria de la Kayton	200	John Baker	141
The Greate Newe Spaynyard	—	—	—
The Second Newe Spaynyard	—	—	—

(Brit. Mus., Rot. Reg. 14, B. xiv.)

56. *Victualling of the Loyse and her bark.*

(Honfleur: 6 March, 1513.)

[For three months, 600 soldiers and mariners.]

Je, Jehan Barbelée, maistre de la grand nef Loyse appartenant à Monseigneur l'Admiral, estant du port de 790 tonneaulx ou environ, confesse avoir eu et receu de sire Jehan Lalemant, conseiller du Roy nostre sire, receveur général de ses finances ès païs et duché de Normandie, et par luy commis à tenir le compte et faire les paiemens des fraiz extraordinaires de ses guerres et armée de mer qui se dresse présentement en ceste ville de Honnefleu, par ordonnance du Roy nostredit seigneur, les victuailles cy après déclarées.

Lesquelles me ont esté fournies et mises en

SHIP OF THE ADMIRAL GRAVILLE (LOUISE, GRAND LOUISE, OR LOUISE AMIRALE), ABOUT 1500.

icelle nef par ledit receveur général, commis susdit, pour trois mois entiers prouchains advenir, de la provision, vivre et despense de 600 hommes, tant gens de guerre que mariniers, ordonnez estre embarquez et mis en ladite nef, et pareillement de 20 hommes qui seront mis et embarquez en la barque Taillevant, qui est du port de 40 tonneaulx ou environ, laquelle a esté prinse pour accompagner et faire service à ladite nef admiralle, que pour les advantaiges de victuailles livrez en icelle nef oultre son ordinaire pour aucunement supporter l'extraordinaire de la despense qu'il y conviendra faire pour la récepcion des allans et venans, à cause que M. du Chillou, lieutenant général du Roy nostredit seigneur en la présente armée, va dedens comme chef et principal conducteur d'icelle pour le service du Roy nostredit seigneur.

Et 1° biscuyt : 16209 douzaines.
Pain fraiz : 279 douzaines $\frac{1}{2}$.
Farines : 8 pippes.
Cildres : 330 pippes.
Bières : 156 pippes.
Vin : 31 pippes.
Chair sallée : 47 pippes.
Chair fresche : 6 bœufz.
Moutons : 22.
Lardz : 704 costez.
Beurre : 3870 livres.
Poix : 10 pippes.
Febves : 5 pippes.
Harenc : 62 barilz.
Chandelle : 1445 livres.
Suif : 1820 livres.
Boys : 2480 busches.
Vinaigre : 3 pippes, 1 poinçon.
Verjust : 24 pippes.

Pippes à eaue : 50 pippes.
Barilz à eaue : 50 barilz.
Sel : 3 pippes, 1 poinçon.

Desquelles parties dessus déclairées je me tiens content et bien paié, et en quicte ledit receveur général, commis susdit, et tous autres, et davantaige en promectz tenir bon et loyal compte où et à qui il appartiendra.

En tesmoing de ce, j'ay signé de mon seing manuel ou marc dont j'ay acoustumé user ceste présente, en la présence de sire Pierre Gaultier, contrerolleur ordonné par le Roy nostredit seigneur sur le fait dudit advitaillement, le 6ᵉ jour de mars l'an 1512.[1]

            Et   P. GAULTIER.

(Bib. Nat., MSS. fr. 26,112, n° 1161.)

57. *Report sent by Th. Spinelly to Henry VIII.*

(Malines : 21 March, 1513.)

[29 men-of-war in Normandy : 2 at Eu ; 7 at Dieppe ; 20 at Honfleur. 10 galleys and 32 or 33 ships at Brest ; 14 other ships expected there. Relief expected from Scotland and Denmark. Robert Barton's ship at Harfleur.]

Joes Pierdux se partit pour le second voyage de la ville de la Vere le 1ᵉʳ jour de mars 1512/3, et tira vers Bretagne par les costes de la mer jusques à Brest —Et alla par Abbeville en Poitiers [Ponthieu] où il trova beaucop de gens de guerre—Item de là alloit il à Heu, en Normandie, petite ville près de la mer, où il trouva deux navires de guerre chacun du port de 300 tonneaulx ou environ, et une autre petite navire de 80 tonneaulx, l'une desdites grandes navires appartenant à M. de Mailly, et l'autre à M. d'Escrip-

---

[1] The year began at Easter.

ture, la 3ᵉ à la ville de Heu—Item de là alloit il à Diepe, où il trouva 7 navires de guerre qui se mettoient en mer le 8ᵉ jour de mars. La plus grande desdites 7 navires estoit du port de 350 t^x ou environ, et les autres de 250, 200, 180, 120, et une de 80 t^x, tous bien esquipez à la guerre—Item de là à Honfleur, auquel lieu il trouva 20 navires de guerre tous prestz pour eulx bouter en mer et aller à Brest, et n'attendoient que le vent. Entre lesquelles il y avoit deux grandes navires, l'une du port d'environ de 600 t^x, et l'autre de 400 t^x. Il vit aussi audit lieu la barcque de M. l'Amiral de Bourgogne chargée de vin, deux autres busses de la Vere chargiés de bois et de vinaigre, et bien 20 autres navires de par deçà, tant de Flandres, de Brabant, Hollande que de Zélande, lesquelz ne povoient partir jusques à ce que les navires de guerre seroient partiz—Item il digna audit lieu avec le capitaine du blochuys, Guillaume L . . ., en son logis, et aussy avec les deux marronniers desdites [bus]ses, dont l'un s'appelle Cornelius Keise, et l'autre Cornelius Ycop.

Item de là à Tocques, à St Sauveur, à Ville-lez-Boscage, à . . . qui est une ville sur une montagne, à Pontorchon, scitué sur u[ng br]as de mer, là où l'on ne peult à présent entrer que par une porte. Duquel lieu estoient partiz, trois jours avant qu'il y vint, 4 navires de guerre bien esquippez, l'une de 200 t^x, et les autres 3 plus petites.

Item de là adevant une grant ville[1] scituée sur la mer, où il ne trouva nulles navires de guerre, mais l'on disoit qu'il y en avoit 2 qui estoient en mer—Item de là à Susières, scitué sur ung bras de mer, là où il ne trouva nulles navires.

Item de là à Brest en Bretaigne, où il trouva 10 galées,[2] 4 brigantines, et disoit on qu'il y avoit

---

[1] Probably St. Malo.
[2] Fray Bernardin's galleys (p. 150).

2 ou 3 galées et . . . brigantines[1] avec 3 ou 4 des autres navires de guerre allés en mer serchier aventure. L'une desdites 10 galées estoit toute neuve, et a esté faicte audit lieu de Brest, et si faisoit on encores une autre neuve galée, laquelle estoit fort avancée—Item audit lieu de Brest n'y avoit pour lors que 32 ou 33 navires de guerre, entre lesquelz y avoit 2 grandes navires,[2] l'une de la Rochelle, du port d'environ 500 t^x, et l'autre grande navire estoit du port d'environ 600 t^x, et les autres de 300, 250, 200, et plus et moins. Lesquelles navires estoient du costé de Oost du chasteau, et les galées et brigantines du costé de Zuyt, tous en ordonnance.

Il dit aussy que une quantité de navires qu'il vit à la 1ère fois[3] à Brest estoient venuz à Honfleur et à Dieppe, entre lesquelles aucunes navires chargées de vin, que l'on disoit par delà estre à Madame de Savoye : ne scet s'il est vray—L'on disoit aussy audit lieu de Brest qu'ilz attendoient encores 14 navires de Bretagne, dont le moindre seroit du port de 400 t^x. Ilz attendoient aussy 5 karakes de Rhodes et 3 galées.

Ilz ont aussy grant fiance et espoir que les Escossoys et ceulx de Denemercque les assisteroient par bon nombre de navires, entre lesquelles y auroit 2 bien grandes navires. Néantmoins dit qu'il ne peult bonnement tout croire ce que [disent] ceulx de par delà, car il luy semble qu'ilz se vantent trop, pourquoy ne scet qu'il doit dire. L'on dit par delà pour vray qu'il y aura en tout 300 navires de guerre, avec les aventuriers, qui n'ont gaiges ne soulde du Roy. Item l'on dit aussy par delà qu'il y aura plus de navires de guerre sans gaiges que à gaiges.

Item, à son retour, trouva que ceulx de St Malo

[1] Prégent de Bidoux had left Brest on 13th March (Doc. 59).
[2] Queen Anne's ships.
[3] Pierducx's first report has not been found.

avoient prins une buysse de la Vere, appartenant à Ghilain Sagere, chargé de vin, desquelz vins ilz avoient mis à terre environ la moitié, et falut qu'il vendit l'autre moitié à leur plaisir—Item de là vint à Herfleur, où il trouva Robert Berton, et parla à luy. Lequel a fait faire une belle navire du port de 300 t^x,[1] que l'on a carpenté audit lieu, et seroit prest pour bouter en mer à Pasques dernier passé. Lequel Robert se vantoit de faire beaucoup de choses, comme les autres font. Il fut aussy arresté audit lieu, mais par la congnoissance qu'il avoit audit Robert fut eslargy.

Item de là vint il à Diepe, et trouva sur le chemin plusieurs navires de guerre qui gardoient les frontières—Item audit lieu de Diepe fut il prins et mis au chasteau, où luy fist on fère serment de dire la raison pourquoy il estoit venu. Les aucuns luy mirent sus qu'il estoit une espie, les autres disoient qu'il estoit Englès, et se n'eust esté qu'il eust trouvé audit lieu Jehan Baillart, capitaine d'une barque appartenant au roy de France, auquel Jehan il avoit congnoissance, il ne fut point esté à sa voulonté.

Item il trouva aussy audit lieu une navire d'An-

---

[1] The Lion, victualled at Harfleur, on 21 May, 1513, and sent to Scotland: 'C'est la déclaracion des achaptz, priz et marchez des victuailles nécessaires de la provision de 300 hommes, tant officiers que mariniers, pour ung mois entier prouchain advenir, lesquelz le Roy nostre sire a ordonnez estre mis et embarquez en la nef nommée le Lyon, estant de présent au havre de Harfleu, du port de 300 tonneaulx, appartenant à Robert Abreton, gentilhomme escossoys, cappitaine d'icelle nef, que le Roy nostredit seigneur a ordonnée estre présentement advitaillée pour le servir à ung voiage où il envoye ledit Abreton de ce royaume en celuy d'Escosse devers le Roy dudit pays touchant aucuns ses affaires. Lesquelz priz et marchez ont esté par nous, Loys de Bigars, chevalier, sieur de la Londe, commissaire sur ce député, faitz en la présence de Pierre Gautier, contrerolleur ordonné sur le fait dudit advitaillement, avec les personnes et ainsi qu'il est cy après declairé. . . . [Total] 823l. 7s. 5d.'

vers, dont le maistre s'appelle Wonter, laquelle estoit chargée de vins, et fut prinse par une navire de guerre de Diepe, disant que la moitié des vins appartenoit aux Englès, et soubz umbre de ce soubstenoient que tous les vins estoient confisquez et de bonne prinse, mais il n'estoit point vray—Il vit aussy audit lieu 9 ou 10 navires aventuriers qui se apprestoient pour aller en mer.

Item de là vint au lieu de Heu et ainsy par Abbeville envers l'ostel. Il vit à Abbeville arrester 4 chariotz chargez de vins appartenant à ung marchant d'Arras, lesquelz furent deschargez et mis en ung sellier et tenuz pour bonne prinse, et semblablement les chariotz et chevaulx, comme le commun peuple disoit.

Et de là est il venu à l'ostel par Auxy, par Mont St Eloy, Lille, etc.

(Brit. Mus., MSS. Calig. D. vi, fol. 88.)

58. *Sir Edward Howard to Henry VIII.*

(In the Downs: 22 March [1513].)

[The fleet leaves the Thames on 19 March; review of the ships. Lack of victual.]

Pleasith Your Graas to understand that the Saterday[1] in the mornyng, after Your Graas departyd from your fleet, we w[ent] downe to have goon into the Deps, but, or we cam at the danger off the entryng into the Depps callyd Gyrdelar Hed, the wynd feeryd owt off the W.N.W. into the E.N.E., wherfor we fain to goo to an ancre for that day. And the same mornyng that I cam toward the Depps, I commanded [some] of the small shipps as wold goo the next way to the Downes, to

[1] Thomas Wyndham is appointed treasurer of the fleet on 15 March.

get them over the landes end, and [there] went that way both the new barkes,[1] the Lesard, the Swalow[2] and an 8 moor off the smal shippes.[3] The residew kept with us thorow the Depps.

And, Sir, al Palm Sonday we stiryd not, for the wynd was . . . heer with us at E. and by S., whiche was the rygth curse that we shuld draw to . . . .

On Monday the wynd cam W.S.W., which was very good for us, and [I assure you] we slept it not, for at the begynyng off the flood we wer all under sayle.

And . . . first settyng off sayle . . . slakyng, when the Kateryn Fortaleza saylyd very weel and . . . Al suche shippes as maad sayl even togydder with her onys over a quarter off a . . . 3 myl saylyng your good shipp,[4] the flower, I trow, off al ships that ever saylyd, rekenyng . . . every shipp, and cam within 3 speer length off the Kateryn, and spak to John Fle[myng], Peter Seman, and to Freman, master, to beer record that the Mary Roose dyd feche her at the tay . . . best way, and the Mary's worst way. And so, Sir, within a myle saylyng left her an flyt . . . at the sterne, and she al the other, savyng a 5 or 6 smal shipps whiche cut . . . the forland the next wey. And, Sir, then our curs chanched and went hard uppon a bowlyn . . . the Forland, when the Mary Roose, your noble shipp, fet the Mary George, the Kateryn Prowe, a bark that had lord Ferys hyryd, the Leonard off Dartmowth, and some off them wer a long myl afor me, or ever I cam to the Forland. The next ship that was to me, but the Sovereyn, was

[1] Greater and Lesser Bark.
[2] The Sweepstake left the Thames only on 22 March (Brewer, i. 4376).
[3] One of them, the Jenett, is at Sandwich on 24 March (*ibid.*).
[4] The Mary Rose

3 myl behynd; but the Sovereyn past not half a myle behynd me. Sir, she is the noblest shipp off sayle [and] grett shipp at this hour that I trow be in Cristendom. A shipp of 100 tone wyl not be soner at her . . . abowt then she. When I cam to an ancre, I called for pen and ynk to mark what shippes [cam] to me, for thei cam al by me to an ancre. The first next the Mary Roose was the So[vereyn, then the] Nycholas, then the Leonard off Dartmowth, then the Mary George, then the Henry off Hampton, then the Anne, then the Nycholas Montrygo, callid the Sancheo de Garra, then the Kateryn, then the Mary J[ames]—Sir, one after another. Ther was a fowle tayle betwen the Mary Roose, and the aftermast was the Marya de Loretta. And the Crist was one off the wurst that day; she may bee . . . sayl, no mor may the Kateryn; I trust we shal remedy her wel inowgh that she shal felow with the best; Sir, she is overladen with ordenauns, besyd her hevy toppes, which ar byg inough for a shipp of 8 or 900.

Sir, we had not ben at an ancre at the Forland but the wynd [turned] upp at the Norther burd so strynably that we cowd ryd no lenger ther withowt gret danger, [and] we weyd to get us into the Downes thorowgh the Gowles. And when we wer in the mydds, betwen the Brask and the Godwyn, the wynd ferd owt agayn to the W.S.W., when we wer feyn to mak with your great shippes 3 or 4 tornys, and God knoweth . . . row Chanel at low water. As we took it, the Sovereyn and the Mary stayd . . . a quarter off a mile off the Goodwyn Sands, and the Mary de Loretta offerd her . . . wold non off it, and was fayne to goo abowt with a for wind bak . . . wher yet she lyth . . . I feched the Downes with many tornys, and thankyd be God I . . . Downes at an ancre in faste.

And I pray God that he send our vital sh[ortly] . . ., for in Cristendom owt of one realme was never seen such a flete as [this. I assure you that] with our barketts com to us, that the first fair wynd that cometh, we mygth be doyng [servys, for you] saw never poor men so in corraag to be doyng as your men bee.

I besech Your Gras not [to be] myscontent that I mak so long a matter in writyng to yow and off no mater off substance, but that ye commanded me to send Your Gras word how every shipp dyd sail, and this same was the best tryall that cowd be, for we went both slakyng and by a bowlyn, and a cool a cors and a bonet, in such wyse that few shippes lakkyd no water in over the lee wales.

Sir, the shipps off Bristow[1] be her with me, I assur Your Gras, gorgeas shipps for ther burdon, one that Anthony Poyngs is in uppon a 180, and another of 160, and another of 140, I had not spoken [of] when I wrot this letter. I understand they lak vital. I have writton to Master Amener for itt and for theyr maryners, Your Gras must command Master Amner to mak a warrant to ble . . . to delyver to Hopton 200 hernes for them, which shall send it down in the vytall[ers].

[I have] no mor news to writ to Your Gras, as att this tyme, but that the next fair wedder . . . lye heer in the Downes, I wyl send furth your two new barkes, the Lysard, [the 2 row] barges, the Baptyst off Herwyche, to play up and down betwen Dover and Caleys . . . purchas will fal in ther handes that we mygth have some news therby owt off [France].

Sir, for Gode's sak, hast your Consell to send us

---

[1] The Trinity of Bristol, the Cristopher Davy, and the Matthew Cradock.

down our vitall, for, iff we shall lye long, the comon voys wyl roon that we lye and kep in the Downes, and doo no good but spend money and vitall, and so the noys wyl ron to our shames, thow Your Gras know well that we can no otherwys do withowt we shuld leve our vitall and felows behynd us. I remit al thys to the order off your moost noble Gras, whom I pray God preserve from al adversite, and send yow as much victory off your enemys as ever had eny off your noble ancetry.

Written in the Mary Roose[1] by your most bownden subject and your poor Admerall

EDWARD HOWARD.

[Endorsed.] To the kynge's noble Grace, from the Admerall.

(Ellis, 2nd series, i. 213.)

59. *Pierre de Rohan to Louis XII.*

(Brest : 26 March, 1513.)

[Fitting out of 3 Queen's and 8 King's ships. The fleet of Normandy expected. Prégent de Bidoux left Brest on the 13th.]

Après l'aryvée de l'artillerie et municions de guerre qui cy ont esté envoyées, tant pour les 8 navires qu'il vous a pleu faire équiper en ce pays que pour les nefz de la Royne, on a fait la meilleure diligence que possible a esté de les remonter et distribuer ainsi que a esté avisé plus expédiant et requis. Sire, ilz se sont aujourduy mis à voille pour, le plus tost que estre pourra, aller rencontrer et se joindre avec vostre autre armée de mer de Nor-

---

[1] The Mary Rose is at Woolwich, 18 March, and at Sandwich, 26 March. No mention is made in this letter of the John Baptist (Gravesend, 16 March, Sandwich, 26); nor of the Gabriel Royal, moored at Plymouth (Brewer, i. 4376).

IN 1512—13

mandie¹ pour myeulx ensemble vous faire quelque bon service.

Avant que j'eusse receu les lettres qu'il vous a pleu dernièrement m'escripre, et dès le dimanche 13ᵉ de ce moys, Mʳ l'Amiral de Levant, très bien en point avec ses galères et brigandins, estoit sorty de ceste chambre de Brest en la rade, dont il partit le lendemain après mydy en intencion d'exécuter quelque bonne entreprinse² qu'il avoit pour vostre service. Et d'empuix n'en ay ouy aucunes nouvelles.

(Bib. Nat., MSS. Dupuy 261, fol. 16.)

60. *The French Admiral to the Captain of Guernsey.*

[Saturday 26 March, 1513.]³

[M. le] Cappitaine de Grenezay, j'ay receu vostre lettre par laquelle [me escripvez que] eussiez bien

¹ 40 ships, according to Spinelly (Malines, 22 March).—M. du Chillou left Honfleur with 13 or 14 only, Philippe Roussel being pilot of the Grant Louyse: 'Guillot Baultier, parroissien de St. Martin de Harfleur, ès parties de Normandie, dit que au moys de mars (1513), estant à Honfleu carsonnier d'une nef nommée la Grant Louyse, veit le sʳ du Chillou, qui lors estoit lieutenant du Roy en l'armée de mer. Lequel, pour le bon rapport et savoir qu'il avoit ouy dudit Rouxel, l'envoya quérir jusques à St. Mallo pour estre pillote en ladite Grant Louyse pour d'illecques la conduire à la coste de Bretaigne. Ledit Rouxel alla audit Honfleur, auquel ledit sʳ du Chillou bailla la charge audit Rouxel pour estre pillote en ladite Grant Louyse, et commanda que ung chacun luy eust obéy. Et de fait on faisoit ce que ledit Rouxel disoit et ordonnoit . . . (*R. O., Chapter House Book* 83, p. 82).

² John Wiltshire wrote, from Middelburg (20 March), that 25 ships and 6 galleys were expecting at Brest 16 sail of Normandy for an enterprise against Falmouth (Brewer, i. 3814).

³ A safe-guard was granted to Guernsey by M. du Chillou, the castle excluded, Sunday the 27 March. A similar one was granted to Alderney, on 20 April, 1513 (Bib. Nat., MSS. lat. 17,064, 254).

'Loys, seigneur de Graville, Milley en Gastinois, le Boys Mallesherbes, conseiller et chambellan du Roy nostre sire, et admiral de France, à tous ceulx qui ces présentes lettres verront, salut

H 2

pris prisonnier le gentilhomme que [ay envoyé] à

> Receue avons l'umble supplicacion de vénérable personne Guillaume Fabien, prebstre natif du duché de Normandie, curé de l'église paroissial assise en N. D. de l'isle d'Aunery, pour luy et les habitans de ladite ysle, contenant que ou temps passé, ainsi que guerres et divisions se mouvoient entre le Roy, nostre souverain seigneur, et ses anciens ennemys les Angloys, lesdits habitans estoient tenus et maintenus en bonne paix, transquilité et union de la part du Roy nostredit seigneur et de ses subgectz durant lesdites guerres, parce qu'ilz avoient acoustumé de toute ancienneté d'eulx apastir et composer à noz prédécesseurs les Admiraulx de France, et mesmes en semblable cas le firent à feu nostre prédécesseur, admiral de Bourbon (que Dieu absolve), requérans, actendu que la guerre est de présent ouverte entre le Roy nostredit seigneur et sesdits anciens ennemys, les Angloys, que les voulsissions recepvoir ausdits apastiz et composition, et leur donner bonne et loyalle sauvegarde et sauconduit pour eulx relever des pertes et dommaiges qu'ilz pourront souffrir et qu'ilz ont jà souffertes au moyen de ladite guerre, au grand détryment et spoliacion des biens de ladite ysle d'Aunery.
>
> Pourquoy nous, ce considéré, voullans entretenir les bonnes et anciennes coustumes de noz prédécesseurs Admiraulx de France, et subvenir aux oppressés de tout nostre pouvoir, avons donné et octroyé, et par ces présentes donnons et octroyons bonne et loyalle sauvegarde, sauconduit et seureté audit Fabien, prebstre, curé de ladite ysle d'Aunery, et à tous les manans et habitans d'icelle pour tous les subgectz du Roy nostredit seigneur et de nous jusques au 1er jour de janvier prochain venant, affin que icelluy curé puisse aller et venir audit païs de Normandie, tant à ses terres que avec ses parens pour ses affaires, et mesmes que iceulx habitans puissent venir en cedit païs de Normandie, aporter leurs marchandises et quérir leurs nécessaires, en eulx adrechans, en quelque lieu qu'ilx arriveront audit païs de Normandie, à noz officiers illec estans, pour par eulx leur bailler hostes et personnes qui les conduisent, tant à faire la vente des marchandises qu'ilz aporteront que à acheter leursdits nécessaires, pourveu qu'ilz ne prennent ne achètent victuailles en plus avant que besoing leur sera pour leurdite ysle, et mesmes qu'ilz n'enporteront hors dudit païs de Normandie aucune artillerie, pouldres, municions de guerre ne choze qui puisse tourner à préjudice au Roy nostredit seigneur ne à la choze publique, et pareillement qu'ilz ne feront durant lesdites allées et venues choze prejudiciable au Roy nostredit seigneur et ne porteront nouvelles, lettres ne gens non ayans bon congié devers ledits ennemys, sur paine de confiscation de corps et de biens et d'enfraindre ladite sauvegarde et sauconduit.'

terre.¹ Je vous faiz assavoir que par raison ne [le dev]yez prandre prisonnier, car il avoit la seureté de la terre. Mais le vostre que m'avez envoyé m'est venu menasser dedans ma nef de par vous et me dire que me feriez savoir que m'en allasse hors d'ycy ou bien que m'en feriez repentir. Si je l'ay retenu, faire le povoye, car il est venu sans seureté ne asseurance, et me porter les paroles susdites. Qui est la cause pourquoy je l'ay retenu, et ne pense point, Cappitaine, avoir reproche en cest endroit.

Au regard de demourer ycy 10 jours, je ne sçay combien je y demourray, tant y a que si j'avoye le temps de y povoir autant demourer, je vous promectz ma foy que vous m'auriez si près de vous que vous n'y auriez nul proffict, et congnoistriez que je ne suis point ung bri[beur] et que la bribe de quoy vous parlez ne m'a point ycy amené. Et si je y reviens, j'espère de vous le donner à congnoistre.

Au regard de vostre homme, envoyez deux nobles et vous le raurez.

Fait ce samedi au soir.

De par l'Admyral de la flote des Françoys.

(Brit. Mus., MSS. Calig. E 1, fol. 131.)

61. *Defence works and levy of mariners in Upper Normandy.*

[Extracts of bills of Antoine and Jean de Clercy.]

(March 1513.)

Pour avoir fait besongner, en ensuivant la charge et commission qui luy fut lors baillée par Monseigneur le Grant Séneschal, lieutenant général du Roy nostre seigneur audit païs de Normandie, à la

¹ An indenture had been concluded on 5 Feb. 1513, with Richard Weston for the defence of Guernsey (Brit. Mus. MSS. Stowe 146, p. 39).

repparacion et fortifficacion du port et havre de Veullectes, qui est au pays de Caux, et sur le rivaige de la mer, illec faire faire rampars et fossez pour tenir ledit lieu en seureté, auquel, sans ladite fortifficacion et augmentacion desdits rempars et fossez, facillement les Angloys, lors ennemys de ce royaume, eussent fait descente ;

Pour avoir pareillement audit lieu de Veullectes fait dresser et mectre en estat ung boullevart et pour celluy parfaire avoir eu et entretenu à ses despens par plusieurs jours grant nombre de gens, tant dudit lieu de Veullectes que des villaiges d'illec environ, qui manouvroient et besongnoient oudit affaire, alloient faire venir et charier boys de toutes pars pour y emploier ;

Aussy pour avoir fait, à troys voyages différentz, par l'ordonnance que dessus, l'assemblée de 5 à 600 hommes du plat pays et d'iceulx avoir fait monstrée et reveues, fait mectre leurs noms et seurnoms par escript, et iceulx conduitz et menez à diverses foys audit lieu de Veullectes, pour illec demourer aucun temps, lorsque le bruyt estoit commun que lesdits Angloix y voulloient faire descente pour tousjours icelle descente empescher.

Pour avoir, au moys de mars 1512, fait l'assemblée d'autres 400 hommes mariniers dudit quartier de Caux, et iceulx avoir menez et conduiz en la ville de Honnefleu pour servir le Roy nostredit seigneur en son armée de mer que lors on dreçoit et équippoit audit Honnefleu.

Tant à faire faire plusieurs rampars au droit du chef de Caux,[1] sur et le long des fallaises de la mer, ès lieux les plus dangereux à faire descente de la part des Angloys, que pour faire assembler les abbés,

---

[1] J. Pelle, keeper of the beacon ('garde du fouyer de guerre d'entre le Chef de Caux et Bléville') had 3 sous daily (Arch. Nat., PP. 110, p. 654).

prieurs et groz personnaiges de l'église du bailliage de Caux et illec leur déclarer que le bon plaisir du Roy nostredit seigneur et de sondit lieutenant général estoit qu'ils eussent à faire conduire vivres de leurs maisons et revenuz dedans les fortes places de la lisière dudit pays de Caux pour la provision des vivres des gens de guerre qu'on y avoit mis en garnison pour la deffence et sceureté du pays,— aussi pour avoir fait assembler 500 hommes compaignons adventuriers et les avoir assis, de lordonnance que dessus, èsdites places fortes ès lieux le plus convenables dudit quartier du Chef de Caux, affin que les Angloys n'y feissent descente—

Item pour avoir esté, au moys d'avril darrenier passé, contraindre les habitans des vicontez de Caudebec et Monstiervillier à porter vivres en la ville de Harfleu, en ensuivant ce que le Roy nostredit seigneur et mondit seigneur le grant sénéschal avoient ordonné pour la municion d'icelle ville qui est en frontière.

Item pour avoir aussi esté sur et le long de ladite coste du pays de Caux depuis ledit Harfleu jusques à Fescamp, Dieppe, le Tresport et en savoir s'il estoit point de nouvelles d'avoir veu en mer l'armée desdits Angloys pour en venir faire le rapport à mondit seigneur le lieutenant général, et pour plusieurs autres dilligences par lui faictes durant le bruyt qui a couru d'icelle armée d'Angleterre.

(Bib. Nat., MSS. fr. 26,113, n°s 1306, 1332.)

62. *Sir Edward Howard to Wolsey.*

(Plymouth : 5 April [1513].)

[Bad victualling of the fleet : no food and drink assured beyond 15 days; all the pursers left at London. Bad state of the Katherine Fortaleza.

The French ready to leave Brest. The enterprise against them must be tried within 5 or 6 days.]

Maister Amner, in my hartiest wise I can I recommende me unto you, certifiing to you that I am now, at the writyng of this my lettre, in Plimowthe rode, with all the Kyng's fleet, savyng the shippes that be at Hampton,[1] wich I loke for this nyght, for when I cam open on the Wighth I wolde not goo in, but sent a shippe of Compton's to cause them to comme in all hast, and the wynd has been ever syns as good as was possible.

And as for our Spainards,[2] that should come oute of Thamys, I here no worde of them. Godde sende us good tydyngs of them.

Sir, I thynke our besynes wil be tried withyn 5 or 6 days at the furdest, for an hulke that cam straight from Brest shewith for a certente that ther be redy commyng forward a 100 shippes of warre, besids the galeis, and be prest uppon the first wynde, and sais that they be very well trymmed and will not faill to comme owte and fight with us.

Sir, thies be the gladdest tydyngs to me and all my capytayns and all the residew of the army that ever cam to us, and I trust on God and St. George that we shall have a fair day on them, and I pray Godde that we lynger no longer, for I assure you was never army so falselie vitailled. They that receved ther proportion for 2 monthes flesche can not bring about for 5 weks, for the barells are full of salt, and when the pecis kepith the nowmbre, when they shuld be peny peces, they be scant halfepeny

---

[1] Ten ships, according to Doc. 64; the Peter Pomegranate was probably among them, as she is not quoted in Doc. 58. Also the Sabyn, as W. Sabyn, her captain, delivers to Th. Wyndham, captain of the John Baptist, 1,000*l.* from the customs of Southampton, 2 April (Doc. 65).

[2] C f. Gonson's letter (Doc. 71).

peces, and wher 2 peces shulde make a messe, 3 will do but serve. Also many cam owte of Themys with a monthe's bere, trustyng that the vittelers shulde bringe the rest, and here commyth none. I send you word for a sewrty here is not in this army, one with another, past 15 dais.

Sir, the Kateryn Fortileza hath troubled me beyonde reson, she browght owte of Themys but for 14 dais vitaill, and no vitelar is comme to helpe her, and so have I vitailled her with beere ever sens, and so bryngs my vitallyng bak, for it is no small thyng that 500 men spend daily, and no provision here for her.

I have sende to Plumouth on myne owne hedde to gete somme vitaill if it be possible, I trust ye will allow for hit. I wolde I had never a grote in England that I myght kepe thies west parties till they and I meate.

Sir, ye Mylords of the Kyng's moost honorable Counsell wrote to me of a proportion that shulde be all redy delyverd. Sir, if some be well vitailled, the moste parte be not, and ye know well, if half shulde lakke, hit wer as good in a maner that all lakked. In consideration to kepe th' army together, Sir, for Godd's sake, sende by post all along the coste that they brew bere and make biskets that wee may have some refresshyng tò kepe us togedor uppon this cost, or els we shal be dryven to come agayn into the Downes and let the Frenchemen take ther pleasure, and Godde knowith when we shall gete us up so high Westward again. I had ever, then that we shulde be dryven to that yssew, to be put all the dais of my life in the peynfullest prison that is in Cristendome.

Sir, the Kateryn Fortileza hath so many leakis by reson of Bedell, the carpynter that worked in her at Wolwiche, that we have had moche to do to kepe her above water; he hath bored an 100 agore hoolis in her and left unstopte, that the water cam in as it wer in a seve. Sir, this day I have all the calkers of th' army on heer. I trust by to morow she shall be more stanche.

Sir, wher ye write to me that ye send hois to take our pipes, Sir, thei ar such men that they wolde throw them that ye sent with the vitaill over boarde, and when the pipes had been brought and they goon from us, they throw them over borde and gotte into Flawnderes. Sir, I know no mannys proporcion but myn awne, nor one capitayn knowith what his purser hath receved, for we lafte all our pursers at London to hast furth our vitall, and nother here of our pursaris nor our vitaillis. And well I note that I have geven such ordre in despendyng of our vitaill that ther was never army so straited, not by one drynkyng in a day, which I knew well hath byn a grete sparyng, but for all this we be att yssew that I shewed you befor.

And wheras ye write that it were no reason that the Kyng shulde pay for his awne good, Sir, I am of the same opinion. But, Sir, or ever I had knowlage of any man, the delyverars of vitell had receved dyvers foists of diverse shippes, and geven the stewards 4d. for every ton drawyng. Wich I thought a parelouse example, howbeit one that Atclif sent for the sealyng of certayn commissions for the takyng and preservyng of the foists showed me that maister Atclif had commaunded them to pay every man 4d. for the drawyng of a ton. And, Sir, if that had not byn, I shulde have seen all delyvered withoute any peny takyng; but, Sir, never man complayned to me of any such thyng.

Sir, all the vitaill that shall com to us, let it come to Dartmouth, for ther it may lie redy for us, and sewre inough. Sir, ther ys moche vitall at Sandwich, and they have no vessels to bryng it to us.

Fill some of your Spanyards shippes ther bellies full, 3 or 4 of them will cary much, and spare not to spende vitaill upon us this yere. For, with Godd's grace, the fleete of Fraunce shall never do us hurte after this yere, and if they be so redy as the hulke hath showed us for a certente, I truste to Godde and St George that ye shall shortlie here good tydyngs. And, howsoever the matter gooth, I will make a fray with them, if wynde and wedar will serve, or 10 days to an ende.

Therfor I pray you recommende me to the kyng's noble Grace and show him that he trust no tydyngs till here worde from me, for I shalbe the first that shall know it if I leve, and I shalbe the first that shall sende hym word. Sir, I pray you recommende me also to the qwene's noble Grace, and I know well I nede not to pray her to pray for our good spede, and to all good ladies and gentlewomen, and to my felowes sir Charles and sir Henry Gilforde, and, Sir, speciallie recommende me to mylorde my father, besechyng him of his blessyng. And, Sir, I pray you to knyt up all, with have me moost humbly recommended to the kyng's noble Grace as his most bounden servaunte as knowith Our Lord, who ever more sende hym victory of his enemyes, and you, my speciall frende, your most hart's desire.

Written in the Mary Rose, the 5th day of Aprile, by your to my litill power

EDWARD HOWARD.

Sir, I neede not to write unto you what stormys we hadde, for you know it well inough. Sir, I saw never worse, but, thanked be God, all is well, savyng the loss of one of our galeis. All ill go with her. Sir, I send you in this paquet a lettre to my wife; I pray you delyver it to her.

(Ellis, 3rd series, i. 196.)

63. Roberto Acciajuoli, Florentine Ambassador in France, to Florence.

(Blois : 7 April, 1513.)

[James IV. sends news of the English fleet ready to sail, and he will shortly equip his own ships.]

Et ultra hoc quella maestà [di Scotia] mostra li apparati di Inghilterra essere grandissimi et essere in ordine per partire al primo vento, di che ci era nuova prima, una parte della armata essere di gia fuora et come la franzese, ne dipoi qualche giorno se ne è inteso alchuna cosa. Il prefato re [di Scotia] fa intendere ancora volere ad ogni modo scoprirsi contra Inghilterra et volere mandare la armata sua che ha presta per congiungersi con la franzese.

64. Antonio Bavarin to Venice.

(London : 9 April, 1513.)

[69 ships sailed out of the Thames in Holy Week, 10 or 12 of 300 to 1,000 t., the others of 100 to 250 t., 10 others were in Southampton. Besides, 6 rowbarges, better for landing than galleys. 16,000 soldiers and 32,000 mariners. Captains, pilots, soldiers, and mariners have jackets and coats of white and green.]

La setimana santa parti de qui nave 69, tra le qual n' è da 10 in 12 de 600 fin 2000 bote ; el resto de bote 200 fin 500. Altre 10 nave erano in Antona, che se hano conzonto insieme, che sono in tutto da 80. Hanno etiam 6 legni longi e bassi come gali e vogano remi assai, che tuti questi marineri Viscaini tengono, per questo mare, sarano meglio che galie per andar a la guara. Oltra i marineri per governo dei navilli, che sono al dopio, vi sono da 16,000 combatenti,[1] tuti bonissimi homeni et ben ordinati de victuaria. El simele, la maestà del Re a tutti i capitanei ha donato una cota de damaschin verde e bianco, che è la sua divisa, et a nochieri penexi i parioni de zambeloto ; poi a tutti marineri et soldati de bon pano verde e bianco.

(Sanuto, xvi. 195.)

65. *The English navy.*

(11 April—25 Sept. 1513.)

Here ensuyth a declaracion taken by sir Robert Southwell, knyght, of sir Thomas Wyndham, knyght, tresorer of our soveraigne lord the King's warres, of his army royall sent to the see ayenst his auncyent enemye the French Kyng, by vertue of our said soveriaigne lord the Kyng's lettres myssyves beryng date the 23 day of October the 5th yere of his reigne to the seid sir Robert Southwell in that behalf directed. That is to say : as well of all and singular such sommes of money as the same tresorer hath receyved of sir John Daunce, knyght, and John Dawtrey, customer of Hampton, by several commaundements of our seid soveraigne Lord to them in that behalf geven, as also of all and almaner of payments by hym made, as well by vertue of certeyn instruccions and other warraunts, signed with the hande of our said soveraigne lord the Kyng to the seid tresorer directed, as otherwise by vertue of severall bylls signed with the hand of sir Edward Howard, late Admyrall of England, and lyke bills assigned with the hand of mylord Admyrall that now is [2]—

From the 15 day of Marche, the 4th year of our said soveraigne lord the Kyng, which day the said

---

[1] These figures were entirely false.   [2] Thomas Howard.

sir Thomas Wyndham, knyght, by vertue of our said soverayne Lord's commission to hym in that behalf directed, fyrst occupied and excercised the seid rome and office of tresorer—

Unto the last day of October then next folowyng. Money receyved of John Daunce, by the commaundement of our seid soveraigne lord the Kyng, the 16 of Marche the 4th of his reigne, as apperith by an indenture made betwene the foreseid tresorer and the seid John Daunce upon this declaracion shewed and examyned. 6500*l*.

John Dawtrey, customer of the port of Southampton, the 2 day of Aprile the [4th] year of our seid soveraigne lord, by the hands of William Sabyn
1000*l*.
the 3 day of Juyn then next folowyng, by the hands of the seid John Dautrey 8500*l*.
the last day of July then next aftyr 4000*l*.
the 24 day of August then next folowyng
2000*l*.
and the 1 day of October then next folowyng
1000*l*.
In all, as by 5 severall indentures made betwene the seid John Dawtrey and the seid tresorer upon this accompt examyned it may appere 16500*l*.
[Sum :] 23000*l*.

Wherof allowed to the seid tresorer for payments made by the seid tresorer, as well by vertue of certeyn instruccions and letters to hym delyverd, signed with the hand and signe of our seid soveraigne lord the Kyng, as by severall bills signed with the hand of the late lord Admyrall, and also by bills signed by mylord Admyrall that now is.
That is to sey for:

i. *The Kyng's owne shippes.*

Ffyrst for the wages, dyets and rewards, as well of the late lord Admyrall as of the lord Admyrall that now is, at 10*s*. by the day; the tresorer of the warres, at 3*s*. 4*d*. by the day; 11 capteyns, yche of them, at 18*d*. by the day, ovyr and beside 9 of the Kyng's speres[1] whiche hadde no wages; 2 clerks of the tresorer, ether of them, 8*d*. by the day; 5211 souldiours, maryners and gonners, yche of them at 5*s*. by the moneth; 444 dedeshares, at 5*s*. the share by the moneth; and for the rewards of 21 maisters gonners, yche of them at 5*s*., 69 mates and quarter maisters, yche of them at 2*s*. 6*d*., and 196 other gonners, yche of them at 20*d*. a moneth,—That is to say for a moneth[2] endyng the 8 day of May, anno 5° regni predicti,—beyng in 21 of the Kyng's own shippes, as apperith in a boke of the parcells and also in instruccions signed with our said soveraigne lord the Kyng's hands and by bills signed by mylord Admyrall upon this declaracion examyned:

1487*l*. 11*s*. 10*d*.

Also for lyke dyets, wages and rewards of mylord Admyrall, the tresorer, his 2 clerks, 10 capteyns ovyr and besyde 9 of the King's speres, 5027 souldiours, maryners and gonners, 424 dedeshares ½, and for the rewards of 20 maister gonners, 68 mates and quarter masters, and 192 other gonners, aftyr the rate abovesaid,—for another moneth endyng

---

[1] 'We have now appointed that the wages of our speres attending upon us shall not be any longer payed for a season by the hands of our servant John Heron, tresorer of our chamber, but oonly of oure warre money' (Brit. Mus., MSS. Stowe 146, fol. 57-58, 71).

[2] Beginning the 11th April. The fleet had left Plymouth the 10th (Doc. 66). The account of the navy from 15 March to 10 April has not been found.

the 5 day of June the 5 yere of our seid soveraigne lord,—beyng in 20 of the Kyng's shippes...
          1433*l*. 18*s*. 2*d*.

Also for lyke dyets, wages and rewards of mylord Admyrall, tresorer, his 2 clerks, 12 capteyns ovyr 8 of the speres, 5640 souldiours, maryners, gonners and one boy, 462 dedeshares, rewards to 21 maister gonners, 63 mates and quarter maisters, and for 206 other gonners beyng in 21 of the Kyng's shippes, for another moneth endyng the 3 day of July...   1605*l*. 9*s*. 4*d*.

Also for semblable dyetts, wages and rewards of mylord Admyrall, tresorer, his 2 clerks, 13 capteyns ovyr 7 of the Kyng's speres, 5710 souldiours, maryners, gonners and a boy, 481 dedeshares, $\frac{1}{2}$, and for rewards to 22 maister gonners, 78 mates and quarter masters and 212 other gonners, beyng in 22 of the Kyng's shippes for another moneth endyng the last day of July... 1631*l*. 6*s*. 8*d*.

Also payed for lyke dietts, wages and rewards of mylord Admyrall, the seid tresorer, his 2 clerks, 12 capteyns ovyr 8 of the foreseid speres, 4995 souldiours, maryners, gonners and oone boy, 443 dedeshares $\frac{1}{2}$, and for rewards to 21 maister gonners, 73 mates, and quarter masters and 178 other gonners, beyng in 21 of the Kyng's shippes, for another moneth endyng the 28 day of August...
          1437*l*. 5*s*. 2*d*.

Also for lyke wages and rewards of the seid tresorer, his 2 clerks, 5 capteyns ovyr and beside 5 of the Kyng's speres, 3549 souldiours, maryners and gonners, 183 dedeshares $\frac{1}{2}$, and for rewards to 12 maister gonners, 20 mates and quarter maisters, and 125 other gonners, beyng in 12 of the King's shippes, part for half a moneth, part for a hole moneth endyng the 25 day of September...
           952*l*. 9*s*. 1*d*.

[In all:] 8547*l*. 19*s*. 11*d*.

IN 1512-13

ij. and iij. *Englishe shippes reteyned into the Kyng's warres.*

Also payed for the wages and rewards of 20 capteyns ovyr and beside 2 of the Kyng's speres, 2698 souldiours, maryners and gonners, 374 dedeshares, and for rewards to 22 mates and 66 other gonners, beyng in 22 shippes, hyred and receyved into the Kyng's warres, at lyke wages and rewards as afore is specified, and for tondage of the seid shippes, amountyng to 3040 tonne, aftyr 12*d.* for every tonne by the moneth, that is to sey for the moneth endyng the foreseid 8 day of May the yere aforesaid 975*l.* 15*s.*

For lyke wages and rewards of 21 capteyns ovyr 3 of the foreseid speres, 2868 souldiours, maryners and gonners, 409 dedeshares ½, for rewards to 24 master gonners, 24 mates and 71 other gonners, beyng in 24 englysh shippes, and for the tondage of the seid shippes amontyng to 3280 tonne, aftyr the rate aboveseid, for the foreseid 2de moneth
1042*l.* 12*s.* 6*d.*

For lyke wages and rewards of 24 capteyns ovyr and beside 2 of the foreseid speres, 2990 souldiours, maryners and gonners, 437 dedeshares, and for rewards to 26 maister gonners, 25 mates, and 74 other gonners beyng in 26 shippes reteyned as aboveseid, and for the tondage of the same, amontyng to 3490 tonne, rated as aboveseid, for the 3de moneth afore rehersed 1097*l.* 6*s.* 8*d.*

For lyke wages and rewards of 24 capteyns ovyr 2 of the foreseid speres, 2983 souldiours, maryners and gonners, 437 dedeshares, and for rewards of 26 maister gonners, 25 mates, and 74 other gonners, beyng in 26 shippes, and for the tondage of the same conteynyng 3490 tonne, rated as aforeseid, for the 4^{the} moneth 1095*l.* 11*s.* 4*d.*

I

For lyke wages and rewards of 24 capteyns, ovyr 2 of the seid speres, 3121 souldiours, maryners and gonners, 469 dedeshares ½, and for rewards to 27 maister gonners, 26 mates and 76 other gonners, beyng in 27 englysh shippes, and also for tondage of the seid shippes amountyng to 3740 tonne, rated as aboveseid for the 5th moneth   1144*l*. 2*s*. 11*d*.

And for lyke wages and rewards of 16 capteyns ovyr 2 of the foreseid speres, 2216 souldiours, maryners and gonners, 337 dedeshares ½, and for rewards to 19 maister gonners, 19 mates and 53 other gonners, beyng in 20 shippes, and also for the tondage of the said shippes amontyng to 2720 tonne, rated as aboveseid, for the foreseid 6th moneth   819*l*. 4*d*.

And for the wages of 32 maryners, 12 dedeshares ½, and also for the tondage of the Vynsent of Ffowey amountyng to 60 tonne, for the foreseid 6th moneth aftyr the rate aforeseid   84*l*. 15*s*.

In all: 6259*l*. 3*s*. 5*d*.

Also payed to dyverse capteyns for the wages and rewards of souldiours, maryners and gonners beyng in dyvers english shippes, and for conduytyng of them towards the see, and also for dedeshares, and tondage of the seid shippes, aftyr the foreseid rate, somme of them for a moneth, somme 2 monethes, some for 14 days afore the foreseid 6th moneth, and within the seid tyme of 6 monethes, whuche shuld have been payed by sir John Daunce, knyght, and was not   882*l*. 8*s*. 11*d*., quadrans.

iiij. *Spanysh shippes reteyned in the Kyng's warres.*

Also payed for the wages and rewards of 3 capteyns, yche of them at 18*d*. by the day, ovyr 3 of the Kyng's speres, which toke no wages, 869 souldiours, yche of them at 5*s*. by the moneth, 181 englysh maryners, yche of 5*s*., 23 gonners at 5*s*. the pece, 40 dedeshares at 5*s*. the share, rewards to 2 maister gonners, ether of them at 5*s*., 2 mates, ether of them at 2*s*. 6*d*., and 19 other gonners, yche of them at 20*d*. the moneth, oone maister and oone pilot Spanyerds, ether of them at 30*s*. by the moneth, 121 maryners Spaynyerds, yche of them at 7*s*. 1*d*., 51 grometts, yche of them at 4*s*. 9*d*., 18 pages, yche of them at 2*s*. 5*d*., and 60 dedeshares, every share at 6*s*. by the moneth, and for the tondage of 6 Spaynysh shippes,[1] wherin the seid persons served the Kyng, amontyng to 1650 tonne, at 15*d*. quadrans ½ the tonne, by the moneth, that is to sey for the foreseid fyrst moneth

517*l*. 2*s*. 1*d*.

For lyke wages, dedeshares and tondage of the seid 6 Spaynyerds shippes for the 2de moneth

516*l*. 7*s*. 7*d*. quad.

For lyke wages, rewards, dedeshares and tondage of the seid 6 Spaynysh shippes for the 3de moneth afore reheresed. 512*l*. 12*s*. 7*d*. quad.

For lyke wages, rewards, dedeshares and tondage of the seid 6 Spayneyerds for the 4th moneth afore specified. 504*l*. 17*s*. 7*d*. quad.

For lyke wages, rewards, dedeshares and tondage of the said 6 shippes for the 5th moneth aforeseid. 504*l*. 17*s*. 7*d*. quad.

And for lyke wages, rewards, dedeshares and tondage of 5 of the seid Spaynysh shippes for the 6th moneth afore rehersed. 419*l*. 3*s*. 7*d*. quad.

In all: 2975*l*. 13*d*. quad.

---

[1] Sanchio de Gara, Erasmus Rosamus Sebastian, Antony Montrigo, Sta Maria de la Kayton, Great New Spaniard, Second New Spaniard (Doc. 55 *in fine*).

v. *Englysh shippes reteyned for vitaylers.*

Also payed for the wages of 543 maryners, every of them at 5s. by the month, 188 dedeshares to the seid maryners, every share at 5s. by the moneth, beyng in 42 vitaylyng shippes, wherof the tondage amontyth to 2584 tonne, every tonne rated at 12d. by the moneth, that is to sey for the foreseid fyrst moneth 312l. 4s.

For lyke wages of 585 maryners, 198 dedeshares and for tondage of 46 shippes amountyng to 2757 tonne aftyr the seid rate for the 2de moneth above rehersed 334l. 9s. 6d.

For lyke wages of 510 maryners, 154 dedeshares, and for tondage of 27 shippes, amountyng to 2313 tonne payed aftyr the foreseid rate for the aboveseid 3de moneth 281l. 13s.

For lyke wages of 550 maryners, 46 dedeshares and for the tondage of 30 shippes conteynyng 2473 tonne payed aftyr the same rate for the 4th moneth aboveseid 295l. 6d.

For lyke wages of 399 maryners, 125 dedeshares and for tondage of 21 shippes amontyng to 1733 tonne payed aftyr the same rate for the 5th moneth aboveseid 217l. 13s.

And for lyke wages of 117 maryners, 45 dedeshares and for tondage of 7 shippes, amountyng to 507 tonne aftyr the foreseid rate payed for the 6th moneth above specified 62l. 12s.

In all: 1503l. 12s.

Also payed to the maister of the Nicholas Benlay of London for the wages of 10 maryners, 3 dedeshares and for the tondage of the seid shippe amountyng to 5 tonne, aftyr the foreseid rate payed, and for vaytells for the said maryners, every of them aftyr 2d. by the day, for the seid 6 monethes

48l. 10s.

IN 1512-13 117

vj. *Spaynysh shippes reteyned for vitaylers.*

Also payed for the wages of oone maister and oone pilate, every of them at 30s. by the moneth, 22 maryners, yche of them at 7s. 1d. by the moneth, 7 gromez, yche of them at 4s. 9d. by the moneth, 1 page at 2s. 5d., 10 dedeshares at 6s. the share, and for tondage of oone shippe conteynyng 150 tonne, at 15d. quadrans ½ the tonne for the foreseid 2ᵈ moneth   25*l*. 5s. 3d.

And for lyke wages of 5 maisters, 5 pilats, 139 maryners, 31 grometts, 8 pages, 47 dedeshares and for tondage of 6 shippes amountyng to 820 tonne, aftyr the seid rate payed for the 3ᵈᵉ moneth wages above specified   102*l*. 11s. 10d. quad ½.

In all: 127*l*. 17s. 1d. quad ½.

vij. *Hoyes and Flemysh shippes reteyned for vitaylers.*

Also payed for the hire of 7 hoyes of severall portages reteyned for lyke vitaylers of the seid army in grace by the space of 3 moneths, that is to say for wages, tondage and all other necessaries to them belongyng   227*l*. 12d.

Also payed for the wages, dedeshares and tondage of the James of Andewarpe, of the portage of 130 tonne, at 3s. 8d. the tonne, for all manner charges for 7 wekes within the tyme aboveseid.

40*l*. 4s. 2d.

viij. *Wages of offices of warre.*

Also payed for the wages aswell of William Symonds, clerk comptroller of the seid navy, as of John Husy, clerk of the ordynance in the seid army, for 140 daye at 12d. by the day   17*l*. 10s.

ix. *Wages of pylotts.*

Also payed to Petyr Seman,[1] pylot of the Kateryn Forteleza, Martyn Sirrea, pilot of the Mary de Loreto, John Daryllio,[2] pilot of the Gabriell Royall, and to other pilots[3] of the Kyng's shippes, for their wages aftyr 36s. by the moneth, somme of them for 5 monethes, and somme for 7 monethes, somme more and somme lesse 50*l.* 19s. 4*d.*

x. *Wages of surgions.*

Also payed for the wages, aswell of 4 maister surgions, as of dyverse other pety surgions under the nomber of 26, awatyng of the seid navy, somme of them by 4 monethes, somme by 2 monethes, somme more and somme lesse, the seid maister surgions takyng by the moneth 13s. 4*d.*, and every other surgion 10s. by the moneth, aftyr the rate approrcionned in the Kyng's lettre missive to the seid thesorer directed. 88*l.* 6s. 8*d.*

xj. *Wages of trompetts.*

Also payed for the wages of 3 tromppetts appoynted to attend upon mylord Admyrall, everyche of them at 16*d.* by the day, appoynted by the Kyng's most honorable Councell, that is to say for 91 dayes.
  24*l.* 8s.

---

[1] 'For 7 monethes, wherof oone was expiryd afore the seid 6 monethes,' *id est* from the 15 March.

[2] 'For 5 of the foreseid monethes.'

[3] 'To the pilot of the Anthony Montrigo, for his wages 2 monethes.'

IN 1512—13 119

xij. *Wages of Sharant, Spanyerd.*¹

Also payed to Sharante, Spaynyerd, for the wages of hymself, at 18*d.* by the day, 4 servants, yche of them 5*s.*, and 2 boyes, eyther of them 2*s.* 6*d.* for the 1ˢᵗ moneth of the seid 6 monethes, and for oone of his seid servants for another moneth, 5*s.*

72*s.*

xiii. xiiij. *Wages and rewards of mylord Ferèrs, his capteyns and peticapteyns.*

Also payed to Mylord Fferers, capteyn of the Trenite Soveraigne, for the wages of hymself, at 5*s.* 2*d.* by the day, resydue of 6*s.* 8*d.* by the day to hym yevyn by the Kyng, ovyr 18*d.* by the day, in full payment of the same 6*s.* 8*d.* in the ordynarye wages allowed, and for the wages of 4 capteyns under hym, ych of them at 12*d.* by the day, and 4 pety capteyns, yche of ye at 8*d.* by the day, that is to sey for the fyrst 4 monethes aboveseid, as apperith by the Kyng's warrant. 66*l.* 5*s.* 4*d.*

Also payed to mylord Ferers for a reward to hym yevyn by the Kyng for costs of his retynew lying on land at Plymouth for lack of vitayle by the space of 6 dayes 40*l.*

xv. *Reparacions of shippes.*

Also payed to soundrie capteyns and to pursers of dyverse of the Kyng's shippes, aswell for the repayryng and amendyng of the same shippes, many maner awayes hurt and erasyd, as for dyverse masts, bords, nayles, and other necessaries bought, occupied and spent for and abouzt the same.

291*l.* 17*s.* 9*d.* ob.

¹ [In the margin] *Stet.* [This article is cancelled.] Cf. p. 143, note 1.

xvj. *Stuff, tacle and abillaments for the warres bought.*

Also payed for arrowes, gonnepowder and other necessaries for the warres bought and prepared by John Shipman for the 3 shippes of Bristoll. 39*l.*

And for ores and cabulls bought for the Kyng's shippes, and for mendyng and stockyng of gonnes
16*l.* 6*s.* 8*d.*

In all : 55*l.* 6*s.* 8*d.*

xvij. *Necessary payments.*

Also payed for a bote bought for the Mary Imperyall, price 4*l.*, and for conveyaunce of prisoners to Portesmouth and to the Councell, with rewards to hurt souldiours, 72*s.* 6*d.*, and also for bryngyng of a Danys bote to Portesmouth, 46*s.* 8*d.*

In all : 9*l.* 19*s.* 2*d.*

xviij. *Bere bought.*

Also payed to dyverse bere brewers of Sandwich for bere of them bought for the vitaylyng of the foreseid flete wantyng drynk, taryng in the Downes for the Scottysh flete,[1] what tyme the vytaylers cold not comme to them 86*l.* 9*s.* 3*d.*

xix. *Pursers costs in tyme of revytaylyng.*

Also payed for the costs of dyverse pursers at soundrie tymes lying on land for the revytaylyng of their shippes, somme by 6 days, somme 8 days, somme more, somme lesse, allowed at the ovyrsight and discression of the seid tresorer 38*l.* 17*s.* 4*d.*

[1] The Scottish fleet sailed along the west coast (July 1513).

xx. *Conducte money homeward.*

Also payed to dyverse and soundrie capteyns of 40 shippes for the conduyte money homeward of their retynuewes frome Portesmouth and Hampton to severall shires where they inhabite, aftyr the dischargyng of the foreseid army havyng lycence to depart, that is to sey every man takyng aftyr the rate of land wages, that is to sey every souldier 6*d*. for 12 myle by the day... 1175*l*. 9*s*. 2*d*.

Also for the wages, dietts and expense, aswell of the seid tresorer, at 3*s*. 4*d*. by the day, as of hys 2 clerks, ether of them at 8*d*. by the day, lying at Hampton for dischargyng of th' army and paying of conduyte money to the souldiours, frome the 25 day of September the foreseid 5th yere of our seid soveragne lord unto the 16th day of October next folowyng by the space of 21 dayes, as also for lyke dietts, wages and expense of the seid tresorer and his seid clerks lying in London and other places, attendyng of the Councell for and abought the fenishing of his accompte, frome the seid 16 day of October to the 15 day of November next folowyng by the space of 27 dayes, and also for costs of paper, parchement and other necessaries concernyng the seid tresorer's office—for the wich he hath no warraunt. 13*l*. 6*s*. 8*d*.

22,560*l*. 8*s*. 4*d*. quad. ½.

(R.O., Letters and Papers Henry VIII, t. v, n° 247.)

66. *Sir Edward Howard to Henry VIII.*

(Before Brest haven : 12 April [1513].)

[The fleet left Plymouth, 10 April, and, on the following day, met 15 French ships which fled into Brest, where the French fleet of 50 sail is blockaded. Prégent de Bidoux went to St. Malo a week ago. Lack of victuals. The letter is sent by a small boat captured at Crozon Bay.]

[Pleasith Your Grace] to understand that on Sonday last, was the 10 [day of Aprill we adv]ancyd owt off Plymmowth with your noble armye, and we . . . nygth.

The Monday last, the wynd roosse soon to N.N.E., that we weer feyn [to] set us in with the Traad, and went in at the brood sownde, wher [w]han we cam afoor Seynt Mathews, ther lay at rood a 15 sayl off men a war, whych, as soon as they spyd us, they, lyk cowards, fled to the Brest water, soo that they war get in or we cowd get as far as Seynt Mathews. And the wynd shot owt to E.N.E., and the e[eb] cam, that with all the turnyng we cowd maak, we cowd get no furder then the mowth off the entry off Brest water, wher we sawe ryd[ing] al the fleet off Frans to the nombre of 50 sayle, which we shulde not have myssyd, iff the wynd and the eeb had not com. And so we [weyd] an ancre in ther sygth, determenyng that the next mornyng, [if] we cowd have wynd to ley itt on a bord, that we wold have . . . them ther they lye. For, Sir, this shipp cannot get in by [the cas]tell, but an hye water and a drawyng wynd. Sir, the wynd has blown soo at E.N.E. that we cannot as yet com n[earer sti]l, we have them at the grettest avantaag that ever men had. God worketh in your caus and rigth, for uppon a 5 or 6 days [afor we came to the] Traad, Peryjohn, with his galeys and foysts, for skant [of wynd went] to Seynt Maloo's, and a 5 or 6 smal barks . . . betwen the fleet. And al ther trust . . . ther shal never come togydder with God's . . . them to leve them . . . hys yssew. Sir, the fyrst· wynd that ever commeth . . . have broken heds, that al the world shal spek off itt.

Sir, . . . shipps resort with our vitalls into the Traad, settyng ther curse on f[ast] along the coost of Ynglend or they hal over. And iff they her news of us ther, then let them com over, on God's naame, commyn at the broode, for they be inough to bet Peryjohn and al hys fleet, I warrant Your Grace havyng them a see bord.

Sir, this Tewsday at nygth, I hard, as I lay at an ancre, that a shipp off 80 lyyng in Croydon[1] bay and 4 small men had ron themself aground, so I sent owt the Lyzart, the Genet, the Bapytst off Harwyche and my shipp boot wel trymmyd, and commaunded them to bryng them away if they cowd, or els to burne [them]. And so, Sir, the shipp of 80 was ron so far a grownd that they cowd not [get] hym off, and my boot set hym on a fair fyr, and mad a goodly . . ., and the resydew of the smalle men wer browgth to me, wheroff [one] was laden with salt, which I have sent to bryng this letter to . . . that he com to off Ynglend.

And, Sir, I have sent a letter to the captains of the shipps off Spayn[2] and vitellers, iff so bee they be com on the coast . . . to Your Gras that ther shal resort hydder with al diligens.

Sir, iff God is so good to send us any wynd, not havyng no part off the e . . . [the ar]mye of Frans shal doo Your Gras litil hurt. At the . . . shal not tary long heer for it, for, Sir, that we w . . . in 2 days, with Godd's gras. And it plesid God, I w[olde] . . . [that] we had done our besynesse with the armye t . . ., also with al Britteyn, for her is . . . that is fel litil, and . . . a land . . . eth at al.

Sir, ther was never such a sort off capteyns that the . . . the see, nor such a sort off soldiour and maryners so weel wyllyng to do. And to be doyng with your enemys, Sir, we loos no tyme, I warrant you, for we thynk uppon none other thyng but how

[1] Crozon.
[2] W. Gonson, J. Iseham and Ric. Barclay (Doc. 71).

we may best greve our enemys. [And] iff vital feynne us, as your men and shipps ar determyned, we shal this yere mak a bar coost al the realm off Frans that bowndeth on the see cost, [which] shal never recover it in our days. Therfor, for no cost sparyng, let pro[vision] be maad, for it is a weel spent peny that saveth the pownd, for . . . was wont to be spent in 3 or 4 yeer on the see with one [e]spens now, we shal doo mor good then in 4 yeer by dreblet. Sir, I remitt al the furder order off this gret mater to your noble wisedom and discret order off your wys Consellours, and I pray God send us [bette]r wynd, that we may doo Your Gras that servys that our hert desirith . . . I pray thus the blissid Trinyte send Your Gras victory off your enemies.

[When] I was writyng off the latter off this letter, the Lyzard, the . . . rowgaleys and row-barges went in to them with the flood rowing . . . t them and caused them to come to ther sayls, and so cam larg . . . we com and fougth with us, and so I weyd and cam to sail . . . mad to them ward with the skant wynd that we had that . . . lked but wynd. God iff we had it com it on th . . . ll is one to us. Sir, Seynt George to borowgh . . . he yet for 10 days heer and . . . have our vitell.

[Endorsed :] To the kyng's noble Gras.

(Brewer, i. 3877.)

67. *Henry VIII. to Cardinal Bainbridge.*

(London : 2 April, 1513.)

[James IV. said to the Dean of Windsor, English ambassador, that he would appeal from the Pope to Prégent de Bidoux.]

. . Scotorum rex nuper iis verbis usus est

decano Wyndesoriensi,[1] nostro apud eum oratori : 'Ego appellabo ab istis executorialibus.' Tunc orator noster respondit illum appellare non posse a processibus papae, qui neminem superiorem habet. Tunc ille : 'Appellabo, inquit, ad Petrum Johannem, pyratham et apostatam, praefectum [galearum] regis Gallorum.'[2]

(Sanuto, xvi. 199.)

68. *Roberto Acciajuoli to Florence.*

(Blois : 13 April, 1513.)

[The English fleet is scouring the coasts of Brittany ; 12 ships of 1,000 t., 20 of 800, 80 of 300, 40 hulks. The French fleet ill provided with soldiers.]

L' armata d' Inghilterra, come per altra si dixe, s' intende essere fuori, et di Brettagna ci fu notitia che andava cercando la Franzese per afrontarla, et che haveva buon vento. Nientedimanco da più giorni in qua non se ne è inteso alcuna cosa, ma se ne sta con grande expectatione. Ritrasi l' Inghilese fare più di 12 nave di 2000 bote, o circa, più di 20, di 800 ; insino alla somma de 80, di 300 a circa, et di più 40 urche da portare vettovaglie. La Franzese anchora s' intende essere gagliarda, ma non si bene provista di fanterie come quella, tamen di natura di potersi difendere.

[1] Nicolas West, 28 March (Brewer, i. 3838).
[2] 'Guillaume Bruce, dit Marche,' James IV.'s herald at arms, left Dieppe, 20 April 1513, on 'Johannet Abreton's' (John Barton) bark, 80 t., sent to Scotland by the Bishop of Murray, Scottish ambassador to Louis XII. (Bib. Nat., Pièces orig. 348, dossier *Bigars*, pièce 41).

69. Sir Edward Howard to Henry VIII.

(St. Matthews : 17 April [1513].)

[The Admiral lands at Crozon Bay. The French ships moored near the Castle of Brest, behind a row of hulks. Boats, small vessels, and row-barges sent to meet Prégent's galleys. No news of the three Spaniards. No more victual, but one day. Arthur Plantagenet, bearer of this letter.]

[Pleasith] Your Gras to understande that the next day after [I have writ]en to Your Graas, I caused al my boots off the armye with the . . . hed to mak a contenans off landyng on the syd that Brest . . . one, for to mak the contrey to resort down to the watersyd, . . d the vitall off the contrey, and to wery off them. And I am [sure there] was within a howr above 10000 men. Such as they be, Sir, my [men wou]ld have landed to have fowght with them, and I dar say we [had no]t in al the boots past 1500 men. For, Sir, to content som what the [me]ns mynds, which ar hardly handeld in the distributyng off [da]yly vitallyng, by reson that as yet our vitallyng is not com to us, a[nd to] kep them owt off murmeryng, whiche is hard to doo without they be set a work with som whatt, I skyrmishyd there the past twoo howrs with our ordenans. And when I spid the contrey sor moved and [to] the watersyd, for fear off landyng, I went over to the other syd off Brest, that New Croydon[1] stod on, and landyd al my boots, and maad twoo batells, and so went over al the nek off land in [the b]ay, and maad our muster so streit afor the castell that they myght see that we wer not aferd to land our men afor ther sygth, to proc[ede] to com forth yea, and to anger them wer burned up al the ho[wses

[1] Crozon.

that] stood in ther sygth on the watersyd to ther grat displesir and the [plesur] off our men.

Sir, ther I vewd how the shipps lay. Sir, they be rone underneth the castell, and they have by, as fer as we can spye . . . al the hulks afor the mowthe off the haven, for bycaus we shuld [doo] them noo hurt. By reson off, for no otherwys, Sir, we dar not put . . . bycaus off lak of vitall. And we be abell to land . . . many hors as wyl cary 2 peces off good ordenauns, with the carts, [with wh]iche thes shipps shal be sonk wher they lye. Sir, it wer to gret a p[eril th]ey shuld ever skaap, seyng that we have them in this danger. I remyt thys to your gret wysdom.

Sir, as for the galeys, we mak gret wa[y with] them, as master Artour can show Your Graas. And, Sir, iff ther com any owther by day or be nygth, the bots and smal vessells and rowgaleys shal ley them sharply abord, and rather then they skap us, I have assygnyd Harper, the Thomas of Hul, my bark, [Trevy]nyan's bark and 2 or 3 smal shippes not to spare to geve them, and thow they shuld ron them agrownd for to mak them [sink]. And, Sir, iff they cam amongs us, they shal not skap clean with good.

Sir, we merveyl soor that we her no word off our thre Spanyards[1] [that] shuld com owt off Temes. We fer that they have ben in some danger (which God defend) in the Deps, for they have had as fair wynds to com unto us as can be wysshyd, and our vitallers to. I shal thynk long to have word from Your Graas off all your ferder plesur how ye wyl ha[ve all] furder orderd. Sir, and our vital com not to us by to morow, we be in great despeyr to have any remedy, for now this 2 days hath blown the fairest wynd that could he devysyd. God send us

---

[1] Doc. 71.

comfort of them shortly! We can doo no mor then is possible, and that wyl we doo to byd you [greate]st payn that ever dyd men, seyng that God hath sent us here in so gret advantage off your enemys, as I am sur Sabien[1] hath informed Your Graas.

Sir [I have] taken all master Artour's folks and bestowed them in the armye wher s[ome lacke]d by reson off deth, by casuelte and otherwys,[2] and, Sir, [I gave hym licen]ce to goo hoome, for, Sir, when he was in the extreme danger . . . from hym, he called uppon our Lady of Walsyngham for help and comfort, [and made] a vow that, and it plesyd God and Her to delyver hym owt off the peril, he wold never eet flesshe nor fyche tyl he had seen her. Sir, I a[ssure you] he was in mervelous danger, for it was merveil that the shipp[3] bey[ng with] al her sayls strylkyng full but a rok with her stam, that she br[oke] not on peces at the first stroke. Sir, we shal have a gret [want of] hym owt off your noble armye, for I know no man dis . . . that, consyderyng hys power, shuld better have served yow iff the fortune had not been, for, Sir, he was wel trymyd, and hath . . . he had in effect. And, Sir, he wuld not have departyd, but [for] that vow he shuld doo heer in a maner Your Gras but smal servyse [and to] hymself gret discomfort to see every man shippyd and to see h[is own]e plas and hys men devydyd from hym. Therfor and bycaus . . . th inform Your Gras what plas we stand in, and to be set . . . d agayn iff Your Graas wyl have to com to us, which wylbe as . . . thyng as is possible

[1] 17 April, 1513: 'To W. Saben that brought letters from the lorde Admyrall to the kyng's Grace: 20*l.*' The letters sent by Sabyn have not been found.
[2] 10 soldiers 'lately in the reteygnew of Artur Plantagenet, esqwyer,' are put in the Great Bark (*R. O., Augmentation Office Book* 315).
[3] Nicholas of Hampton.

IN 1512-13

whersoever ye wyl command hym, I have sent hym [to Your] Graas, besechyng Your Graas to be hys good and gracious lord. [I assu]r yow he shal do Your Graas good servys whersoever ye . . . both for his good order and herdynes. And, Sir, he is the sore . . . man I ever saw and no man heer can confront hym. Therfore I beseche agayn Your Graas to geve hym comfortable words to be his good [lord].

I besech Your Graas to send me word how ye [do hear of] Scotland to [sen]d a spyal off hys shipps.

And Our Lord send yow victory ever of your enemys.

Written to Seint Mathews, the 17th day off Apryll.

Your bounden servant
EDW[ARD HOWARD].

[Endorsed :] To the kyng's Grace, in al possible hast.

From mylord Admerall.

(Brewer, i. 3903.)

70. *Roberto Acciajuoli to Florence.*

(Blois : 20 April, 1513.)

[The English fleet is 8 leagues from Brest; battle is expected daily.]

L' armata Inghilese si truova in Brettagna, vicina a Bres dove è la Franzese, a 8 leghe, e duo giorni sono ci furono nuove che si erano accostate si presso che si expecti l' affrontamento un pezo. Di poi si intende ad causa de' venti contrarii che la Inghilese si era alargata qualche poco, pure si potrà ogni hora udire qualche grande percossa.

71. *William Gonson to Wolsey.*

(Queenborough, 24 April [1513].)

[W. Gonson, with the smallest of three Spanish ships and his bark, is ordered to convoy the victuallers to the fleet off Brest. Iseham and Berkeley, with the two other Spanish ships, will remain between Dover and Calais for the safe conduct of the Zeland fleet. The three Spanish ships are only sent to sea for two months. The sale of the Great Nicholas.]

Ryght worshypfull Syr, my dwty consyderyd, acertenyng your mastershyp thatt the 21 day of thys present monthe I receyuyd a letter ffro the kynges Grace, writen the 18 day off the same, in the wyche he comaundythe me thatt in one off the Spanyards shyps takyng wit me Ygyngam in hys ship[1] I shall conducte and wafftt hys vytellars to hys grett army in the water of Brest.

To wyche letter I incontynentt made hys Grace answer acertenyng the same thatt Ygyngam was departyd fro Qwynboro 8 days affore my comyng thydur, and bycawse thatt he was gon I wolld go my sellfe in the smallist of the 3 Spanyards sentt fforthe wit me and take wit me my barke, and leffe John Ysame and Rychiard Barkeley in the other 2 Spanyarde shyps to wafftt over the Zeland fleett, wyche ys a thyng off grett importans, and so to kepe betwene Douer and Cales tyll my comyng to them ageyn, wyche I trust, wit God's hellp shall be shorttly.

And, Sir, I beseche your mastershipp to haue in remembrans thatt I and my company wer sentt to the see butt for 2 months begynnyng the 5 day of thys monthe, wyche will consume fast and yeff hytt

[1] The Germaine.

shall please hys Grace thatt partt or all shall tary
lenger fforthe, hytt wyll be nedffull that knolege
theroff shall be shortly gyvon, or ells hytt wyll not
be possebull to putt hytt in couenyentt aredynes and
to knowe your pleasure, I send herwit on of my
vytellars and the other remayns weytyng vpon
John Ysame and Rychiard Barkley ffor ther nedys.
Yeff we myght haue taryed all togythur, I wolld
haue trustyd we sholld haue doone some seruys to
your pleasure, to wyche I shall ever indevor my
sellffe, wit God's hellp.

Allso, Sir, wher the Kyng gaffe to John Bruges,
Rychard Page and me lysans for to shyp euery man
100 sake wolls past the streytts off Maroke, att the
byyng of the Greatt Nycholas off vs, payyng the
custom theroff att 3 yers and 3 yers, and hytt pleasyd
your mastership to cawse my partt theroff to be
asygnyd to my greatt avauntage, ffor wyche and
other I am bound nextt the kynges Grace to owe
you my servys, hytt is so the day of my comyng
fforthe I bowght off the sayd Rychiard Page hys
partt, trustyng thatt hytt wyll please you to contynu
so good master to me as to cawse the kynges Grace
to asygne hytt, ffor ells I shall lese all the mony thatt
I haue payd ffor hytt. And sir John Hopton shall
delyuer your mastershyp the lysans wyche I beseche
your mastershyp cawse to be asygnyd.

Allso, Sir, the 22 day of thys month, hythur
came ouer Rychiard Thurcull who sayd thatt he
come fro the kyng's Grace and that he comandyd
me to se wit partte of our shyps certen hoyse condutyd owtt of Zeland into the Teamse, and he
hathe shewyd suche tocons thatt I suppose hys talle
to be trwe. Wherffor, having no contrary comaund-
mentt, I haue gyuon order thatt John Ysame and
Rychard Barkley shall se them saffly condutyd wit
God's help.

Syr, here we ly nott very myre seyng our tyme spend so ffast and can haue no wethur to bryng us fforthe off the Teamse. I beseche God soone to remedy hytt, as yet all the vytellars be not come down to vs.

Ageyn, Sir, I beseche you to haue in remembrans thatt we war sentt fforthe butt ffor 2 months, begynyng the 5 day hereoff, wyche ffast spend.

Also, Sir, thys day come hythur 20 men fro Sir John Shellton, butt afore ther comyng, consyderyng thatt we had apoyntyd as fewe men to eny shyp as myght convenyently be, and trustyng to haue bene shorttly att the see, I putt in to every shyp hys holle nomber and clothyd and harnesyd them thatt lakyd my sellfe, so thatt I have harnesyd off myn own cost in theys 4 shyps 74 men.

And thus I beseche Jhesu to send your mastershyp muche honowr and vs a convenyent wynd to doo suche seruys as we be bound to doo.

Writen aboord the shyp, rydyng affore Qwynboro, the 24 day off Aprill, wit the hand off yours wit hys seruys

WYLLIAM GONSON.

[Endorsed] To the ryght worshypfull hys syngular good master awmner to the kynges Grace.

(Brewer, i. 3946.)

72. *Prégent de Bidoux to* [*Florimond Robertet ?*]
(Conquet : 28 April, 1513.)

[He has not written for a long time, on account of the wind having been foul for the passage to England, ever since he left Brest on 13 March, and also of the sickness and mortality on board his galleys.

When he was at Portrieux he heard from M. du Chillou that the English fleet was out. He sailed as soon as possible to join him at Brest. When he came to St. Pol de Léon, the English were at St.

Matthew's. Being stopped at Beurat by bad weather, he rode to Bertheaulme, to confer with the Grand Master of Brittany, who authorised him to hire 200 of the country-folk for rowers, in the room of those who were sick or dead. He then went to Brest, where M. du Chillou and other captains supplied him with seamen. He returned to Beurat; was obliged by bad weather to stay three or four days at Bar-le-Duc; and 30 or 40 ships came there to hinder him proceeding. On Friday, 22 April, he put to sea in a calm; but the wind got up, and at the Croix-Porzmoguer, he found himself to leeward of them, in a very disadvantageous position. There were 45 or 50 English ships, and 4 or 5 of them, with two row-barges, came within a spear's leng'h of the galleys, and for two hours there was a very sharp fight. The English then fled, losing four of their great ships, which were sunk, as also two store ships.

The Grand Master and M. de Laval gave him, and ordered the country people to give him, all necessary assistance. They also supplied him with two culverins and two falcons.

On Monday, 25 April, he was attacked by 30 ships, and 25 or 30 barks. Howard, in the first row-barge, boarded him, with 45 or 50 men. The row-barge was cut adrift, and all the men, except two, were slain or thrown into the sea. The second row-barge then attempted to board, but was thrust off, as also three barks, with great loss on both sides. The other barks fled, returning to the great ships at St. Matthew's; and the next day the galleys went to Conquet.

Of the two prisoners, one, a Fleming, was badly wounded and died. The other was an Englishman. They both stated positively that the Admiral was in the first row-barge, and they described his armour. Prégent found the Admiral's body on the afternoon of the 28th, and told the Grand Master and M. de Laval, who directed him to acquaint the King and Queen, and take their pleasure as to how the body was to be buried. Meantime, whilst waiting for their answer, it is to be embalmed. He has had it disembowelled and salted, and the apothecary will embalm it the next day. He should like to keep the heart for himself, and hopes this may be allowed.

There are 13,000 or 14,000 fr. due to him; he begs that the Queen may be spoken to about them. He has lost some 400 men, and desires that the number may be made up with convicts from the prisons of Paris or Blois.

The Queen gave Prégent a whistle. He now sends her the Admiral's whistle 'of command.' It weighs less than the one she gave Prégent, but is richer for her service. He sends the Admiral's clothes to Mme. Claude. He will have the scene of the battle painted.

The Grand Master and M. de Laval have hardly changed their shirts since the enemy arrived; and MM. du Chasteau and Tavarant have been with Prégent night and day. He has written to the King.]

Mgr., je me recommande à vostre bonne grace tant humblement que faire puis.

Mgr., il y a longtemps que je n'ay escript à cause du temps contraire que j'ay eu pour passer en Angleterre depuys le temps que je partis de Brest, qui fut le 13ᵉ jour de mars, et aussi pour les maladies et mortalitez que j'ay eux aux gallères. Pour quoy n'ay voulu escripre aulcunes nouvelles.

Mgr., moy estant en la riviere de Pourtriel, euz nouvelles de M. du Chillou, par lesquelles il me mandoit que la flotte d'Angleterre estoit partie dehors. Ainsy, tout incontinent que euz temps, me levay pour m'en venir joindre avec M. du Chillou. Quant fuz à St Pol de Léon, sachez pour vray que l'armée d'Angleterre estoit au canal de St Mathieu. Je feiz mon effort de venir, et comme feuz auprès de Beurat, le temps me fut contraire, et passay audit Beurat. Et incontinent montay à cheval et vins à Bertticaulme,[1] où estoit M. du Chasteau-pourry, et que l'on m'avoit dit que M. le Grand Maistre s'y debvoit trouver. Et le trouvay monté à cheval, et luy dis que j'avoye plus de 200 hommes de ranc[2] malades, et pareillement de ceulx de bonne voille[3] mallades et mors. M. le Grand Maistre a ordonné que je feusse secouru des gens de rive en les payant. Et feiz prendre des gens du pays, et en recouvray jusques à 200, qui est environ ce qu'il me falloit. Et pour recouvrer des gens de cap, M. le Grant Maistre fut d'oppinion que je allasse avec luy à Brest devers M. du Chillou, vis admiral de Bretaigne et les cappitaines, les supplier qu'ilz me voulsissent secourir de leurs gens. Ce qu'ilz firent soubdainement.

Et incontinant avoir eu lesdits gens, partis dudit Beurat pour sercher de m'en venir joindre à Brest avec le demeurant de l'armée. Et en venant j'euz temps que ne peuz venir d'une traicte, et fuz contraint de prendre à Bar le Duc, et demouray 3 ou 4 jours, et là incontinent vindrent devant moy 30 ou 40 navires pour me garder de venir en avant.

Le vendredy, veille de St George, me sembla que le temps estoit calme, et partis pour m'en venir. Et quant je feuz party, le temps me fut contraire, et me trouvay au dessoubz d'eux du grand vent, et me trouvay au Croyx Primoguet en ung très mauvais lieu pour mon avantaige. Là se trouvèrent de 45 à 50 navires devant moy pour me venir assaillir, et soubdainement virent que le vent ne leur servoit pas bien pour venir à mon bort. Mais les deux galliasses et 4 ou 5 navires vindrent passer à une picque loing de l'esperon des gallées, en façon que deux heures

---

[1] Bertheaulme.   [2] Convicts.   [3] Bonevogli=volunteers.

[durant] on ne vit jamais donner tant de coups l'un à l'autre d'artillerie et des arbalestres et dars, qui ne fut sans grant perdicion de gens d'un costé et d'autre. En effect ilz feurent contrains leur lever honteusement et, en se levant de là, visiblement, s'en alla au fons devant nous une bonne nef de 300, et une auctre derrière la poincte, et deux aultres en allant la nuyt: qui furent quatre. Ausquelz navires il y avoit 4 ou 5 basteaulx chargez de gens et d'artillerie, desquelz il en alla deux au fons.

Cela passé, M. le Grant Maistre [et] de Laval se rendirent incontinent à terre pour me donner le secours qu'ilz me eussent peu donner, et avoit mandé M. le Grant Maistre à noz gens du pays qu'ilz se vinssent rendre à la marine pour me faire toute l'ayde qui me seroit possible. Et M. du Chastel a esté ordinairement de l'un des costez, et M. de Tavarant de l'autre, en la façon que toutes celles gallées où j'estoye estoient toutes advironnées de repères. Et M. le Grant Maistre y fist mener une coulevrine bastarde et une moyenne, et M. du Chasteau fist mectre de son costé deux faucons siens en quelques repaires que nous fismes faire.

Le lundy ensuyvant, qui fut le jour St Marc, me vindrent assaillir 30 navires avec 25 ou 30 basteaulx, desdans lesquelz estoit l'admiral millord Harvat, et estoit en dedans la $1^{\text{ère}}$ galléasse qui me vint aborder, pour ce qu'elle avoit le vent à plaisir, cuydant me faire sortir de dedans la gallée de playne arrivée, avec 45 ou 50 hommes. Quoy que ce soit, ladite galléasse fut désabordée, et partie de ceulx qui estoient dedans furent tuez à coups de picques et les aultres gettez en mer, à la façon qu'il ne feut prins que deux en vie par inconvénient, car l'ung fut getté dedans d'ung coup de picque de leur compaignie et fut getté dedans ung remer et fist le mort, mais il fut repoussé en mer et estoit en habit dissimullé.

Et firent de grandes armes à merveilles. En faisant cela, l'autre gallée aborde. Et croyez, Mgr., que si Dieu ne m'eust aydé, sans comparaison ilz me debvoient effondrer, mais elle fut désabordée à coups de picque. Après ces deux galléasses vindrent trois navires, et tous abordèrent sur ma gallée tant seullement, faisant leur compte que, s'ilz m'avoient, qu'ilz auroient bien le demourant. Et jamais ne viz gens venir si désespérément comme ceulx là. Mais toutes trois furent désabordées comme les galléasses. Et sachez, Mgr., que ce n'a point esté faict sans grant perdicion de gens. Et quant les autres navires virent que ces cinq ne nous avoient rien fait, ilz prindrent la voille dehors et eurent parlement ensemble, et subitement comme gens confus prindrent leur chemin à eulz en venir trouver les grosses navires devant Saint Mathieu, et nulluy ne demoura devant moy. Ilz avoient acoustumé de demourer tousjours de 25 à 30 navires.

Je réparé ce soir le moins mal que je peu, et le matin euz temps pour partir et m'en vins incontinent au Conquest, où suis à présent. Des prisonniers, y avoit ung Flamant, qui autresfoys m'avoit servy et m'avoit faict quelque mauvais tour, et estoit fort blecé et se mouroit, je luy ay fait avancer son chemin, et l'autre, Angloys. Et tous deux me certifièrent que sans point de faulte l'Admiral estoit à la 1ère galléace, qui estoit sorty en gallère, et me devisèrent les armes et habillemens qu'il portoit sur son harnoys. J'ay prins peine de faire pescher les mors, et ay tant fait que je l'ay trouvé. Ce jour duy, environ midy, il m'a esté apporté. Incontinant j'en ay adverty M.M. le Grant Maistre et de Laval qui sont à St Mathieu. Incontinent M. le Grant Maistre s'est monté à cheval et m'a dict qui luy sembloit qu'on en devoit advertir le Roy et la Royne pour sçavoir de quelle sorte on le doibt enterrer.

Mgr., si d'un an Dieu ne m'eust donné grace de faire service au Roy et à la Royne, d'un an je n'eusse escript. Et puisqu'il a pleu à Nostre-Seigneur de me donner ceste grace, il me semble que je luy puis bien rescripre et qu'il prendra quelque plaisir à veoir de mes nouvelles. Et aussi ce qui me garda de rescripre à la Ière route qu'ilz eurent, ce fut que M. le Grant Maistre me dit qu'il vous en rescriproit.

Mgr., M.M. le Grant Maistre et de Laval ont esté d'oppinion de faire embaulmer le corps jusques à tant qu'on sache le bon plaisir du Roy et de la Royne comme ilz veullent qu'il soit enterré, et ainsi sera fait. Et m'a promis M. le Grant Maistre de me faire venir incontinent l'apoticaire ores lendemain soubdainement, et l'ay fait ouvrir et vuider, et mettre du sel en attendant le baulme, et ay fait mettre le corps à part embaulmé de baulme artificiel que avoys. M. ledit millort Havart estoit grand seigneur, comme ilz disoient. Se c'est le plaisir du Roy et de la Royne que je retienne le cueur par devers moy, j'en feray leur profit, je leur en supplie très humblement.

Et pour ce que, Mgr., de ce voyage je suis arrière de 13 ou 14000 francs, j'en escrips auxdits seigneur et dame. Je vous supplie très humblement qu'il vous plaise en voulloir rescripre audit seigneur, à Mgr. le général de Beaulne[1] qu'il en vueille parler à la Royne.

Mgr., il fault adviser d'avoir des gens par force, car j'en ay plus de 400, tant mors que malades, que tués, que noyés, que blessés, qui ne pourroyent jamais servir. Par quoy, Mgr., je vous supplie très humblement qu'il vous plaise en advertir ledit seig-

---

[1] About Jacques de Beaune-Semblançay, cf. A. Spont, *Semblançay; la bourgeoisie financière au début du xvie siècle* (Paris, Hachette, 1896).

neur et mander en extrême diligence que j'en soye secouru, et n'y aura pas grand peine de les faire venir, car ceulx de Paris,[1] on les pourra faire venir par eaue jusques à Rouen, et ceulx du cartier de Bloys jusques icy. Et à cecy, Mgr., fault extrême et grande diligence.

Mgr., Vostre Seigneurie a sceu comme il a pleu à la Royne me donner ung siflet avec la chayne. En récompense, je luy envoye celuy dudit Admiral, non pas son siflet d'honneur, mais est celuy de quoy il commandoit, il ne poyse pas tant comme celluy que ladite dame m'a envoyé, mais il me semble qu'il est plus riche pour son service que n'est l'autre.

Je envoye à Mme Claude[2] la despoulle dudit admiral millort Harvart.

Je ordonneray ces jours icy de faire paindre le lieu où a esté ledit combat et l'envoyray au Roy incontinent. J'espère, avec l'aide de Nostre Seigneur, que le bon recueil qu'on leur a fait les gardera que une aultre fois ne seront point si oultrecuidez.

Et vous advise que M.M. le Grant Maistre et de Laval se sont tousjours tenus montés et armés, et croyez, Mgr., que depuis que les Angloys sont arrivés, ilz ne se sont despoullés, si ce nest pour prendre chemise blanche, car à toutes heures de la nuyt ilz avoient mille alarmes. Et M.M. du Chasteau et Tavarant n'ont jamais bougé d'auprès de moy ne nuyt ne jour.

Mgr., j'ay escript au Roy comme je vous escriptz bien au long, il vous plaira veoir les lettres que je luy escrips, les luy donner et l'advertir bien au long.

Mgr., je prie au benoist filz de Dieu que par sa grace vous doint bonne vie et longue, vous

---

[1] Sentence of death commuted to service in the galleys, July 1513 (*Arch. Loire Inférieure*, reg. Chancery, xxi. fol. 225).

[2] Louis XII.'s daughter, married to Francis, Duc d'Angoulême, in 1506.

suppliant qui vous plaise me mander de vos nouvelles et de vos bons plaisirs pour les accomplir.

En galère, au Conquet, le 28ᵉ jour d'avril.

Vostre humble et obéyssant serviteur.

PRÉGENT.[1]

73. *Roberto Acciajuoli to Florence.*

(Blois : 30 April, 1513.)

[Prégent with his ordnance sunk two English ships, and lost a brigantine. The English tried to land, but were repulsed by the country people, and did little damage; it is thought that they have come on the coast of Brittany in order to detain the French there, and so leave the sea near Calais open.]

Tre giorni sono ci fu adviso di Brectagna come Pregianni si era riscontro nella armata Inghilese et con le artiglierie havea messo in fondo 2 nave et lui havea perso uno brigantino, et ritiratosi con uno soccorso datoli da terra ad salvamento. Nè dipoi è seguito altro.

Hanno li Inghilesi da quelle bande più volte tentato in diversi luoghi scendere in terra, et in ogni loco da' paesani[2] sono stati rebuttati in mare,

---

[1] We know the names of only two of Prégent's companions: his nephew, Pierre de Bidoux, sʳ de Lartigue (afterwards vice-admiral of Brittany), and Dominique Séguier, of Marseilles (Ruffi, *Histoire de Marseille,* 349–350).

[2] Jean de Rieux, Marshal of Brittany, sent the following message to the local officers of Lamballe, Moncontour, Dinan, Jugon, St. Brieuc and St. Malo (Kerahès, 28 April) :

'Dès piéça les Anglois ayant fait congrégation et assemblée de gens de guerre en manière hostile, tendans, si faire le peuvent, endommager cestui pays, gens et sujets dudit seigneur, comme vraisemblablement appert par l'amas et congrégation des navires de guerre qu'ils ont puis naguères fait assembler et congréger en la coste de cestui pays, et divisément ès parties de Brest, St. Malo, le Conquest, Crauzon et en plusieurs autres endroits de cestuy pays et duché, et doutans qu'ils ne veuillent, en ensuivant leur damnable enteprise et mauvaise délibération, faire descente par sourprise et clandestinement en plusieurs endroits de cestuy

et hanno facto pochissimo danno, perche li paesani sono tanto animati a defendersi che da quella banda non sono per fare gran progressi, perche s' intende in su quella armata non sono più che 12,000 homini da porre in terra. Ma si crede che quella armata si vadia intractenendo nella costa di Brectagna per tenere impegnata quella armata Franzese, et potere verso Calese et Picchardia havere libero il mare, et porre qualche gente in quella provincia dove per ancora non vi è scesa alcuna quantità di gente.

74. *W. Sabyn to Wolsey.*

(Under sail : 30 April [1513].)

[Sabyn showed the King's letter of credence to the admiral. The strength of the French is too great in Brittany. There are places on the coast or islands that can be destroyed. The attack on Prégent's galleys was imprudent. Convicts should be sent for the galleys.]

Right honorabill and my singuler good mayster, I reco[mm]end myself to youre good maysterchyppe, besechyng Jhesu to preserve you to God's p[lesur.]

As so that accordyng to the Kyng's commandement and yours, I scho[yd to] mylorde Admyrall all soche credens as I was commandyd by the Ky[ng and] you, and sins hys departyng, I have schoyd yt to mylorde Fer[rers and] other off hys Consell to se yff yt had byn possybyll to a destroyd [owre] sovereyn lord's enmys. Sir, I cannot se be them nor yt by my pore r[eson] that the Kyng's Grras can have eny vantage off hys enymys [nor] we be abyll to londe, for they be in ther gret strenght apon [yt] with ther ordennas and gret nomber off pepoull, and make ever gret provysyon. Wherfor, Sir, by my sympyll reson and as me thyn[ks, if] the kyng's

pays et divisément ès ports et havres des éveschez de St. Malo, Dol et St. Brieuc . . .' (Dom Morice, iii. 906).

Grras wyl not sende men to londe, yt wyl be hard to d[o them] dysplesur. Also ther be other places to do dysplesur, and men wyll p[ovt them]selfe to it, besydes the Trade, for me thynks to ly alwey in on betyng and remove not to sum other places, we shall do [no more] good, bot only to kepe in owr enymys, and as long as we [are on this] coste off Breton, they wyll never comm to the coste off Yngland, [unless] that we schold porsew them. Sir, ther is in the maine lo[nde of] Breton places to lande in, yf we wyll, and owre enymy sch . . . We wylle not venter so far with the army, and to us more avan[tage]. Also ther be places in France lyke wyse to londe in, yff men w[yll] do ther dylygens and do the kyng's Grras good servys, and l[et] not spende the Kyng's money and vetellys, bot that we [wyll] do hym some servys for yt. Also besides the mayne londe off Fra[nce], ther be serten hylands pertenyng to France that may be destro[yd at] owre plesur.

And, Sir, whereas yowre maysterschippe gaff me commandement to scho my pore advyse, I have don yt, and I do yt to the utterest off my power. And whereas yt wyll p[lease] yowre good maysterschyppe that he so be owre hed and governor, [and if] he wyll accept my pore advise, I schall never gyff hym [one] but that schal be to the honer off my soveren lord the Kyng, and I schal be ever the fryste man be londe and be wa[ter] myselfe in the fryste danger in any soche consell [to] gyff, yff I se yt may be don with reson, and I beseche you [to be so good] mayster, unto me that he so be owr Admyrall that I m . . .

Sir, as for the enterprys on the galles, had not been don aft[er the] manor, yff I myght have had my mynde, God knowi[th. My] lorde Admyrall had skyrmyshyd with the galles afore I ca[m].

Whan I se them ly in so gret a strenght be w[ater and] londe, I comm unto mylorde Admyrall and schoyd hym [credens] and myne advyse. The wyche he was so sore set apon [me] be a Spanyarde[1] that I cowde not torne hys mynde. [The] Spannyarde poot hym in so gret comfort and sayd th[at there] were nothyng in manor that my lorde dred noth[yng]. More pyty yt was, howbeit he dyed lyke a vallyent [knyght]. And he was informyd by the same Spannyarde he ... Jhesu have mersi, for now we be bodys withowte a hed [to the] dyscomforte off us all.

Sir, I movyd mylorde Admyrall [last] Crystemmes to scho the kyng's Grras, for soche enterprys as [he wold] have to do, ther be many tall men in Yngland in convyct[yon] and that be worthy for to dy be the Kyng's lawys, as fe[lons] and other, that myght better be loste than other m[en],[2] they wolde by my reson rather to venter ther lyvys then [have] ony schamfull dethe, and yff they dyd well, to have ther gawardon therafter. Sir, he that intends the warrys m[ust] ymagin that thyng to destroy hys ennymys as they m[ust] lyke wyse unto us, for, yff we schold make a raffe, thes scholde stonde us in good stede, for the flete off France wy[ll a]lway resorte into the chamber off Breste, and ther yt ys [not] possybyll to be don by owre londyng and be the menys the raff. And whereas other men wyll m . . . ., thies men wyll make lytyll danger for savyng off [ther lyvys].

[1] Charran, captain of a carrack, apparently the Gabriel Royal (Brewer, i. 3762) : 15*l.* 16*s.* 11*d.* for the hire of the ship from Spain to England (8 Feb. 1513). Cf. p. 77, note 3; p. 80, note 1.
[2] 'En icelles gallères,' says the Chancellor of Brittany, 'y a continuité de exercice auquel guères de gens ne se veullent constituer de franc vouloir' (*Arch. Loire Inférieure*, reg. xxi. fol. 26).

I pray God we may do well in tyme to comm and to [do] that my be to the honer of owre soveren lord. He [schold] preserve hys ryall astate and preserve yowre good maysterschippe. [Pleasi]the besech you to pardon me, for I am a pore secr[etar]y.

Wryttin under sayle, the laste day off Apprylle
by yowre trew b[ounden servant]
WYLLYAM SABYN.

[Endorsed:] To hys moste honorabyll maister Armoner to the kyng's Grras, be thys letter delyveryd in haste possybyll—WILLIAM SABYN.

(Brit. Mus., MSS. Calig. E. i. ij. iij., fol. 1.)

75. *Roberto Acciajuoli to Florence.*

(Blois : 3 May, 1513.)[1]

[Attack on Prégent's galleys. Death of Admiral Howard, whose body has been found with a golden whistle round the neck. 50 English killed.]

Dixi per l' altra mia come l' armata Inghilese era in Brettagna et come si era ricontra in Pregianni, el quale con l' ajuto di terra si era ritracto salvo. Dipoi decta armata si è messa intra l' armata Franzese che si truova a Brest et Pregianni, per impedire che Pregianni non si unisca con l' altra Franzese, et l' ha tenuto più giorni come obsediato, et ultimamente con le nave grosse si eron parati avanti alle nave Franzese, et con le piccole erono andati a trovare le galee sottili di Pregianni, et observando il fluxo et refluxo lo haveron serrato in modo che è suto a gran pericolo. Tandem, con lo havere messi cierti cannoni in terra et con lo essersi

---

[1] That letter was read in the Council, at Venice, on 20 May (Sanuto, xvi. 274).

portato virtuosamente si è insino a hora difeso. Et ultimamente volendolo strignere, una delle nave Inghilesi si accostò tanto animosamente per intrare tra lui et la terra che lo mise in gran pericolo, et bastò l' animo a forse 50 homini, che vi erono su, venire alle mane con lui: e' quali alla fine furon tutti morti, et in tale numero per molti riscontri che vi sono essere suto lo Amiraglio di decta armata, huomo di gran conditione, perche dicono li nimici havere facto demandare instantamente se havessino tra prigioni un tale, vestito con tale habiti, el che monstrava essere huomo di che tenessino gran conto. Et per tale cagione havendo Pregianni facto ripescare e' morti, ne hanno trovato uno vestito in quella forma con uno fischio d' oro a collo, lungo un mezo palmo, et per tale riscontro giudicono che sia l' Amiraglio o homo di buona sorte.[1]

76. *Edward Echyngham to Wolsey.*

(Hampton : 5 May, 1513.)

[Prégent broke through the English fleet (22 April). Landing near Conquet (24). Attack on the French galleys and death of the Admiral (25). Cheyne, Cornwall and Wallop go on shore to ascertain the death. Bernardin at Bordeaux. Sickness. Return to Plymouth (30 April). Necessity of galley-convicts. Narrative of Echyngham's journey, from 13 to 19 April, with the victuallers.]

Sir, for to write unto you the newes of theis parties, they be so dolorous that vnneth I cane write them for sorrow ; how be it I have founde you soe good maister unto me that [it] heth pleasit you to cause the kynges most noble Grace to write unto

[1] Cf. Sanuto, xvi. 242, 248, 269.

me which hathe encoraged me for to send you in writyng of those thynges that I have sene.

Upon Ffrydaye, the which was the 22th day of Aprill, 6 galyes and 4 foysts came through parte of the Kynges navie, and there they sanke the ship that was maister Compton's, and strake through oone of the Kynges new barkes, the which sir Stephyn Bull is capiteyn of, in 7 placys, that they that was within the ship hade much payne to hold her above the watre. Then the ship bootes toke oon of the ffoystes, and the residew of the gallyes and ffoystes went into Whitsonbaye, besyde Conkett, and there thaye laye Satterdaye all daye.

Upon Sondaye, mylord Amirall appoynted 6000 men for to land betwene Whitsondbaye and Conkett, and so to come vnto the backside of the galyes. And as we were landing, mylorde Admyrall espyede Sabyn commyng under sayle. And than that purp[ose] was loste, for euerye capiteyn hade put his men into vyttellers, and mylorde Admyrall sende M[r] Ffythwilliam unto all theym that ware capiteyns of the greate shypes for to retorne into the Treade where as the greate shipes lay before the havyn of Brest, and soo for to abide still before the haven of Brest th[at the] armye of Ffraunce shuld not come oute, whillist that the small shippes s[hould run] upon the galyes. And the small shippes and the greate laye 4 myles...

Upon Saynt Markes daye, the which was the 25 daye of April, mylord Admyrall appoynted 4 capiteyns and hymself for to borde the [galyes. A]t 4 of the clok in the afternone, my saide lorde went into [one of the galeys] hymself with 80 men with hym, and in thother [mylord] Ferris, with suche companye as hym semyd best, and . . . with 2 small crayres, in oon of the crayres w[ent] Wal-[lop], and in thother went sir Henry S[herburne] and William Sidnaye. And theise were they that enterprysed for to wyn [the] ffrenche galyes, with helpe of the bootes, for there couth no ship comme [to] theyme for lack of water, for the said frenche galyes laye in a baye [betwene] rockes, and on both sides of the galyes was made bulwerkes [where] laye full of ordynaunce, that no boote nor vessell couth comme unto them, but that they must comme betwene the bulwarkes, the which [were] soo thick with gonnes and crosbowis that the quarrelles and the gonstons came together as thick as it hade be haylestones.

Ffor all this Mylorde wold needes borde the galyes his owen p[ers]on for there couth no man counsayle hym the contrary, and at the owre above wreten he bordit the galye that Preyer John was in. And as sone as he was aborde of Pryer Johns galye, he le[ped] oute of his owne galye unto the fore castell of Pryer Johns galye, and Charran, the Spanyart, with hym, with 16 other persones. S[ir, by] advice of mylorde Admyrall and Charran, thay hade cast theyre ancre in to . . . of the french galye, and fastened the cabull unto the capsten, for this con-[sideration] yf it happened . . . any of the galyes to have bene on fyre, that they myght have vered the cabull and have fallen of. But, Sir, how so ever it fo . . . the Frenchmen did hew asondr the cabull, or els somme of our [said] maryners in our galye lete slip the cable, when mylorde Admyrell [went] into the frenche galye, and all for fere of thordy-naunce that w[as on] the galyes and from the lande, and so they lefte this [poor Admerall in the] handes of his enymyes, wheras by divers mens say[ing] the Morris pickes. Sir, ther was a maryner that . . . the which is woundit in 18 placys . . ., the whiche by adventure recouered unto the boye of the galye, and soo the bote of the galye toke hym up, and he saythe that he sawe my lord Admyrall thras[ted] up agaynst the rayls of the galy with Morris pikes.[1] Also Charran's boye tellith a tale in like maner, for when his maister and mylorde Admyrall were entert the galye, Charran bade his boye fetche hym his hande gonne and when he came up with the hande gonne to delyuer to his maister the oone galye was gone of from thother, and he saith he see my lord Admirall wayvyng with his handes and cryeng to the galye : ' Comme aborde agayne ! Comme aborde agayne !' And when mylord saw the galye couth not comme to hym agayne, the boy saide he sawe hym take his whistill from aboute his neck, and wrap it together, and hurlid it in to the see, and thus he lost the sight of my saide lorde Admyrall.

Sir, for to knowe the more suretie whither he ware alyve or not, we sende in a bote to the shore a standart of peax, and in the bote went Thomas Cheyne, Richard Cornewale and Wallop, for to have knolege whither they hade takyn any English men prysoners or not. And whan they came to the shore, there came unto them 2 gentilmen of Ffraunce, and askid theym what they wold h[ave], and they saide they came to speke with th'Admyrall of Ffraunce.[2] And then these 2 gentilmen bade theym comme on lande, [and they woul]d warraunt theym for thaym and thayres, but thay [would] not without they hade 4 gentilmen of Ffraunce . . . And so theise 2 gentilmen torned agayne, a . . . men and send theym in to the bote. And . . . Cheyne and his companye came oute and went unto londe where the Admyrall of Ffraunce was. And there Thomas Cheyne mett with . . . acquayntance of the quene of Ffraunce court. And, thus, as they [were] talkyng and makyng chere yche to other, came

---

[1] Large pikes (Halliwell).   [2] M. du Chillou.

Preter John, ridyng [on] horsbak. And soo they askid if they hade takyn any prisoners english or not, for Thomas Cheyne saide he hade a kynsman that [was] outher takyn or slayne among theym, and if they hade hym, [that] they wold assigne hym to his ransom and he wold paye it, or [else] that he myght be well kept and they shuld be richly rewardid [for] his kepyng, And then Pryer John stept forthe hymself and [said] to them : ' Sirs, I ensure you I have no prysoners english within [my] galye but one, and he is a maryner, but there was oon that lep[t] into my galye with a gilt targett on his arme, the which I caste ouer borde with Morris pikes, and the maryner that I have prysoner told me that that same man was your Admyrall.'

Sir [I have] forgoten to write you of the galye that my lord Fferris was in [with the] other companye. Sir, there came in my lord Fferris with his galye . . . fell among the other galyes, and there he shott all his ordynance both pouder and stone that he hade within borde, and he shott 200 sheif of arrois among theym in the galyes . . . was my lord Fferris had none of his owne f . . . but there was many in the same galye slayne and . . . When he sawe that the galye that my . . . of and all his own ordynaunce . . ., then the lesser rowbarge came unto likewise, and at her commyng her master was slayne, and than came Thomas Chayne and Wallop in theyre crayre and they shott theyre ordynaunce such as they hade. And then came sir Henry Sherborne and sir William Sidnaye, and they russhid aborde of Pryer Johns galye and brake parte of his oris on the one side. And so when they saw euery gone of from theym, and they last alone wenyng to theym that mylord Admyrall hade be still in the english galye, they came of foloyng our galye, and so they retorned all into the Treade, whereas the greate ships laye without any more doyng, for they knew not perfitely where mylord Admirall was.

Sir, when the holl armye knew that mylord Admirall was outher takyn or slayne, I trow there was neuer men more full of sorrow then all we ware, ffor there was neuer noble man so ill lost as he was, that was of so greate courage and hade so many vertues, and that rowled so greate an armye so well as he did and kept so good order and trew justice. Sir, I assure you as for now there is in this armye but small regarde takyn to any man of th'armye, [if it] shall please the kynges most noble Grace to admytt an Admyrall or . . . capiteyn generall over us, the which may be somme noble man . . . may be discrete, wise and sadd, and also that he may . . . feared and loved, for there was never armye that hade . . . We have at this tyme for to kepe good order and . . .

Ffrere Barnardyn [1] is at Burdeos and there [are with hym] [t]en galyes, the which the Frenchmen . . . to Brest haven, howbeit ty . . . in a calme, or els that they haue the londe to be theyre . . .

Thies be the newes of thes parties, savyng that my lorde Fferris [is the one we] have chosen to our Admyrell, and sir Weston Brown with other of t[he Coun]saile hath yeven me and Harper [2] in commaundment for to go to Hampton for to wafte the vytlers unto theym, for I was chosen for 3 consid[erations], furst bycause my ship is so good with a sayle, the second bycause I haue [a] gretter store of vitaile within borde then any other ship in th'armye, the third was all my men ware holl without any siknes.

Sir, I certifie you that there be many men slayne

---

[1] Inventories of the galleys of Fray Bernardin, at Marseilles, 11 April—1 May, 1513 : Ste. Marthe, Ste. Lucie, Ste. Barbe, Madeleine-Limose, Anguille, &c. (*Arch. Bouches du Rhône*, B 1232, fol. 19-29). [2] Captain of the Baptist of Harwich.

at this small skyrmysh, and there is also in th'armye many seke men, and that is not in one ship but in euery [one of] th'armye, and many dethe of the measilles and other siknes that is among us, and as in my ship I hade neuer oone dede but one yet, I hade . . . and I thanke God I haue recouered theym by the [way] of suche spices . . '. as I have within borde.

Sir, upon Satterday, the last daye of Aprill, [the] holl navye came to Plymouth, and on Sonday I se my selfe a bote of sikmen [la]nd out of a ship of th'armye, and two of those men, assone as they felt . . . the erth, they fell down and dede. Sir, as me semyth, yf the [kyng's] noble Grace will have his galyes and his rowbargis to do any harme to the Fren]chmen], he must put into theym somme gentilman that is of god corage . . . capiteyn and of the best maryners and most hardiest that be in his realme . . . the rowers in the saide galys must be tyed fast with cheyns or ells . . . when men shall have most nede of them and that they must . . . And also they must be well manyd with archers and with . . ., and they that shall be capteyns and maryners in the saide galys, ye [must give] theym greate rewarde if they do well, and th . . . and frely to sett on theyr enemys, or els noman . . . [en] due the payne. Sir, ther was neuer oon of . . . of theym the which lacketh no . . . be foresene that the . . .

[Sir, after] departyng out of Yngland, upon Wedynsday [13 day of] April I spiede a sayle thwart of Bechif,[1] the which I reknyd a Frenche[man]. We chasid him 2 or 3 owres, and so at the last she stroke sayle and so it . . . a hulk of Ffreselonde, and so we departed from her and drewe westward along [the coast of the] sees all that day and nyght.

[1] Beachy Head (?).

And on Thursday in the mornyng we spiede 15 sayle [com]yng towards us, and somme of my companye reknyd theym for Frenchemen, howbeit . . . de I wold see whither they were Frenche, Ynglysh or Duche, for I trusted my ship [so good] with a sayle that I ffered theym not all. And so, when we came nere theym, we [discove]red they were Spanyartes. Sir, then incontynent after our metyng, the wynde w[as contr]ary for us.

And upon Ffryday in the mornyng we aspied 3 Frenchmen of [war]re that made unto us warde, and then I comfortid my folk & made theym to harnes, and bycause I hade no rayles upon my dek I coyled a cable rounde a[long] dek, brest hye, and likewise in the waste, and so I henged upon the cable [mat]rasses, dagswayns & such beddyng as I hade within borde, and settyng out my [morr]is pikes and my ffyzghtyng sayles all redy to encontre theise 3 French barkes, [and] such pore ordynaunce as I hade. And than they saw that I made unto theym . . . so god a will and wold not shrynk for theym. Then they put theymselves [to] fflyght and I chasid theym till they came to the abbay of Feckam,[1] [which ly]ith harde by the see side, and so they gate theym under the walls of . . . [in] the havyn, and we ffolowed theym till they shott theyr ordynaunce onto us. I seyng there was no remedy to comme to theym, torned . . . That day & nyght we travest the sees.

The 16 day of Aprill . . . on, for the wynde was so at S.S.W. that we couth none . . .

[The 17th] day of Aprill I came from Camborow[2] in the mornyng and . . . ne.

The 18 day we spied a sayle in the mornyng . . ., in conclusion it was a ship of Armue[3] and . . . pilott of the same ship, and I toke hym as . . . of

[1] Fécamp.   [2] Cherbourg (?).   [3] Dartmouth.

the clok in the afternone we came . . . that durst go no fferder for . . . . .¹
. . . .
to bryng theym to the armye.

The 19 day we . . . and at 10 of the clok in the mornyng we aspied the French galeys amongst the rocks, and at that tyme I was chasyng a Bryton and . . . vytlers lying on the see borde of me, and assone as I perceived the galy, I . . . rownd to the vytlers and left my chase, or ells the vytlers had bene t . . . everychone. Then, when we came to the vytlers, we espied 22 sayle . . . withyn 2 myle of the galys, wherfore we reknyd theym the French [flete]. Sir, ye saw never men so feared as the Spanyarts were, for they s[aid]: 'Now is the day comyng that we shal be fayne to go to the hospital.' Then they in the top spied another company of ships lyeng in the . . . And so we made about unto them saylyng through the brode so[unde] 10 myle out of our course, and came into the Treade the same day, the Kynges most royall army beyng in Brest water, with the vytlers in my company. And then I came aborde to mylorde Admyrall, and then I trow there was never knyght more welcome to his soveraign lady [then] I was to mylord Admyrall and unto all the holl armye, for by[cause I] brought the vytlers with me, for of 10 days before ther was no . . . all the armye that hade but one mele a day and one drynke.

. . . thus an ende of this symple lettre, and I prayng God to sende . . . honorable fortune.

Writen at Hampton, the 5 day of M[aye].
Yores to his power
EDWARD ECHYNGHAM.

I eftsones besech you to be so gode master

¹ One line wanting.

unto me as . . . Hampton by the next that comyth betwene of the Kyngs . . . shortly retorne to the flete, and also Harper or . . . to play us a whyle.

EDWARD [ECHYNGHAM].

(Brit. Mus., Calig. D vi, fol. 107.)

77. *Thomas Howard to Henry VIII.*

(Plymouth : 7 May, 1513.)

[Why the fleet left Brittany without order: lack of victuals, fear of Prégent's galleys and ordnance. List of men slain and hurt. Danger of Sir Edward Howard's enterprise. If the King does not send a sufficient force, there is nothing to be done in the Trade, and something may be attempted towards La Rochelle.]

Please it your most noble Grace to understand yesternight I cam unto Dertmouth at 9 of the clok, and this daye at oon of the clok I cam hydder as wery a man of rydyng as ever was any. At which tyme I assembled in the Mary Rose my lorde Ferrers and all oder noblemen and capeteynes and most expert masters of your army, and ther rehersed unto them your commandement yeven unto me, and after that I enquired of them the cause of their comyng from the parties of Breten without your commandement. Unto which they answered with oon hole voyce and all in oon tale they did it upon dyverse and resonable groundys. Oon was they had grete defawte of vyttell and had not in their borde for 3 days, notwithstandyng that Sabyan brought with him 9 crarys ladyn with vittells. And such vittellers as were appoynted for them, came from London hydder and to Dertmouth, and here remayned till the cummyng hidder of your armye, without cummyng to them.[1] Oon other cause was,

[1] 'The wynde contryved that nowther I nor the said vitells

all your capiteynes and masters generally sey, that, and they had contynued there and oon day of calme had cum, if the galyes being within 3 myle of them wold have doon their werst unto them, as it is to suppose they wold have doon, they shuld not a fayled to have sonke such of your ships as they list to have shot ther ordinance unto : which ordinance, if it be such as they report, is a thynge mervelous. Without that your said armye could in anywise have anoyed them. Whereupon [I] resoned with your masters, seying if the galyes had cum forth and that your 2 gallies and 2 rowbarges with the help of the boats had sett on them, what they thought they had been able to have doon to the said galies. And with oon accorde they answered me that oon of the galies in a calme wolde distresse your 2 galies and rowbarges and to drown with their oorys as many bootys as cam within the reche of them. And also all the masters saye that, if the wynde had blowen streynably at S.W., or W.S.W., or W. and by S., ther had been no remedy, [and by] force they must have renne into Croydon Baye, wher they shuld have ly . . . nere, the shorys of both sidys beying allredy soor bullewerked, that, without [they] had been able to have betyn the Frenchmen from the londe, the said French[men with] their ordenaunce myght have destroyed all your fflete lying ther. And as [accordyng] to the actuell ffeitys of all such noblemen and gentylmen as were pr[esent], my broder, the Admyrall, was drowned (whom Jesu perdon!) I assure your [Grace] herforth as I can be anywise understande, they handelid them self as [well as ever] men did to opteyne their Masters pleasure and favor.

Syr, ther w[er with my brother] 175 men, of

cam not to my said lord in the Trade in Breten till on St. Marks daye' (Brewer, i. 4376).

whome wer left on life but 56,[1] and of those [beyng wyth] my lord Ferrers, men 25 slayne and 20 hurte, and may galye had not fallen on grounde beyng nere the shoore, then the od[er in like]wise borded as the oder dyd and of lyklyhode ferre had escaped. . . . Sherborne and sir William Sydney borded a galie, they beying in a small [crayer], and yet by fortune had but 3 men slayne and 7 hurte . . . Thomas Cheny and Wallop beying in a littell crare borded in lykewise and yet they had no man slayne nor hurte. William Tolly and his broder Sir Robert B . . . of all men and had 12 men slayne and above 20 hurte. Wiseman m . . . borded not, but he had all his men slayne or hurte. Sir Wystan Bro[wne had] 3 men slayne, and dyverse oder bootys had many men slayne and hurte. [Please] your Grace that, as ferre as I can understand by any mannys report, [it was] the most daungerfull enterprise that ever I harde of, and the most manly handeled of the setters on, insomuche that I see no lyklyhode [nor] possybillyte to brynge the maryners to rowe the galies or bootys to s[hore without] other bargen. Sir I had forgetyn 2 men that did aswell as was possibl: [it] was Gurney beying in the Jenet Purwyn, and good Lewes with the oon . . . in the Elizabeth of Newecastell, as well apperyd by the slaughter of . . . and bowgyng of their ships. And all oder gentilmen which had [part] of the enterprise ar the most angrye men in the worlde that they ha[ve . . . therof.

Also, Sir, plees it your Grace to understande I have declared . . . unto all the capitaynes and masters howe your Grace wold I shuld [with the] armye retourne unto the Trade, demaundyng of

---

[1] John Soome, petty captain of the Lezard, was 'soor hurte' in Brittany (Brewer,'i. 4376); also Oliver Awerey (*R. O., Warrants for issues*, bundle 80: Richmond, 25 January, 1514).

them what servyce . . . shall be possible for us to do your Grace ther. And as well the capitaynes [as the] masters have answerd me that, consyderyng the gret fortifycation out . . . the gret daunger of the galies if a calm cum, the great daunger o[f the] wyndys afore rehersed, if they fortune to blow streynably, they all [beyng of one] mynde say precysely they see no lyklyhoode nor possybyllite but that o[ur retourne] there shall rather tourne to our great reproche, losse of ships and [men than] oderwyse. And also they all thynke it not possyble, the premysses consi[derd] anythynge that may redounde to the honour of your Grace, your re[alm and] oure poore honesties, oonless that your Grace wold so furnysshe us with [all, that] we myght be able both to kepe our shippes and also to defend [them against] your enemyes for 5 or 6 dayes: which doon, all the expert cap[teyns and] masters thynk veraly your Grace shall not oonly cause us to d[estroy the ships] of Fraunce with the galies, but also put your enemyes to the . . . that ever they had in Bretyn.

Sir, I haue not wretyn vnto [your Grace] the premysses, but that the noblemen and capiteynes of [the navy] signed with their handys the copy of the same. And nowe, Sir, in my most humble [waye], I beseche your Grace that with all possyble diligens I may knowe howe your pleasure shal be, that I shall order myself, and that I may have answer from your Grace by Wednysdaye at nyght, before which tyme it shall not be possyble for me to departe hens, consyderyng that your army wold not have their vittell in before that tyme, and also a great part of your armye is sparkylled abrode on the londe, and slayne, and departed from the armye I am sure not so fewe as 500. At which tyme, if I have no worde from your Grace, the wynde servyng with Goddys grace, I shall see the Trade. And if I can perceyue any thynge that may be doon, I shall accomplyssh the same to the best of my power, and if it may stande with your pleasure that I shall seke along the cost of Breten beyond the Trade howe I maye most anoye your enemyes, I beseeche your Grace I maye be advertised thereof, for, Sir, if your pleasure shal be to send us no gretter nowmbre of men, as ferre as I can perceyue by all your masters, the gretter displeasures that we may do your enemyes shal be beyonde the trade to Rochell ward, wher if your Grace woll that we shall medill with the yles patessed,[1] as they have doon with yours, I dowte not to do them great hurte. And as towchyng the flete that lyeth at Brest, they dare not come forth toward the west parties of your realm, for, and they did, that wynde that shuld serue them shuld serue me to clap betwene them and home, which I pray God to geve me grace onys to see. And as for vittelers, your seruantys from Hampton beyng come to me I dowte not to be well furnesshed [for] 2 moneths. And if they wold go to Normandye warde, then I wold trust your Grace shuld shortly haue your pleasure of them. Syr, I can saye no more unto your Grace. Myn poore advise shalbe, heryng so moche as I have herd, that eyther your Grace shall send us a sufficient company to londe, or ells to let us seke oure best ad[vantage], for in the Trade, if your masters may be trustyd, is nothyng to be doon, and in the letter wich I send Master Awlmesner, your Grace shall understande [more] and thus our Lord preserue your most noble Grace.

Wryten in the Mary Rose, in Plymouth havyn, the 7 day of May, at 11 a clok at nyght.

Your most [bounden servant].

[1] Cf. Doc. 60 and note.

IN 1512—13

[Endorsed :] To the kyng's Grace.
Delyverd the post at mydnyght.
MY LORDE ADMYRALL.
(Brit. Mus., Calig. D, vi, fol. 104.)

78. *Thomas Howard to Wolsey.*

(Plymouth : 7 May [1513].)

[The English army demoralised and in great fear of Prégent's galleys and ordnance. The King's letter has discouraged captains and men].

Myn owne gode Master Awlmowsner, all such matier as I have wryten to the kyng's Grace off, I woll leve unwriten to you, assewring you that I have here fownd the worst ordered armye and furthest owte of rewle that ever I saw. This day when I cam hither, I am sewer ther wer more then half the armye on lande, and I fere me, by hering say, ther is a grete nomber stolen away. At my commyng to Exeter, I herd of their departyng and so have sent thorow all the contre to bryng them agayne. Never man saw men in greter fere then all the masters and maryners be off the galies, insomoche that in a maner they had as leve go into Purgatory as to the Trade. But that notwithstandyng, iff the kyng's Grace send me not contrary commandement, I trust to be there by Fryday at the furthest. Also the Kyng's lettre sent to the captayns hath gretly trobled and discoraged them, for they had trusted to have had grete thanks, and undowted as many jentilmen as wer warned theroff, did as valiauntly as was possible. And as for the galies myght have be brent, but my brothir (whom God pardon) was so feise that he wold suffer no man to cast in wyldfier, and the said galies dyd our men but litell hurt. But both the shorys wer so well bulwarked and so innewmerable ordinance therin that it is to wonderfull to here the report of them that saw it.

Gode Master Awlmosner, cause the kyng's Grace to wryght unto the captayns som favorable lettre, ffor I assewre you it is nedefull, and iff any of them wolde make labor to awayte on His Grace when he goth over see, for Godd's sake stope it, for and one shuld go, all the resydew wold desire the same.

Here is 2 men that, as I here sey, did their part very ill that day my brother was lost: the one was Coke, the qweny's servant in a rowe barge, and the other Freman, my seid brother's howshold servant. Iff it be off trewth, I shall ponyshe them that all other shall take ensample, I assewring you that I see very few or none, grete or small, that with their wills wold go agayne to the Trade; what the course is, as yet I cannot say, but shortly I trust to see jff the danger be so grete as I am enformed off. Besechyng you that the kyng's Grace take no displesure with me that I tary here so long, for I assewre you no man is so wery theroff as I, and before Thursday shall not be possible for us to depart, what for takyng in off vitell, wherof a grete part as yet is uncome, and also I fere we shall moche ado to get our souldiors aborde. Also the Anne Galaunt[1] is in suche case that she shall not be able to go to the see this yere, she lieth here on dry grownde, and in her stede I have takeyn another.

I wold wright to you off many other causys, but that I woll not tary the post no longer, and iff the

[1] 'Whereas Walter Loveday, beyng capitayne of the Anne Gallant, haled the said ship on grounde at Plymouth to amend such hurts as the same ship toke upon the rocks in Breten, and when she was in the havyn of Plymouth, the said ship sanke' (Warrant of Thomas Howard, 9 July 1513). The Anne Galant is replaced by the Katherine of London.

Kyng's lettres come to Plymouth when I am gone, I shall leve one to bryng them after, with Godde's grace, who kepe you.

Scrybeled in gret hast in the Mary Rose at Plymouth, half our after 11 at night, the 7 day off May.

Your owne
THOMAS HOWARD.
(Ellis, 3rd series, i. 154.)

79. *Robert Acciajuoli to Florence.*

(Blois: 7 May, 1513.)

[The English fleet has returned to England. Prégent's galleys are safe, but destitute of rowers, and are not expected to do any service for several weeks.]

L' armata Inghilese si truova in Bretagna dopo che hebbe tentato di strignere Pregianni. Dopo non molto proficto si è partita ne si sia ancora dove sia per posarsi. Questi dicono essersi tornata in Inghilterra.

Le galee di Pregianni sono tutte salve, ma sono in modo restate sfornite di gente, parte per essere periti li homini di peste, parte per quelli assalti diminuito il numero, parte per essere suto liberi li homini che vi erono su per forza, che non si crede che intra molte septimane possa fare molte factioni.

(*Firenze, Arch. di Stato, Reformazioni, Dieci di Balia. Responsive, Filza no.* 114.)

80. *W. Knight to Henry VIII.*

(Valladolid: 12 May, 1513.)

[Ferdinand the Catholic dissatisfied with the news from Brittany and with the sale of the Katherine Fortaleza.]

Where it was soo that newys were broughte unto this courte upon St Mark's day that Your

Grace's royall armye by the seeys had discomfetied the frensh flete, yt apperid both by thair countenances here that the saide victorye contentyd not thayr mynde,[1] and by their other demenure, for they did as moche as lay in them to contrarie and destroye the fame of the sayde newys and victorie, as Don Petro Belis de Guyvara, I doubt not, will shew right shortli unto Your Grace.

Over thys, aftyr the fame of the saide newys, where we laboured instauntly unto His Grace for Domyngo de Losa, whose movables beth excheted for selling of a carrack unto Your Highnes, contrarie to the statutes of this contree, we fownde His Grace so sore moved with the selling of the said carrack that yt apperid that he was grevid that his shippes shuld be parte of the occasion of the saide victorie, for, before the forsaide tydyngs were broughte, His Grace gave to us always comfortable aunswere in the saide cause and promised to put a remedye in hytt, soo that Your Highness and your moost honorable Counsayle may forsee and put remedy if the King of Arragon wolde entende aftyr his cautelous maner the revoking of suche his shippes as be in Your Grace's wages.

The forsaid newis were so joyfull unto us, Your Grace's subgetts here, that we desired to know of the king of Arragon what certaynte he had thereof. Which aunswerd that he did know nothing thereof. But aftyr 3 daiys, when the same dyd more largeli increase, he shewed unto us that he was enformed owte of Fraunce that the Frensh king gave in expresse commaundement to the capitains of his navye, that, in case thei were not able to have the ovyrhand of the Englishmen, that thei shulde rather fyer thaire owen shippes then suffre them to be taken. Wherein

---

[1] On the other hand James IV. deplored Edward Howard's death, Edinburgh, 24 May (Ellis, 1st series, i. 77).

his meanyng was, bi all that I cowde perceyve, that if there were any shippes distroied by the frensh flete that yt was doone by themself, because of the commaundement of their King, and not by Your Grace's royall armye.

(Ellis, 2nd series, i. 203.)

81. *Thomas Howard to Wolsey.*
(Plymouth: 15 May, 1513.)

[The wind is contrary. The fleet will shortly leave for Southampton. The King must forbid landing without licence. The truce between France and Spain. The rebellion of Brest castle.]

Master Almoner, I hertly recommande me unto you, and, thanked be God, the wynd is wher I wold wishe it, howbeit it bloweth so sore that I with the Peter and diuers grete shippes can not get out of this water called Katt water, also here be many small men off vittellers that can not get out, the wynd blowyng thus strenable; but I trust agaynst nyght this W.N.W. wynd will ly, and then we woll forth with warpyng, and otherwise we can not, for till we be past the poynt of the Castell, the wynd is full in our way, as every shipman can shew you. Wherfor I hertly desire you to call vnto you some maryner that knowith this coste and then I doute not yo shall know there is no thyng vndone that may be done here.

In folowyng the Kyng's plesure also, the Souereyne and all the carrykkes and all the grete shippes ryde under Seint Nicholas Ilond and with this wynd may go wher they woll, and so I haue comanded them to go forth and ryde in the Sownde, and as sone as this letter is wryten, I shall go myself into Ashe water and send all the vitellers there forth to Hampton warde and with them Antony Poynes,

Wisman and Draper for wafters. And if it be possible that the wynd be any thyng peasable, this nyght with all the resydew off men of war and vitellers, I woll to Hampton [war]de.

At wich tyme I require you I may have a streite letter directed to [me comma]ndyng me to suffer no man, captayne nor other to go on [londe, al]so another to the captayns not to go on londe without [lycence]. Sir, I am loth to complayne and also it is no ty[me] all, howbeit I asseure you I am dissayued . . . wynd came westerly and I had . . . .

. . . . .[1] to bryng them to their shippes which be sparkled 12 [miles] abrode in the contre, I haue yeven no lenger day but . . . to be aborde, and I have made a pair of galows at the waterside, wher I fere me some woll towter tomorow, [for I] rather hang half a dozen knavys than any oftener to . . . this desplesure all captayns do not amys, but I asseure you . . . moste part in this behalue. Wherfor I require you to cause the sharp [letter] to be directed and make your ground that the Kyng is [infor]med that the souldiers be abrode in the contre and robe [and] stele and do moche hurt. Towchyng this matier I say [no] more: sapienti pauca.

Also I send you a wryting [of a] Spanyshe wich a merchant of Bristowe yave me this day and [came] hither this nyght, and was at Calys in Spayne 10 days past and . . . the same proclamed[2] and for his savegarde if he h[ad] to mete with Frenchmen broght the same with him. I [think] the Kyng shall spede the better, if the Kyng trust his owne [people].

Also, Sir, I am sewerly informed by Sabian that at the [same] tyme Brest castell was won by M. de

---

[1] A line or more missing.
[2] About the truce with Spain, cf. *Arch. Loire Inférieure*, reg. Chancery xxi. fol. 84 (21 April, 1513).

Rohan and M. de Shamperous, the French king's lieutenant, then . . . obteyned it by this ways. Ther was many Brytens [in] the castell wich had their londs lying in the contre adioynyng and the seid french captaynes gave warnyng that, onles they yelded them, the[y wold] wold borne and distroy the hole contre and [cut] their tymber trees by the myddes. W . . especiell fellyng of their trees . . . they yelded the keys with . . . .
. . . .[1] send us 2 or 300 axis.

Also I beseche you that, at my coming and sir Charles to Hampton, we may fynde ther mylord off Wynchester to debate with him such enterprises as we have to do and I trust to rype him well in every cause, for, when I am not occupied, it is my most besynes to be instructed of them that can skyll, most hertly desyring you to beseche the kyng's Grace not to thynk no lacheousnes in me ffor our long abode here with the vitellers, ffor I asseure you the fawte is in the wynde and not in me, as I am sewer every skylled man can shew you. And wheras I wright unto you often and peraventure every cause I wright off be not of grete grauyte, yet I require you ascrybe not the same to my defawte, for I asseure you I had rather the posts toke payne in sparryng their horses then I shuld be fownd to slow in wryting or workyng when tyme shall require, and till I see you, I shall not forget your words ad captandam benevolentiam and our lord hold the wynd wher he is, and on Tewsday at nyght ye shall not fayle then to have the vitellers at Hampton and the men of war about the row and the Wight . . . apoynted ships here for . . . broke and sir Piers Egecombe . . . for a moneth of prouysion . . . tre and wafters for . . . broke wold kepe his . . . not he is to blame and thus our lord kepe you.

[1] A line or more missing.

Scrybeled [in] hast in the Mary Rose at one at after, when the w[ynd] . . . tofore if God wold otherwise.

Yours asseuredly
THOMAS HOWARD.

[Endorsed:] To Master Almoner, with the kyng's Grace.

Delyverd to Plymmouth, this Witsonday before 2 at afternoon.

82. *Wolsey to Thomas Howard.*

(About 25 May, 1513.)

[The fleet must be revictualled at Southampton for a month or six weeks before returning to Brittany, but the Admiral must punish those who burnt the empty casks.]

My lorde Admirall, with all myne herte I comende me on to you. I haue resseyuyd yor moste louyng letters datyd at Plymowth the 21 day of thys monthe, by the conteyne wherof I do perceyue howe that ye trust to be at the Wyt within schort tyme, wych I assure yow shal be glad tydyngs to the Kyng, for as soon as hys Grace shall haue worde therof, he wold nott fayle within schort whil after to be with yow there. And wher as yor vittell ys so nere expyryd and that ye must bee substancielly vitailled for 6 weeks or a moneth at the leest befor yor departing vnto Brytayn, mylord, I assure you it is not possible to furnishe yor revitailling if ffoystes bee not more plentuously brought from the navye to Hampton than they be, whiche is a grete lak and default, for ye cannot be prouided elleswher of any ffoystes for money, And if the ffoystes amonges the navye bee not kept and reserued, but wastefully brent and broken as I here saye they bee, ye cannot bee sufficiently revitailled to tarye any longer on the see, ffor wheras some shippes haue receyued 10 wekes passed 756 pypes, they have redeliuered scantly 80 ffoystes of thaym. Whiche as it appereth is doon by some lewde persons that wold not haue the King's navye contynue any lenger on the See. And therfor, Mylorde, for Goddes sake, loke wel to this matier so that suche substancial order may bee taken that th' empty ffoystes may be contynuelly reserued and with all diligence sent to Hampton and that suche persons as haue brent any of thaym maybe punisshed by yor discrecion in example of al other, in eschuyng the grete inconveniences and displeasures that for lak of ffoystes mought ensue at this tyme to the hinderaunce and lette of yor entreprises upon yor enemyes as is aforesaid, ffor if the ffoystes bee not reserued, but lost and brent, for lak of good ordre taken therein, it wold bee to yor reproche. Whiche causeth me the mor plainly to write you for yor discharge herin, ffor without the said empty foystes ye cannot tarye any longer on the see, though ye wold neuer soo fayne and than suche as bee accustomed to speke evyll wol averte the blame vnto you and saye that ye wol not out of the havons, but lye ther spendyng wastefully the King's vitaill and money And therfor as oon that wold ye shuld doo wel I eftsones require you to regarde this matier accordingly for yor honor. And this moost hertily fare ye well.[1]

(Brewer, i. 4139.)

83. *Thomas Howard to Wolsey.*

(Hampton : 5 June [1513].)

[False reports against Sir Edward Howard. The enterprise against Brittany was countermanded yesterday. The admiral hopes that the Scottish navy will join the French ; if not, it will be better to discharge all the hired ships, both Spanish and English.]

[1] 16,000*l.* are sent to Southampton for the 'revitailing' of the King's army (5 June) (*R. O., Chapter House Book* 215, p. 257).

Master Almoner, with all my hert I recomande me unto you. Gode master Almoner, I have fownd you so kynd unto me that me thynk I can do no les than to wryght to you fro tyme to tyme of all my causis. So it is, though I be unable therfor, it hath plesed the kyng's Grace to yeve this grete rome and auctorite more mete for a wise expert man then me. But sith it hath plesed His Grace to admytt me thereunto, as fer as my pore wit can extende, I shall endevor myselff fro tyme to tyme to do all maner of servyce when I shall thynk to deserve his most desired favor. And, gode Mr Almoner, as my most synguler trust is in you, send me both now and at all other tymes your gode advyse and consell, assewring you that never pore jantilman was in greter fere to take rebuke and ill report that I am of suche as knowith not what may be done, wich generally be the grettest nombre, and for many causis, of wich I shall reherse a part.

Furst I well perceyve what reports both this yere and the last was made off my brother (whom Jhesu pardon), because ther was none other servyce don, consyderyng what grete charges the Kyng was at in kepyng so grete a navye on the sea. And I well knowe that I nor no man hath better will nor more hardely serve his master then he, as the proffe hath shewed; and as for experience I am yet fer fro that he had, and yet his fortewne was not to have at all tymes the best report, many men puttyng fere what he durst do: wich opynions the day of his deth he well proved untrew.

Alas, Mr Almoner, I se not now how I shall eskape such reports, for I cannot se how I may do any pleasant servyce to my master, for I se no ways but one of the too.

The one is that at my goyng to Brytaynge my fortewne myght have be so gode that either I myght

IN 1512-13

have brenned the shippes at Brest castell, or els to have dystroyed the havyn there with drownyng of shippes, as I have before wryten unto you. Wich enterprises beyng debated before His Grace, and such danger as I thought myght therof ensew by me declared before His Grace, I shewed His Grace I durst not enterprise the seid feats, onles that His Grace wold discharge me iff any misfortewne fell by the same. And then His Grace bad me not spare to adventure the same, and to go with his armye into the grete water at Brest. And now, sith his departure hens, Mylord of Winchester[1] and Mylord Lizle hath devysed upon the seid enterprises, and yesterday called me unto them and commaunded me in the Kyng's name not to enter the water of Brest till I knew further of the Kyng's plesure, for grete causis wich they wold advertise the Kyng and his Consell off.

And so, this matier takyng none effect, I se no way how I shall deserve thank onles the Skotts[2] and

---

[1] For letters of the Bishop of Winchester, cf. Brewer, i. 4056, 4073, 5757.

[2] Robert Barton left Harfleur on 22 May, 1513, for Scotland with his ship Lion (300 t., 300 men), victualled for one month (Bib. Nat., MSS. fr. 26,113, Nos. 1189, 1306). In the same time M. de la Motte went on board the Petite Louise to Brest :—
'Jehan Cinquart, au moys de may [1513], estant lors cappitaine d'une nef nommée le Sacre de l'armée du Roy avec plusieurs aultres navires estans lors à Conkerneau, eut charge de debvoir passer le s' de la Motte, qui estoit ambassadeur du Roy audit navire nommé le Sacre pour aller en Escosse, et pourtant que en sa compaignie avoit ung autre navire nommé la Levrière, ledit sieur de la Motte voulut estre en iceluy, en laquelle estoit pillote Philippes Rouxel, lequel ledit sieur de la Motte avoit amené avecques luy de Brest pour le conduyre èsdites parties d'Escosse. Prindrent la mer pour faire ledit voyage ; mais pour l'impétuosité du temps et tourmente qui survint sur la mer leur convint eulx retourner à St. Mahé, où illecques estoit ung aultre navire nommée la Petite Louyse. En laquelle fut mys ledit s' de la Motte et ledit Rouxel, retenu et mis pour pillote en ladite nef pour passer

Danes joyne with the Frenchmen, without whom I never thynk we shall fynd the Frenchmen abrode; and therfor I beseche God that shortly they may joyn: which onely may be the savegarde of my gode name. And, gode Mr Almoner, iff ye se sewerly that the Skotts and Danes come not, let me have licence to discharge all the armye, save only the Kyng's shippes, with whom the navie of France wol not fyght this yere. And as for the Spanyards here, I assewre you they wolde fayne be at home ever sith they here of the trewes.

And thus most hartly I beseche you, iff my mysfortewne shal be to do no acceptable servyce, to be menys for me to the Kyng and his Consell to consider that never man endured more payne then I shall do to se all other wher they may do gode servyce if they woll, and I can do none, but his enemyes wol adventure as well as I. And, for Godd's sake, let His Grace and his Consell commande me to some herd enterprise to se if I woll folow the same, being in dispaire, save onely off the Skotts and Danys comming.

Mr Almoner, all the premisses and all other my causis I remit to your wisdome, ffully trustyng that ye woll not onely fro tyme to tyme yeve me your gode advice and consell, but also with your frendly words withstonde all ill reports undeserved made of me, as my singuler trust is in you.

And thus Our Lord have you in his tuicion.

Scribled at Hampton, the 5 day off Juny.

Yours asseuredly
Thomas Howard.

(Ellis, 3rd series, i. 157.)

ledit s^r de la Motte, qui alloit quérir les navires d'Escosse pour venir au secours dudit sieur. Et par commandement du s^r du Chillou et d'iceluy ambassadeur, ledit Rouxel conduisit et mena ledit ambassadeur audit lieu d'Escosse ' (*R. O., Chapter House Book* 83, p. 67).

84. The English fleet (4–31 July, 1513).

King's ships.

Name of the Ship	Tonnage	Captain	Master	Soldiers	Mariners	Dedshares	Gunners	Total of Men
Trinity Sovereign [1]	1000	Ferrers	F. Clerk	439	239	38	40 (1 master, 1 mate, 4 quarter masters)	720
Gabriel Royal	1000	W. Trevillian	Hervy	345	240	37½	20	607
Maria de Loreta	800	Cornwall and Courteney	Rutter	338	228	37½	20	589
Katherine Forteleza [2]	700	J. Flemyng	Edm. Freman	251	229	27½	40	522
Mary Rose	600	Th. Howard	Th. Spert	200	179	27½	20	402
Peter Pomegranate	450	Wistan Browne	J. Clog	136	130	20½	20	288
John Baptist	400	Th. Wyndham (and 2 clerks)	J. Kempe	150	135	20½	15	304
Nicholas Rede	400	W. Pyrton	Th. Morgan	147	135	20½	15	299
Great Bark	400	H. Shernburne and W. Sydney	J. Browne	147	100	20½	12	263 [3]
Mary George	300	Morice Berkley	Rob. Spodell	137½	88	19½	12	239½
Mary James	300	Rauffe Ellercar	—	146	85	19½	15	249
Christ	300	Th. Cheny	J. Mytchell	114	85	19½	15	216
Less Bark	240	Stephen Bull	Rob. Spert	84	88	19½	12	186
Lizard	220	Cristofer Coo	Rob. Longwode	58	32	19½	8	100
Jenet Purwyn	70	Th. Gurney	Freman	10	43	19½	5	59
Barbara of Greenwich	160	Ed. Yelverton	Bert. Wynall	74	45	19½	5	126
Henry of Hampton	120	W. West	J. Haryson	85	40	19½	6	133
Sweepstake	80	W. Tolley	—	—	62	16½	4	68
Swallow	80	Th. Carrewe	J. Peryn	20	46	16½	4	72
Bark to the Mary Rose	80	—	W. Davison	—	59	16½	6	66
Bark for the Katherine Forteleza [4]	80	—	W. Kenwode	—	59	16½	6	66
Mary and John [5]	—	—	Edm. Cony	71	66	19½	12	151

[1] Vacant for 5th month (August, 1513).   [2] Petyr Seman, pilot, 6 months ending 28 Aug. 1513.
[3] Ten men late in the retinue of Arthur Plantagenet (warrant of Th. Howard, 19 June, 1513), 'The Kyng's Grete Barke callyd the Henry of Grenewych.'   [4] Rose galey or Rose Henry.
[5] Warrant of Th. Howard, 16 July, 1513, to pay one month's wages for 150 persons to Roger Rothwell, purser of the Mary and John [8 July–4 August].

English hired ships.

	Tons	Captain	Men
Trinity of Bristol	160	Ant. Poyntz	130
Christopher Davy	160	Edm. Wiseman	157
Nicholas Draper	160	Rob. Draper	148
Matthew Cradok	240	Mat. Cradok	195
Elizabeth of Newcastle	120	Lewes Southern	132
Rosamus of London	160	Rich. Mercer	136
Jermyn	100	Roger Bridges	98
Sabyn	120	W. Sabyn	101
Margaret of Topsham	120	James Knyvet	100
Baptist of Calais	120	Ch. Clyfford	101
Mary of Walsingham	120	Philip Barnard	97
Mary of Brixham	120	Rich. Calthorp	92
Gybbes' ship	120	W. Gybbes	120
Julian of Dartmouth	100	George Whitwombe	103
James of Dartmouth	120	Rob. Appulyew	103
Margaret Bonaventure	120	Rich. Berdisley	101
Christopher of Dartmouth	120	Th. Vowell	98
Thomas of Hull	80	W. Ellercar	76
Baptist of Harwich	70	W. Harper	61
Leonard Frescobaldi	300	Alex. Manachen	245
Michael of Plymouth	80	Rich. Courtenay	70
Mary Christopher	140	W. Symons	120
Matthew of Bristol	150	W. Mygenall	131
Mary Katherine of London	160	Walter Loveday	125
Peter of Fowey	120	Edm. Tylney and J. Hansard	86
Mary of Falmouth	90	Roger Aldred	84

Spanish hired ships.

	Tons	Captain	Men
Sancho de Gara	[320]	J. Wallop	271
Rosamus of San Sebastian	250	Fr. Pygott	192
Antony Montrego	240	James de la Vere	186
Santa Maria de la Cayton	200	J. Baker	125
Great New Spaniard [1]	360	George Throgmorton	318
Second New Spaniard [2]	280	Edw. Echyngham	218

[1] Sta. Maria of [ ] 5th month. [2] Sta. Maria Semago, *id.*

85. *F. Joubert, lieutenant of the admiral of Guyenne, to Louis XII.*

(Rochelle : 20 July, 1513.)

[100 crossbowmen, lately sent to Prégent de Bidoux, have stolen some arquebuses. Acts of piracy committed against Spaniards,[1] notwithstanding the truce concluded between Louis XII. and Ferdinand.]

... Ces jours passez, en ensuyvant autres voz lettres, ay envoyé 100 arbalestriers au cappitaine Prégent, et aucuns d'iceulx, le jour devant que embarcher sur mer, auroient prins à quelque prebstre quelques arbalestres et harquebutes. Dont partie furent rendues, et autre partie fut impossible de recouvrer parce que ceulx qui les détenoient s'estoient embarquez. Je en ay escript audit cappitaine Prégent leurs noms et surnoms pour les mectre avecques ceulx qui sont forcez.

Ces jours est venu à une lieue prez de vostredicte ville de la Rochelle ung nommé Adam Leclouston, contremaistre de la Marie de Honnefleur, qui a pillé et prins ung navire Espaignoul, combien que par les officiers de M^r l'Admiral auquel la congnoissance en appartient luy ayt esté envoyé remonstrer la publicacion des tresves faictes de longtemps entre vous et le roy d'Espaigne. Aussi ay esté adverty que ledict Leclouston avoit pillé certains Flamans qui sont de vosdicts subjectz. Dont lesdicts officiers de mondict seigneur l'Admiral ont fait faire informacions et discerné les provisions contre ledict Leclouston en telz cas appartenans. Dont de ce adverty, à l'instant auroit fait voysle. Au moyen de quoy impossible a esté de le pouvoir appréhender.

---

[1] Cf. *Arch. Loire Inférieure*, reg. xxi. of Chancery, fol. 165 (11 Sept. 1513). The truce was better observed by the King of Spain : 'Dyverse of your subjectys,' writes J. Style (Valladolid, 17 June), 'of late beyng on hys cost of Byskay by the ze have taken of your ennymys of France and Bretayne, the whiche be redelyverd ayen and put at thayr lybertys by the commaundement of the Kyng, your goodfader, for the kepeyng of hys trewys wyth France' (Brewer, i. 4267).

Mon souverain seigneur, par tieulx pirates[1] de mer plusieurs inconveniens peuvent arriver, et l'entrecours de la marchandise en seureté ne se peult faire, au grant détriment de voz deniers, perte et dommaige de voz subjectz. A ceste cause seroit le grant bien et proffit de vosdicts subjectz que de vostre grace il vous pleust mander à mondict seigneur l'Admiral ou à sesdicts officiers, et pareillement au maire de ladicte Rochelle, que doresenavant, quant tieulx pirates de mer viendront faire tieulles pilleries et oppressions, incontinant ilz dressent navires et gens pour les prandre, si possible est, et de ma part me y acquicteray selon qu'il vous a pleu et plaira me commander.

(Bib. Nat., MSS. Dupuy 261, fol. 148.)

[1] The fishing boats of Zeland were particularly harassed in 1513: 'Tout ainsi que les marchans de son pays de Zellande s'estoient assemblés avec grant nombre de navyres à voyle chargés de harens et autres poissons et marchandises en leur manière accoustumée, pour icelles marchandises mener et conduire en France comme en pays seur et neutre, et ramener en leursdits navyres vins et autres marchandises en eschange, les François leur ont donné bon espoir de ce faire, les laissant paisiblement entrer en leurs portz, et en iceulx vendre et descharger leurs marchandises, acheter vins et autres denrées à eux utiles et nécessaires en eschange. Lesquelles ilz ont chargées en leursdits navyres après avoir payé les drois accoustumez. Que sont signes de seurté. Et sitost qu'ilz ont eu affrété leurs navyres avec lesdits biens pour leur retour, lesdits François se sont assemblez sur la mer, et illec piglié, emblé et ravy aux povres marchans zellandois leursdits navires, au nombre de 60 et plus, ensemble leurs biens et marchandises y estans, comme dit est, de la valeur de 200,000 escus, sans que d'iceulx ilz veuillent faire aucune restitution' (Leglay, *Documents inédits*, i. 577).—The Portuguese were also captured by the French: George Lopez, Albano Pimentel and Diego Fernandez, of Lisbon, complained, 8 Oct. 1513, in the Court of Chancery at Nantes; also Lopez de Baillie, sent by the King of Portugal to Charles, Prince of Spain and Flanders, in the Christopher of Antwerp (2 Dec.). These were taken near Loctudi and Benodet (*Arch. Loire Inférieure*, reg. xxi. of Chancery, fol. 219, 268).

IN 1512-13 175

86. *Victualling of the navy in Normandy.*
(Honfleur: 1 Aug.-30 Nov. 1513.)[1]

[Wages of Philippe de la Primaudaye, controller, 40s. daily.]

Loys, par la grace de Dieu, roy de France... Faictes paier et bailler comptant à nostre cher et bien amé Philippe de la Primaudaye, commis au contrerolle d'icelle armée de mer, la somme de 244 l.t. Auquel nous l'avons ordonnée et ordonnons par ces présentes, pour ses vaccacions d'avoir esté et continuellement vacqué, luy 2e de personnes et chevaulx, en nostre ville de Honnefleur et ailleurs en nostredit païs de Normandie, à faire et exercer sadicte commission, depuis le 1er jour d'aoust derrenier passé[2] jusques au 30e jour du moys de novembre ensuivant, l'un et l'autre jour comprins, qui seront 122 jours entiers, à raison de 40s. par jour.

Donné à Bloys, le 15e jour de décembre l'an de grace 1513, et de nostre règne le 16e.

LOYS.

Par le Roy,
GEDOYN.
(Bib. Nat., MSS. fr. 25,719, n° 215.)

87. *Louis XII. to the Grand Master of Brittany.*
(About 12 Aug. 1513.)

[The Scottish fleet expected at Brest. The Grand Master must equip seven men-of-war and send them with the others to Honfleur.]

[1] Charles de la Chastre was Commissioner of the Ordnance from Jan. to Nov. 1513 (Blois, 16 Dec. 1513).
[2] The French fleet has unloaded all the ordnance at Honfleur (Spinelly to Henry VIII, Brussels, 20 June, 1513). Hector de Vicquemare says (9 July) that Louis XII.'s fleet is 'poor and ill-manned' (Brewer, i. 4273, 4329).

Mon cousin, j'ay eu présentement nouvelles de mon bon frère et cousin, le roy d'Escosse, par ung de ses héraulx qu'il a envoyé devers moy, qui partit le 27ᵉ du moys passé, par lesquelles il me fait sçavoir que sans point de faulte son armée de mer est partie d'Escosse,[1] pour venir de par deçà à mon service, et m'attens que de ceste heure elle soit arrivée à Brest. A ceste cause et qu'il est question maintenant de me faire quelque bon service, je vous prie que à toute dilligence vous faictes apareiller, avitailler, armer et équipper les troys grans navires de la Royne qui sont là [2] de tout ce qu'il leur fera besoing pour servir, et pour les acompaigner, choisissez en quatre du nombre de huit qui ont servy l'année passée en mon armée de mer. Le tout faictes tenir prest et en ordre pour faire voille incontinant avecques ladite armée d'Escosse [3] et vous joindre avecques les navires de Normandie [4] qui sont toutes prestes, à celle fin de

---

[1] The Scottish fleet left Leith, on 25 July, 1513 (Tytler, *History of Scotland*, ii. 138) : 13 large ships and 10 smaller. (Cf. Sanuto, xvi. 585, 630 ; Fr. Michel, *Les Français en Ecosse*, i. 327-330 ; *Exchequer Rolls of Scotland*, t. 14, lxxvii.) The English ships were 'tarying in the Downs for the Scottish flete' (cf. *ante*, p. 120). The Mary Rose is at Sandwich, 12 July ; and the Katherine Forteleza, 15 July. Then part went northwards to Scotland (Brewer, i. 4535), part returned to Southampton (where the Katherine was on 29 July).

[2] Nefs de Brest, Rochelle and Bordeaux.

[3] 34 ships, according to a Venetian, Lodovico Fioravanti (Amiens, 20 Aug. 1513, Sanuto, xvii. 24).

[4] The St. Michel ('grant nef d'Escosse') had Philippe Roussel as pilot : 'Pheilippe Rouxel eust charge de par le roy d'Ecosse de la grant neff d'Escosse, comme pilotte, pour icelle amener et conduyre à Brest. ... Eulx arrivez audit Brest avecques ladite grant neff, en laquelle estoit le grant amyrall d'Escosse. Lequel présenta à M. le Grant Maistre de ce pays et duché ledit Rouxel, luy disant qu'il s'estoit bien acquité en sadite charge d'avoir conduyt ladite grant neff, et qu'il estoit homme de bien, et que le feist bien paier et récompenser. Et à ce que ledit Rouxel voullut prendre congié dudit admyrall d'Escosse, il en fut reffuzé, et luy fut dit qu'il conduyroit ladite grant neff d'Escosse jusques ès

faire quelque bonne exécucion sur mes ennemys. Car vous entendez qu'il fault que ce soit prompt, aultrement la saison s'en va passée. Pourquoy vous prie y faire bonne dilligence, et le général de Beaulne auquel j'ay donné charge de cest affaire donnera ordre à vous faire fournir argent pour la soulde et les fraiz qu'il y conviendra faire, ainsi qu'il vous fait sçavoir.

Et à Dieu, mon cousin, qui vous ayt en sa garde. Donné etc.

(Bib. Nat., MSS. fr. 5501, fol. 274 v°.)

88. *The Louise waiting for the Scottish fleet.*[1]
(Villerville : 17-31 Aug. 1513.)
[Warrant of the King's commissioner for the wages and victuals of 100 mariners.]

Jehan Lalemant, receveur général des finances du Roy en Normandie, et par luy commis à tenir le compte et faire les paiemens des fraiz extraordinaires de ses guerres et armées de mer audit païs.

Paiez, baillez et délivrez à messire Loys le Brun, chevalier, seigneur de Sallenelles, cappitaine de la nef Loyse Admiralle, la somme de 112*l.* 4*s.* 10*d.t.* que nous luy avons ordonnée pour le rembourser de pareille somme par luy paiée pour la nourriture et despense de 100 hommes mariniers, faisant partie du nombre de 120 hommes de la qualité dessusdite, que avons ordonnez estre mis et embarquez en ladite nef et

parties de Normandie, à Honfleu, avant que avoir sondit congié. ... Ce que il fist, et ... se y acquita bien et honnestement, et de son service fut grandement loué dudit admyral d'Escosse, lequel fist prière au Grant Sénéschal de Normandie qu'il feist paier et sallarizer ledit Rouxel de ses peines et gages ' (*R. O., Chapter House Book* 83, p. 37).

[1] Receipt of Admiral Graville, owner of the Louise [1 July —31 Dec. 1514] (Bib. Nat., MSS. fr. 26,114, n° 46).

illec demourer à la rade de Villerville où nous l'avons fait conduire et mener de ce havre de Honnefleu dès le 17ᵉ jour d'aoust dernier passé par lesdits mariniers, à qui a esté baillé la charge de la garder seurement soubz ledit cappitaine, en actendant que l'armée des Escossoys¹ fust arrivée audit Honnefleu.

Fait audit lieu de Honnefleu, le 1ᵉʳ jour de septembre, l'an 1513.

BRESZÉ.   LOYS DE BIGARS.   PRIMAUDAYE.

89. *Victualling of Robert Barton's Lion.*²

(Honfleur : 24 Aug. 1513).

[Victuals for 260 soldiers and mariners for two months.]

Je, Robert Abreton, escuyer, gentilhomme escossoys, capitaine et à qui appartient la nef nommée le Lyon, du port de 300 tonneaulx ou environ, confesse avoir eu et receu de sire Jehan Lalement, conseiller du Roy nostre sire, receveur général de ses finances et par luy commis à tenir le compte et faire les paiemens des fraiz extraordinaires de ses guerres et armées de mer en Normandie, les victuailles cy après déclairées, lesquelles me ont esté fournies et mises en ladicte nef par ledit receveur général susdit, pour deux moys entiers prochains advenir de la provision et despence de 260 hommes, tant gens de guerre que mariniers, ordonnez estre mis sus et embarquez en ladicte nef pour le service du Roy nostredit seigneur.

---

[1] Cf. 'The Aventures of Meldrum in Forein Lands' (Pinkerton, *Scottish Poems*, i. 150).

[2] Cf. the Trinité and her bark (200 men), capt. Ant. de Conflans (Honfleur, 22 Aug.), the Tyran, 110 t. (90 men), capt. Artus de Fatonville (Honfleur, 27 Aug.), the Françoise de Dieppe, 100 t. (90 men), capt. Jacques d'Estemauville (22 Sept.), etc.

Et premièrement biscuyt : 4332 douz.
Pain fraiz : 52 douz.
Farines : 1 pippe 1 baril.
Cildres : 87 pippes.
Bières : 43 pippes.
Vin : 4 pippes.
Chair sallée : 12 pippes $\frac{1}{2}$.
Chair fresche : 1 beuf $\frac{1}{2}$.
Moutons : 5.
Lars : 194 costez.
Beurre : 80 livres.
Poix : 2 pippes.
Febves : 1 pippe 1 baril.
Harenc : 7 barilz.
Maquereaulx : 7 barilz.
Chandelle : 314 livres.
Suif : 520 livres.
Boys : 694 busches.
Vinaigre : 1 pippe.
Verjust : $\frac{1}{2}$ pippe.
Pippes à eaue : 14.
Sel : $\frac{1}{2}$ pippe.

Desquelles parties de victuailles contenues et cy dessus déclairées je me tiens content et en quicte ledict receveur général, commis susdit, et tous autres, et davantaige en promectz tenir bon et loyal compte où et à qui il appartiendra.

En tesmoing de ce, j'ay signé ceste présente de ma main, en la présence de Philippe de la Primaudaye, contrerolleur ordonné sus le fait dudit advitaillement, le 24ᵉ jour d'aoust, l'an 1513.

    ROBBART BARTON, captan de Léon.
PRIMAUDAYE.

(Bib. Nat., Pièces originales 4, dossier *Abreton*.)

90. [*Antonio Bavarin*] *to Francesco Gradenigo.*

(London : 3 Sept. 1513.)

[Two French ships captured.]

L' altra victoria è la sua armada stata a le man con questa di Franza, e prese do gran nave francesi.[1]

(Sanuto, xvii. 188.)

91. *Equipment of four ships at Dieppe—Rose, Françoise, Sacre, and Levrière.*

(Honfleur : 7 Sept. 1513.)

[Order to levy 180 officers and mariners to take the four ships from Dieppe to Honfleur and to victual them for ten days.]

Loys de Breszé, chevallier de l'ordre, conte de Maulevrier, grant séneschal et lieutenant général du Roy ès pays et duché de Normandie, à nostre très cher et bien amé Martin Lacaille, escuier, seigneur d'Aultretot et du Tronquay, et Charles Blancbaston, bourgeois de Dieppe, salut.

Comme le Roy nostredit seigneur ait ordonné mectre présentement sus une grosse et puissante armée audit pays et duché de Normandie, garnie de nefz, barques et autres vaisseaulx, vivres, gens de guerre, de marine et telles choses requises à

---

[1] No mention of this capture has been found in French or English documents; but we read in a letter of Peter Martyr to L. Furtado (n° 529) : 'In Galli regis auxilium multi capacem struxerat Scotus rex navim, ad supplementum classis quinque aliis additis. Majorem vi tormentorum Angli discerpserunt demisereque in profundum. Reliquas ceperunt. Prehenderunt unam Daccarum regis qui Dinamarca dicitur, aliam et ipsam ingentem : ea ut Scotae classi jungeretur in Angliam vehebatur' (Valladolid, 25 Oct. 1513). A 'Danys bote' can be traced at Portsmouth (Cf. *ante*, p. 120).

ladite armée, et nous ait ledit seigneur donné la principalle charge et commission pour faire les monstres, veues et reveues des cappitaines, gens de guerre et de marine et des officiers qu'il conviendra lever et mectre sus pour le fait d'icelle armée, et aussi ait ledit seigneur fait commectre et deppucter le seigneur de la Londe son commissaire sur le fait et provision des vivres d'icelle armée, et Philippe de la Primaudaye pour contreroller la despence d'icelle, tant en vivres, que souldes et autres fraiz, acoustumez de faire en tel cas.

Et soit ainsi que avons ordonné, en ensuyvant l'estat sur ce expédié, prendre au port et havre de Dieppe les nefz de la Roze, Françoise, Sacre et Levrière qu'il est besoing d'équipper de 180 hommes,[1] tant officiers que mariniers, pour amener et conduire dudit Dieppe en ceste ville de Honnefleu lesdites nefz, où nous avons ordonné qu'ilz seront promptement admenées, et fournir de vivres nécessaires ausdits compaignons pour 10 jours seullement qu'ilz pourront séjourner à venir dudit Dieppe en ledit lieu, oultre le principal ordonné de leursdits vivres qui est tout prest et appareillé de leur livrer à leurdite venue audit Honnefleu. Où ne pourrons, ne semblablement lesdits seigneurs de la Londe et Primaudaye, commissaire et contrerolleur dessusdits, aller, estre présens ne vacquer pour icelles monstres, veues et reveues faire, ne passer prix ne marchez desdits vivres, ne iceulx contreroller, à cause que nous et les dessusdits sommes continuellement occuppez en cestedite ville où se dresse la grosse et principalle force d'icelle armée de mer.

---

[1] Rose : master, Michel le Honchen, 50 men (expense for ten days' victual, beginning 15 Sept.= 47l. 10$s.t.$); Françoise : master, Raoullet Havyden, 50 men (47l. 10$s.t.$); Levrière : master, Gervais Sochon, 40 men (38l.); Sacre : master, Guillaume Dumur, 40 men (38l.) (Bib. Nat., MSS. fr. 26,113, n° 1,217).

Par quoy soit besoing que commectons en l'absence de nous et des dessusdits quelques gens de bien seurs et féables pour servir le Roy nostredit seigneur en cest affaire.

Nous, à ces causes, confians à plain de voz sens, vertus, expériences, loyaultez et bonnes dilligences, vous avons commis et depputez, commectons et depputons par ces présentes, de par le Roy nostredit seigneur et nous, de, en nostre absence, faire ce qu'il ensuit : c'est assavoir, vous, seigneur de Haultretot, les monstres, veues et reveues desdits 180 hommes, officiers et mariniers, qui seront mis et embarquez ès navires dessusdits, recevoir d'eulx et prendre les sermens, ainsi qu'il est requis et acoustumé en tel cas, faire les prix, marchez et ordonner de leur vivre et despence durant lesdits 10 jours, dont cy dessus est fait mencion, selon le contenu audit estat, et vous, Blancbaston, de contreroller les paiemens et souldes d'iceulx officiers et mariniers, ensemble la despence qui sera pour eulx requise estre faicte à la cause dessusdite.

Et vous avons donné et donnons par ces présentes à chacun de vous pouvoir de faire, signer et expédier tous et chacuns les rolles et autres acquictz qui seront pour ce nécessaires pour servir et valloir descharge et acquict à Jehan Lalemant, conseiller du Roy nostredit seigneur, receveur général de ses finances et par luy commis à tenir le compte et faire les paiemens des fraiz extraordinaires de ses guerres et armées de mer audit pays de Normandie. Lesquelz rolles et acquictz qui seront ainsi par vous signez et expédiez en nostredite absence et celle des dessusdits nous voullons valloir et servir à l'acquict et descharge dudit receveur général, tout ainsi que si par nous, lieutenant général, et lesdits de la Londe et Primaudaye, en vertu de leursdites commissions, avoient esté signez et expédiez. De ce faire vous avons donné et donnons povoir, auctorité, commission et mandement spécial par cesdites présentes, mandons à tous les officiers, justiciers et subjectz du Roy nostredit seigneur que à vous et chacun de vous en ce faisant obéissent et entendent dilligemment.

Et pour ce que de cesdites présentes on pourra avoir affaire en plusieurs et divers lieux, nous voullons que au vidimus d'icelles fait soubz scel royal foy soit adjoustée comme au présent original.

Donné audit Honnefleu, le 7ᵉ jour de septembre, l'an 1513.

BRESZÉ.

(Arch. Nat., K 79, n° 12.)

92. *Louis de Rouville appointed Admiral of the Franco-Scottish fleet.*

(Corbie : 17 Sept. 1513.)

[The fleet of Normandy and Brittany did nothing last spring, because the English were stronger. But now the King of Scotland has sent some men-of-war.]

Loys, par la grace de Dieu roy de France, à tous ceulx qui ces présentes lettres verront, salut.

Comme pour courir sus à noz anciens ennemys les Angloys, lesquelz, comme il est notoire, sont piéça descenduz en nostre royaume à grosse puissance et armée, pillant et destruisant les anciennes places et pays de nostredit royaume, et s'efforcent encores faire, et pour iceulx noz ennemys, avec leurs adhérans et alliez, grever et endommaiger par la mer, nous eussions, dès le commencement de ceste année, fait préparer, armer, advitailler et équipper plusieurs navires de noz pays de Normandie et Bretaigne. Mais, à l'occasion de ce qu'ilz n'estoient pas assez puissans, eu regard au grant nombre de navires que nosdits ennemys avoient, ne peurent faire guerès d'exploict, et les convint retirer en por jusques à présent que nostre cher et très amé frère cousin et alyé le roy d'Escosse, en ensuivant l'amytié, confédéracion et alliance qui est entre nous, nous a envoyé à nostre secours et ayde certain nombre de navires de sondit royaume bien armez et équippez pour se joindre avec les nostres. Et à ceste cause avons fait préparer nosdits navires de Normandie et Bretaigne et joindre ensemble pour essayer de faire quelque bon exploict contre nosdits ennemys.

Pour laquelle armée de mer mener et conduire soit besoing bailler la charge à quelque bon, notable et vertueulx personnaige qui soit pour nous y servir, qui nous soit agréable, et duquel ayons fiance.

Savoir vous faisons que nous, ce considéré, et la parfaicte et entière confiance que avons de la personne de nostre amé et féal conseiller et chambellan Loys de Rouville, chevalier, seigneur dudit lieu, grant veneur de France, et de ses sens, souffisance, loyaulté, conduicte, expérience et bonne dilligence, icelluy, pour ces causes et autres à ce nous mouvans, avons fait, constitué, ordonné et estably, faisons, constituons, ordonnons et establissons par ces présentes nostre lieutenant et chef en nostredite armée de mer que présentement mectons sus, où est joinct ledit navire d'Escosse. . . .

Donné à Corbye, le 17e jour de septembre, l'an de grace 1513, et de nostre règne le 16e.

Loys.

Par le Roy : l'évesque de Paris, les sires de Graville, admiral de France, du Bouchage, les gens des finances et autres présens.

Gédoyn.

(Arch. Nat., K 79, n° 13.)

93. *Lorenzo Pasqualigo to his brothers.*
(London : 18 Sept. 1513.)
[Pestilence in England and in the English fleet. Every one leaves London. No trade possible.]

Qui se pol dir esser grandissima peste, e zià tutta la nazion hanno preso casa in paese, e molti sono fuziti, el simel faremo noi, che per Dio si sta qui con gran pericolo ; sì dize morirne da 200 al dì. È la peste è intrada su l' armada de mar de Inglesi.[1] Iddio meti sanità ! E qui non si fa fazende al mondo de niuna sorte ; avisandovi, quando podesse ben vender robe a tempo a boni prezi, non le venderia.[2]
(Sanuto, xvii. 232.)

94. *The Scottish fleet in Normandy.*
(Amiens : 23 Sept. 1513.)
[The Scottish ships paid for three months and victualled for two ; the ships of Brittany victualled for three weeks. Levy of 400 mariners in Normandy.]

---

[1] '1 Sept. 1513—To John Dawtrey for revitailing and waging of the King's navy apon the see this wynter' (at Southampton), 3000*l*. (*R. O., Chapter House Book* 215, p. 267). 'The names of such shipps as be appointed to come into the Thames straight from Hampton : Sovereign, Mary Rose, Peter Pomegarnade, Hopton's ship, Nicholas Rede, Barbara.' 'The names of the ships that shal be discharged and delivered to their owners at Hampton : Charite, Magdalene, Saraguse, Peter of Fowey, George of Falmouth, Gabriel of Topsham. To kepe the see this winter (part eastward, part northward, part Dover and Calais) : Mary and John, Mary George, Anne of Fowey, Cristofer Davy, Nicholas Draper, New barke, Jenet, Henry, Margaret of Topsham, Sabyn, Lezard, Dragon, 2 row-barges, Elizabeth of Newcastle, Pemberton's ship, Nicholas of Hampton' (Brewer, i. 4474). For the expenses of the navy, Nov. 1513—April 1514, cf. *R. O., Chapter House Book* 12, pp. 487-651.

[2] Cf. a letter of the Privy Council to the vice-admiral, Thomas Wyndham, Richmond, 13 Sept. 1513 (Brewer, i. 5762). 'Si moriva da peste da 3 in 400 al zorno' (Sanuto, xvii. 317). 'La pestilentia fano ancora dano assai,' London, 6 Dec. 1513 (*ibid.* 445).

Loys, par la grace de Dieu, roy de France...

Comme pour essaier de courir sus, grever et endommaiger les Angloys, anciens ennemys de nostre royaume, qui sont venuz assaillir et faire la guerre en nostredit royaume, nous ayons fait partir les navires et vaisseaulx que nostre cher et très amé frère, cousin et allyé, le roy d'Escosse, nous avoit envoyé à nostre secours, du port de Brest en Bretaigne où ilz estoient, avecques ceux que y avions fait équipper, advitailler et armer, pour iceulx faire venir et approcher de nostre port et havre de Honnefleu, en Normandie, affin de eulx joindre avecques nostre armée de mer dudit pays, et tous ensemble faire voile pour aller rencontrer nosdits ennemys. Lesquelz navires et vaisseaulx, tant d'Escosse que de Bretaigne, il sera besoing à leur arrivée audit Honnefleu raffreschir de vivres, renfforcer d'artillerie et autres armeemens, faire adoubz tant aux corps d'iceulx que ès mastz, voilles, cordages, encres et autres appareilz, pareillement faire paier les gens de guerre, mariniers et autres estans en iceulx vaisseaulx de leurs souldes pour le temps qu'ilz ont servy et serviront cy après, et plusieurs autres grans fraiz mises et despences qu'il fauldra pour ce faire.

Nous, à ces causes, qui voullons à ce pourveoir en manière que faulte ne inconvénient n'en adviegne, vous mandons et expressément enjoignons que par nostre amé et féal conseiller et receveur général de nosdites finances en nosdits pays et duché de Normandie, et des deniers qui luy ont esté ou seront ordonnez pour convertir au fait de sondit office et commission, vous faictes paier, bailler et fournir toutes les sommes de deniers qui seront nécessaires pour lesdits reffreschissements, advitaillemens, renfforcemens, armeemens, adoubz, appareilz et souldes desdites navires et vaisseaulx tant d'Escosse que de Bretaigne, estans en nostredit service, venans audit port de Honnefleu, et lesdits gens de guerre, mariniers et autres estans et servans en icelles.

C'est assavoir la soulde des Escossoys pour troys moys, lesquelz nous leur avons ordonnez, tant pour leur venue, séjour en nostre service que retour en leur pays, au feur et prix que noz autres gens de guerre et mariniers de nosdites armées de mer sont paiez, et aussi la soulde de 400 hommes, gens de guerre et mariniers dudit pays de Normandie que avons ordonnez estre mis de renffort èsdites navires d'Escosse, et l'advitaillement d'icelles pour deux moys du jour qu'ilz arriveront audit Honnefleu,—et les autres gens de guerre et mariniers desdites navires et vaisseaulx de Bretaigne paiez de leurs souldes à ladite raison et advitaillez pour troys sepmaines à commencer dudit jour de leurdite arrivée, oultre ce que ilz ont eu à leur partement dudit pays.

Le tout par l'ordonnance, assavoir est, quant ausdits souldes de gens, achaptz d'artillerie, cordages, voilles, mastz, adoubz desdites navires et vaisseaulx, et autres appareilz d'iceulx, de nostre cher et amé cousin le conte de Maulevrier, nostre grant séneschal et lieutenant général dudit pays de Normandie, et lesdites vivres et advitaillemens par l'ordonnance de nostre amé et féal conseiller et chambellan Loys de Bigars, chevalier, seigneur de la Londe. . . .

Donné à Amyens, le 23ᵉ jour de septembre, l'an de grace 1513.[1]

Loys.   Par le Roy.
                              Gédoyn.

(Arch. Nat., K 79, n° 14.)

---

[1] Cf. Sanuto, xvi. 266 (Amiens : 15 Oct. 1513).

95. Dacre to Henry VIII.

(Harbotill: 13 November [1513].)

[Return of the Scottish fleet, but the three largest ships remained in France.]

Th' Erl of Aren, admirall of Scotland, is commen home[1] with the shippes of Scotland and a french knight[2] with hym, which hath broght writtings and credence from the French king and the Duke of Albany.

Thre of the grettest shippes of Scotland[3] er left in Fraunce to the spryng of the yere, to th' intent thei mei assist the French navyes as it is supposed. The grett shipp of Scotland was ron on grounde, but she is recovered, as thei say, or theire Admirall departed. The Scottische soldiours which be commen home make ill reaport of the French king, sayng thei were not well entreated there.

(Ellis, 1st Series, i. 93.)

96. Antonio Bavarin to Venice.

(London: 6 Dec. 1513.)

[Failure of the Franco-Scottish enterprise against England; the fleet destroyed by a dreadful storm.]

I giorni pasati, se trovavano in mar de molte nave de Franza con homeni assai, con fantaria da meter sopra questa isola in qualche loco e far danno, che tenimo hariano auto fatica per esser tuto benissimo provisto. Ma Dio non ha voluto abino

---

[1] *The Acts of the Parliaments of Scotland*, ii. 281-2 (Perth, 26 Nov. 1513).

[2] M. de la Bastie.

[3] Warrant of Louis XII. undated (end of 1513 or beginning of 1514), for the payment of 4,000 francs to the masters of these three ships (Bib. Nat., MSS. fr. 647, fol. 57 v°).

tanta pena, che 'l giorno da poi dita armata uscite di Bertagna, fece una fortuna per modo li ha anegati tuti,[1] e in questa compagnia si è dito anco esser negato alcuni di pregioni ; non sapiamo se la è vera, ma per giornata saperemo meglio e vi si dirà ; sichè vedete tuto va contra Franza come merita. Dio pregamo a l' alteza del nostro Re doni victoria.

(Sanuto, xvii. 445.)

[1] 'Durant ce temps se fist à Honnefleu une assemblée et grosse congrégation de navires de France pour aller empescher le roy d'Angleterre qui s'en retournoit en Picardie. Mais, quant ilz furent prestz, survint si grosse tempeste que l'entreprinse fut rompue, et y eut aucuns navires périz' (Alain Bouchart, *Chroniques de Bretagne*, fol. 274). The 'voyage d'Angleterre' is mentioned in a warrant of Louis II. de la Trémoille, dated Dijon, 5 Jan. 1514 (*Arch. of the Duc de la Trémoille*).—W. Gonson cruised three months between Dover and Calais, with the Mary Howard, the Nicholas Draper, the Mary Barking, &c. (*R. O., Chapter House Book* 215, pp. 264, 266-7).

III.

97. *Receipt of the postmaster at Honfleur.*

(Honfleur: 1 January–31 July, 1514.)

[Letters sent by Louis de Brézé, High Seneschal of Normandy, to the captain of the noblemen at Hogue, to the captains of the ships of Brittany, and into Upper Normandy.]

En la présence de moy, notaire et secrétaire du Roy nostre sire, Jehan du Quesne, naguères tenant la poste à Honnefleu, a confessé avoir eu et receu de sire Jehan Lalemant, conseiller du Roy nostredit seigneur et receveur général de ses finances ès pays et duché de Normandie, la somme de 122*l.* 10*s. t.*, à lui ordonnée par M. le Grant Sénéschal, lieutenant général du Roy nostredit seigneur audit païs et duché de Normandie, pour ses peines, sallaires et vaccacions, tant de lui que d'un sien serviteur et deux ses chevaux, qu'il a ordinairement entretenuz audit Honnefleu durant sept mois entiers, commençans le 1ᵉʳ jour de janvier 1513/4 et finiz le dernier jour de juillet dernier passé, pour faire les dilligences de porter au poste estant semblablement assiz par l'ordonnance de mondit seigneur le Grant Sénéschal à Toucque, les lectres que mondit seigneur le Grant Sénéschal escripvoit continuellement, tant au seigneur d'Estouteville, cappitaine des nobles du ban et arrière ban dudit païs estant en garnison au lieu de la Hogue, que à M. le Grand Maistre de Bretaigne, et aux cappitaines et conducteurs de l'armée de mer que le Roy nostredit seigneur faisoit armer et équipper en icellui païs, en tant que estoient les navires, barques et autres vaisseaux dudit païs de Bretaigne, aussi pour plusieurs courses et traverses par lui faictes durant ledit temps à porter lettres de mondit seigneur le lieutenant général ou païs de Caux, Rouen et vers Bernay, Lisieux et Falaise, à plusieurs gentilzhommes et officiers du Roy nostredit seigneur, affin de les advertir de ce que estoit nécessaire de faire pour tousjours empescher la descente que lors s'efforçoient et voulloient faire les Angloys celle part, et pour plus souvant sçavoir des nouvelles les ungs des autres, affin de non estre surprins, et advertir le Roy nostredit seigneur des entreprinses d'iceulx Anglois. Pour lesquelles choses faire, tant pour les peines et sallaires dudit Jehan du Quesne que d'un sien serviteur, que pour la nourriture de sesdits deux chevaux, luy a esté tauxé par mondit seigneur le lieutenant général 17*l.* 10*s.t.* par mois, qui sont pour lesdits sept mois, ladite somme de 122*l.* 10*s.t.*[1]

(Bib. Nat., MSS. fr. 26,113, n° 1288.)

98. *Warrant of Louis XII. directed to the treasurer of the navy.*

(Blois : 13 Jan. 1514.)

[Astremoine Faure has been appointed commissioner to the payment of the navy in the place of Jean Lalemant.]

Loys, par la grace de Dieu, roy de France . . . Nous voullons et vous mandons que par nostre amé et féal conseiller Jehan Lalemant l'aisné, receveur général de nos finances en noz païs et duchié de Normandie, et des deniers qui luy ont esté ordonnez pour convertir et emploier au fait de

[1] Cf. a similar receipt of Nicolas Vibert, postmaster at Villedieu [1 March—12 July] (Bib. Nat., MSS. fr. 26,113, n° 1283).

son office, vous faictes paier et délivrer comptant à nostre cher et bien amé Astre[moine Faure, esleu du bas païs] d'Auvergne et par nous commis à tenir le compte et faire le paiement de l'armée de mer que faisons de présent [mectre sus en nostredict païs de] Normandie, la somme de 40,875*l.t.*, auquel nous l'avons ordonnée [et ordonnons] pour convertir et emploier au fait de sadicte commission. Et par rapportant cesdictes présentes signées de nostre main avec quictance sur ce suffisante dudict Astremoine Faure, nous voullons ladicte somme de 40,875*l.* estre allouée ès comptes et rabatue de la recepte de nostredit conseiller et receveur général par noz amez et féaulx les gens de nos Comptes à Paris, ausquelz par ces mesmes présentes nous mandons ainsi le faire, sans difficulté. Car tel est nostre plaisir, nonobstant quelzconques ordonnances, rigueur de compte, restrinctions, mandemens ou deffenses à ce contraires.

Donné à Bloys, le 13ᵉ jour de janvier, l'an de grace 1513, et de nostre règne le 16ᵉ.

  Loys. Par le Roy,
        Gédoyn.

(Bib. Nat., MSS. fr. 25,719, n° 220.)[1]

99. *R. Wingfield to Wolsey.*

(Calais: 13 January [1514].)

[Orders should be given to look out for the French privateers which infest the narrow sea.]

Upon the 12th day, the barke of Boloyne toke a bote of Dover, the whiche was sent over for the conveyance of the budget, but the sayd budget was cast over the borde of the sayd bote before the taken of hyt, as two of the marynars hayth schewyd

---

[1] 12,314*l.* 11*s.* 9*d.*, 15 May, 1514 ; 6000*l.*, 7 Sept. 1514 (Bib. Nat., MSS. fr. 25,719, nᵒˢ 251, 274).

me, the which be lycencyd to seke theyr ransomes. And, Sir in the sayd bote were taken fyve Esterlyngs and two marchantmen of London, the whyche remayne prisonars at Boloyne . . . Hyt shoulde be well done of the kyng's Grace to gyve a strate command unto suche hys capytaynes as be in wayges and havyng charge the kepyng of the narrow see that they shulde otherwise endeavour theymselff in that behalff. For assuerydly, Sir, there haith bene mo dyspleasures don of late in thys narrowe passaige then haith bene herde of heretofore in many yeres. (Brewer, i. 3659.)

100. *Andrea Badoer to Venice.*

(London : 7 Feb. 1514.)

[The French fleet has attempted to burn the English ships.]

Pocho a manchato che l'armada di Franza non habbi brusata l'armada di quel Re, qual era [1] . . ., et vene per far lo effecto, ma fo remediata.

(Sanuto, xviii. 13.)

101. *Wingfield to Henry VIII.*

(Calais : 3 March, 1514.)

[At Honfleur : six galleys, the great ship of Scotland, the nef de Dieppe. At Dieppe : 14 or 15 Scottish or Breton ships.]

Le vendredi 3ᵉ jour de mars en l'an 1513/4, de l'ordonnance de M. le depputé de Calais, a esté interrogué Baudouin Pucher, agé de 18 ans ou environ, et natif de la ville de Béthune en Artois, si comme il dit, sur les points et articles qui s'ensuyvent.

[1] Cf. a letter of Wingfield to Wolsey, Calais, 10 Feb. [1514] (Brewer, i. 4743).

1°. Interrogué combien il y a qu'il partist dudit Béthune et où il a depuis demouré, dit et respond . . que 3 ans a ou environ qu'il partist de ladite ville de Béthune, et pour gaigner de son mestier de cuveur ou tonnelier il s'en ala besongner en la ville de Diepe en Normandie . . Est le bruyt tout commun audit lieu de Diepe que le Roy françois appreste bien 300 navires à hunes toutes équippées à la guerre, lesquelles il entend envoyer en Angleterre, sans 6 gallées que cet exposant dit avoier veues ung an a ou environ devant ledit Diepe, et pour l'heure il a oy dire qu'elles sont à Honnefleur.

Dit encores que journellement on besongne audit Diepe à la façon de plusieurs navires de guerre, et a l'on délibéré d'en faire jusques à 20, qui sont quasi toutes prestes, et ne reste fors à les vitailler et emplir de vivres, et dit que pour ce faire plusieurs navires marchandes dudit Diepe vont chacun jour quérir des vins à Bordeaulx et ailleurs où ilz en peuvent mieulx rencontrer.

Interrogué quelles navires il y avoit audit Diepe lorsqu'il en partit, et dont elles sont, dit qu'il y eut le jour d'hier 8 jours qu'il partit seul dudit Diepe . ., et dit que . . y avoit dedans le havene ou hable dudit lieu 14 ou 15 navires de guerre bien garnies d'artillerie, dont le[s uns] estoient navires d'Escoce et le reste Bretons, et les alloit veoir ès jours de festes, en quoy faisant il povoit au vray entendre et sçavoir quelles navires c'estoient, et ne scet point que en ladite ville de Diepe ne au hable d'icelle il y eust aucunes autres navires que celles par luy nommées.

Et oultre qu'il scet pour certain que audit lieu de Honnefleur, à sondit partement de Diepe, ung grant navire de guerre, appellé la grant nef d'Escoce, dont il a oy [parler par] Laurens Sandrin, demourant à Diepe, lequel le dép[osant congnoit], car il l'a veu estre maistre de la grant nef de [Diepe], laquelle nef de Diepe est à présent audit Honnefleu, à cause qu'elle ne peult entrer au hable dudit Diepe. Et dit que la grant nef d'Escoce est la plus grande et la plus forte qui soit en France, comme l'on dit, et ne la peult on vaincre que par feu, selon que le bruit et commune renommée est audit Diepe.

(Brit. Mus., Calig. D vi, fol. 90.)

102. *Levy of mariners at Harfleur, Fécamp, Dieppe, Tréport and Eu.*[1]

(Honfleur : 6 March 1514.)

. . . . A Jehan de la Masure, seigneur de Font[aines] . . . . mondit seigneur le Lieutenant Général pour . . . . de février et de mars de l'année de ce . . . . et dillec tout le long de la coste de . . . . les mariniers d'icelle coste et leur enjoindre . . . . ledit moys de mars, affin d'en faire monstre . . . . monstre demourer illec pour estre embarquez ès na[vires] . . . . avoit ordonné estre mise sus allencontre des Angloys vacqué lespace de 22 jours entiers, qui audit feur . . . .

A Grégoire le Francoys, la somme de 18*l.t.*

[1] At the same time convicts were sent from Paris to Prégent's galleys.

'A nostre cher et bien amé Jehan Rousset, l'ung des lieutenants de nostre amé et féal Prégent de Bidoux, chevallier de l'ordre de Jhérusalem, admiral de la mer de Levant et cappitaine général de noz gallères, la somme de 435*l.t.* Auquel nous l'avons tauxée et ordonnée par ces présentes, tant pour fournir aux fraiz, voicture et despence de bouche de 250 hommes prisonniers que faisons par luy présentement prendre ès prisons du Palais et Chastelet de nostre ville de Paris, pour iceulx mener et conduyre par eaue en icelles noz gallères estant de présent en la mer du cousté de Normandye pour nous y servir à l'encontre des Anglois et aultres noz ennemys, que aussi pour l'achapt et payement de 125 fers et 125 manilles de fer pour les mectre et attacher en plus grande seurté, et pareillement pour le salaire de plusieurs personnes que luy conviendroit avoir pour la garde d'iceulx et aultres fraiz' (Bib. Nat., MSS. fr. 647, fol. 500).

pour ung voyaige par luy fait partant de Honnefleu, le 6ᵉ jour du moys de mars audit an 1513, allant à Harfleu, Fescamp, Dieppe, le Tresport et Eu, devers les seigneurs de Fontaines et d'Aultretot qui avoient charge de mondit seigneur le Grant Sénéschal, lieutenant général du Roy nostredit seigneur audit pays de Normandie, de trouver et assembler tous les mariniers qui estoient sur et le long du ryvage de la mer ès portz et havres dessusdits, leur porter lettres de mondit seigneur le Lieutenant Général pour faire dilligence et assembler iceulx mariniers et les faire tenir prestz et en ordre affin que.... les manderoit pour venir en ladite ville de Honnefleu [joindre l'armée] de mer que l'on faisoit illec armer et advit-[ailler] pour faire le voyage d'icelle armée[1] que

[1] While the French fleet was thus being prepared in Normandy, bad news was received from the Mediterranean. The whole duchy of Milan had been lost by Louis XII. in 1513, and the last trace of the French dominion beyond the Alps, the castle of Godefa, at Genoa, was actually threatened by the Holy League. On this account two ships fitted out at Marseilles, 'pour aller dans les mers du Ponent,' were discharged on 2nd and 8th March: Barthélemy du Poulx, *dit* Sermain, and Adam Rondelline had received 3500 francs each for the freight (*Arch. Bouches du Rhône*, B 1450, fol. 127–131). At the same time la Trémoille's ship, which had not left the Mediterranean for the last two or three years, and was now under orders for Normandy, was also discharged. On the other hand, the Trinity of Honfleur was sent (20 April, 1514) to Genoa, and received for the freight 25 sous per ton and per month; she belonged to Jean de la Chesnaye, sʳ de Boully. 'Par l'ordonnance dudit feu seigneur, fut prinse en ceste ville de Honnefleu pour son service et esquippée pour aller dudit lieu à Gennes porter aux gens de guerre estans enfermés dedans le chasteau de Godefa lez ladite ville de Gennes certaines victuailles et municions pour leur fortifficacion et rafreschissement. Auquel chasteau ladite nef ne peut aborder, à cause qu'elle estoit guectée par certains navires et gallères esquippés pour la guerre, et convint à ceulx de l'esquippaige d'icelle nef faire voille vers la mer, de peur d'estre prins, et venir à Aiguemorte et Marceille; où illec ilz deschargèrent lesdictes victuailles et municions de guerre. Auquel voiage icelle nef a nollisé et vacqué, partant dudit Honnefleu, tant allant, séjournant que retournant, depuis le

SHIP OF THE XVIth CENTURY.
(Roscoff Church.)

] . . . Auquel voyage faisant séjournant, a . . . et reveues et avoir rapporté les . . 24 jours entiers . . somme de . . . .
(Bib. Nat., MSS. fr. 26,113, n° 1353.)

103. *Lorenzo Pasqualigo to his brothers.*
(London : 16 March, 1514.)
[The French fleet does not dare to set sail.]
Li Canali sono neti da' corsari per l'armada di la majesta di questo Re, che sempre sto Re a per tutta, e Franzesi non osa ussir fuora, che dubita di loro.[1]
(Sanuto, xviii. 158.)

20 jour d'avril 1514 jusques et y comprins le 13 jour de déc. ensuivant, lequel jour ladicte nef, par tourmente et fort temps, frappa en terre et se perdit dedans la rade des moulins de Malgue [Malaga]' (Bib. Nat., Pièces orig. 737, dossier *Chesnaye*, p. 3).

[1] This is quite untrue. The Normande (Capt. Maheuf) and the Volant (Capt. Guillot), both 'of Dieppe, captured the Nicholas of Lubeck and a Dutch ship (Gosselin, *la Marine Normande*, pp. 21, 69). On 20 Feb. 1514, M. de Brézé delivered to Gilbert Coppelan of Dieppe letters of marque against the merchants of Vere and Middelburg (Bib. Nat., MSS. fr. 5,086, fol. 148 v°). Philippe Roussel, on the other hand, fitted out his bark Rochellaise, 60 t., and left St. Malo, on 16 March, together with the bark Espagnole, belonging to Noel le Maignan, with a view to plunder some English ships before joining the King's fleet at Honfleur : ' Disoit ledit Roussel, avant aller audit Honfleur, qu'il eut rangé la coste de Bretaigne et d'Angleterre pour gaigner ung pot de vin sur les Angloys, et qu'il avoit du temps assez pour se trouver à l'armée qui estoit audit Honfleur.' When they were off Bréhat, a fisherman told them that they would find five English privateers towards the Sept Iles. ' Comme ilz furent en l'endevant de Bréhat à bien 14 lieues de St. Malo, trouvèrent ung pescheur qui leur dit qu'il y avoit des navires d'Angleterre qui pilloient et prenoient à la coste vers les Sept Isles.' They only sailed by night: 'tenoient la mer la nuit et le jour venoient se renger à la terre.' But on Saturday, 18 March, about 10 A.M., a sudden storm constrained them to take refuge at Port Blanc.

104. *John Wiltshire to the Bishop of Lincoln.*

(Calais : 30 April [1514].)

[The Frenchmen are threatening Calais and Guines. Prégent de Bidoux is at Dieppe. The Duke of Albany is ready to leave for Scotland.]

Mylord, as ffor newys, her ys none, bout ouer neightbre the Ffrenchemen maketht manie fforwards and profers, sayng they wyll loke upon us and at Gynes bothe. They have causyd us to kepe goode

Although they showed red and yellow flags (Louis XII.'s colours) in sign of friendship, they were fired at by a Florentine trading ship moored in the harbour. In consequence of this an inquiry was held by the Chancery of Brittany, which is still preserved at the R. O. (*Chapter House Book* 83). Roussel had a crew of about sixty men dressed in red and blue jackets, whose victualling was valued at 120 or 140*l.* per month. His ship carried a heavy armament : ' Deux longs passevollans garnis de deux boistes chacun, et une grosse pièce d'artillerie de fer, et plusieurs autres pièces d'artillerie.' He had spent about 140*l.* for canvas. The Rochelaise was divided in four shares or ' sillages ' belonging to four ' carsonniers ' (10*l.* each share): ' les sillaiges, qui est argent avancé aux carsonniers de la barque pour despartir aux compaignons pour les avoir et tenir subjects à servir ; autrement on ne peut avoir les compaignons.' The Rochelaise left Port Blanc for Honfleur on 26 March, but a truce was concluded with England, and she did little service.—The description of the flags is interesting : ' En aprouchant du Port Blanc, en entrant en iceluy, Phelipes Rouxel desploya et fit desployer les enseignes et estendartz qui estoient en la barque, appellez banczoins, portans les armes et coulleurs du roy, savoir de rouge et jaulne, et des pavoys autour du bort, avecques fleur de lis et croix blanche. Qu'estoit pour signiffier à ceulx de la terre qu'ilz ne voulloient que paix et n'estoient malveillans du pays, ainsi que l'on a accoustumé faire en telz cas. Iceulx estendartz trainoient depuis le haut des deux hunes de ladite barque jusques à la mer. Et y avoit ung estendart carré de mesme coulleur où y avoit une grant croix blanche, qui estoit en la grant hune, que signifie asseurance, et deux autres estendartz carrez, de mesme armoyés de fleur de lis et marqués de croix blanches, estans en deux lances sur la poupe au derrière de ladite barque, en signification de plus grande asseurance.'

wache and too be in aredynes dyverss tymes and
soo we shall contenew. Twyss or thryss I loked
suerly ffor them, thei wer asembeld upon a 800
horsmen and 4 or 5000 ffotmen, whyche wer sene
and descerneid, doyng noo harme (thanked be God).

And yt lycke your lordshepp, sens thys letter
was closed, the meyer and counsell of Sent Homere
sent me a letter and ther parseuant whyche cam
streyght ffrome Depe. He was ther upon Tusday
last past, whoo hatht shewed me ffor a trought that
Prejon was redy with 9 gales[1] at Depe to depart, and
8 mor was a Honflett, as he saytht, they should a
departed owght of Depe on Sont Jorges evyn, had
nott the grett storme a bene, one of the said gales
was lost at same tyme within Depe havyn. The
said pursevant spake with the said Prejone, a said a
wold come to Cales with his gales and bourn ouer
shepps in the havyn : whiche I beleve nott. Yt wer
ryght nes[es]ary to take gode hede to the Kyng's
shepps and that gode vache may be keptt in every
plase. Mylorde, for surte they have an enterpryse
in hands. Wher, I cannott ascerten yow.

And over, that the plane sayng at Depe and
Honflett ys that the Ffrenche Kyng will sende a
20000 men laniskneitts and other into Skotland.[2]

(Brewer, i. 5021.)

---

[1] Prégent had a yearly pension of 600*l*. (Bib. Nat., MSS.
Clairambault 825, p. 119). The King issued a warrant (Blois,
3 Feb. 1514) for the payment of 5875*l.t.* to Prégent (receipt dated
14 Feb.) ; the larger galleys ('bastardes') cost 450 golden crowns
per month, and the smaller ones ('subtiles') 300.

[2] Robert Barton, on returning from Scotland with his ship
the Lion, was driven by a storm to Corunna (Spinelly to
Henry VIII. Malines, 3 March, 1514). Cf. Brewer, i. 4824, 4869,
4902, 4951.

105. *Louis XII. to M. de la Fayette, captain of Boulogne.*

(Paris: 3 May [1514].)

[Warlike preparations of Henry VIII. Ordnance sent to Boulogne.]

M. de la Fayete, j'ay receu voz dernières lettres et entendu par icelles les nouvelles que me mandez. Je vous prie continuer et tousjours m'advertir de ce que vous pourrez sentir de noz ennemys et principallement de ce grant appareil[1] qu'on dit que fait le roy d'Angleterre pour passer la mer et venir en çà.[2] Car selon cela que vous m'en escriprez, je feray, combien que pour ceste trève ne pour autre chose qu'on me puisse dire je n'ay laissé de donner provision à tout ce que je pense estre nécessaire pour le receuillir, s'il dessent.

Au surplus, en tant que touche l'artillerie[3] que vous demandez, j'ay envoié quérir, comme vous savez, le maistre de l'artillerie, et l'ay, deux jours a, dépesché pour aller par delà, tant pour veoir et visiter voz fortiffications et réparations que pour vous pourveoir de ladite artillerie. Pourquoy, j'espère que bientot vous serez satisfait quant à cela. Et au surplus, si autre chose vous fault, mandez le moy, et je y pourverray.

[1] 'Si aveva inteso la bellissima armada maritima ha questo Re contra Franza, e dil prender di certa nave francese' (London, 15 May, 1514) (Sanuto, xviii. 350).

[2] According to Roberto Acciajuoli (Paris: 30 April, 1514), Henry VIII. intends to cross in June: 'Li apparati, per uno uomo che nuovamente è venuto dell' isola, s' intendono essere molto maggiori che l' anno passato, et che quella Maesta debbe venire con tutto lo esercito per tutto giugno al più forte.'

[3] Warrants for ordnance, 13 Feb., 1 April, 1514 (Bib. Nat., MSS. fr. 25,719, n°s 232, 240).

Et à Dieu, M. de la Fayete, qui vous ait en sa garde.

Escript à Paris, le 3ᵉ jour de may.

   Loys.   Robertet.

[Endorsed.] A M. de la Fayete,
 cappitaine de Boulongne.

      (Bib. Nat., MSS. fr. 2,888, fol. 11.)

106. *Louis XII. to M. de la Fayette.*

    (St. Germain-en-Laye : 22 May [1514].)

[Desires him to send news of the landing of Englishmen at Calais ; also news of what Prégent and Clermont are doing. To send the bastard of Stanley to the Duke of Suffolk.]

M. de la Fayette, j'ay veu les lettres que vous m'avez escriptes, et pareillement celles que vous avez envoyées à M. de Piennes et général de Normandie.[1] Et quant à ceste dessente qu'on dit qui a esté faite à Calays et du bruyt qui y est de la venue de Tallebot, je vous en prie vous en bien informer et à la vérité, et me mander ce que vous en trouverrez. Car se ainsi estoit, il seroit requis donner ordre à toutes choses et promptement pourvoir les villes de la frontière par façon que inconvénient n'y advint.

Au surplus je vueil que vous m'envoyez le bastard de Stanlay pour le mectre ès mains de M. de Suffort qu'il demande, et pour ce faictes le partir incontinent et amener en bonne seurecté comme vous saurez bien faire.

Pareillement vous prie me faire savoir des nouvelles du cappitaine Prégent[2] et de ce qu'il aura fait, car j'en entendroye bien voulontiers et pareillement de celles de M. le Visadmiral.

[1] Thomas Bohier had left Paris, 8 May, for Calais.
[2] Cf. a similar letter, St. Germain-en-Laye, 27 May (Bib. Nat., MSS. fr. 2,888, fol. 29).

Et à Dieu, Mr de la Fayette, qui vous ait en sa garde.

Escript à Sainct Germain en Laye, le 22e jour de may.

LOYS.   ROBERTET.

[Endorsed.] A Mr de la Fayette,
 Cappitaine de Boullongne.

(Bib. Nat., MSS. fr. 2,934, fol. 7.)

107. *Thomas Howard to the Privy Council.*

(In Dover road: 27 May [1514].)

[Ten sail tried yesterday to get between Boulogne and Prégent de Bidoux. What Prégent intends to do. Admiral Howard has appointed twenty sail to try again to capture the galleys; 6,000 men necessary.]

[Please it] it yor lordshipes to understand I came yesterdaie unto Sandwich, [suppo]syng to haue fownde the shippes[1] in the Downys, but they

---

[1] The English fleet remained at Portsmouth until the 23 April, 1514 (*R. O., Chapter House Book* 12, pp. 537 and 599). The victualling of ships (2 April-12 August, 1514) will be found *ibid.* Book 2, pp. 265-303. The King had 25 ships (25 April-22 May): Trinity Sovereign (Th. Wyndham), Gabriel Royal (Trevenyan), Catherine Fortaleza (Poyntis), Mary Rose (Sherburne), Peter Pomegranate (Echyngham), John Baptist (Rauf Ellercar), Great Nicholas (Fleming), Great bark (Pyrton), Great Barbara (Wallop), Mary George (Wiseman), Mary James (William Ellercar), Christ (Vowell), Mary and John (Mygenall), Lesser bark (Stephen Bull), Barbara [of Brikelsey] or Lesser Barbara (West), Anne Gallant (Th. Denys), Lizard (Coo), Jennet Purwyn (Lawrence Fartley), Sweepstake (Cooke), Swallow (Rob. Mounteney), Black bark (Christ. Thwaytis), Rose galley (J. Watkyn), Catherine galley (Kenwood), Henry Grace à Dieu (Edward Dunne), Great Elizabeth (Wiston Brown). Add 3: King's victuallers: Henry of Hampton, Mary Imperial, Dragon. The Maria de Loreto had been probably returned to her owner; she lay at Portsmouth until 22 April, 1514 (*Chapter House Book* 12, p. 541). We meet four

were [not] there. And so by 7 a cloke I came unto Dovour, and before my commyng, about none, the viceadmirall, by the advice of the most experte capitaynes and maisters on the coste of Boleyne, sent ouer sir Henry Sherborne and sir Stephen Bole and 10 sayles of smale men with the rowbarges, galies and other well manned, and this was ther order wiche was as good in my mynde as was possible. The wynd was at N.N.E and was so grete an hase that skant [one] might see a myle, and so upon the flood they drewe over with Scalis Clyves, and then with the ebe they came with a good blower towards Saint John's rode, and sent before them 4 or 5 myles [sir] Stephen Boole, Thomas Vaughan, and 3 other smale men, to th'en-[tent] to have gotten betwene the galies and Boleyn haven, and the r[est] of our shippes kepte them owte of syght, and so our 5 saile made as mouche as they myghte toward the haven. And Prior John with 5 galies, 3 foystes and 2 barkes rode at the poynt of Saint John's rode towarde Calayes 5 myles fro Boleyne, and as [soon] as our men wer in sight, wiche war but 5 sayle, awaie went all the Ffrenchemen with sailes and oweres all that they myght and wone the poynt of the haven under the bulwarke. Wiche our men perceyving and that it was vnpossible to come unto [them] ther without utter confusion, shott at them ther ordinance and . . . at them. And then our men perceyvyng the wynd drewe northwarde, they haled oute into the rode and cam to . . . ancre before the galies, without that the said galies sawe [no] more of our shipes but those 5,

new ships : Great Barbara, otherwise Mawdelen of Hull, bought from Edward Madeson (Brewer, i. 4425, 5721); Mary Imperial, otherwise the Bark of Sherborne (*Chapter House Book* 12, p. 535); Great Elizabeth, otherwise Salvator of Lubeck (Brewer, i. 5776), bought from John Tylman ; Black bark.

and wolde never wey to come [with] them. And than aboute mydnyght the wynd was so . . . our men myght no lenger abyde there, but came ther w[ay] . . . and none of them but 2 myght recouer Dovar rode, but w[ent] as fere as Cambernas. And my cousyn Wyndam in like . . . 20 sayles with hym, and at this oure I see hym with them . . . comyng agayne vnto us. . . .[1]

Mylordes, I have written as . . . unto you herof, because I wolde ye shuld perceyve aswell [the] good handlyng of our men as also to consider what Pri[our John] intendith, wiche after my mynde is to make a trayne . . . within the danger of ther bulwarkes, supposyng t[hey could do what] they did the last yere, or elles to watch for a ca[lm] . . . to do some displeasure to some passenger if he can . . . for the best I cane, and have written unto maister . . . · he shall suffer no passenger to come over in no calm w . . . thym to go ouer seebord Goodwyn wiche is as short waie . . . within 4 myles and out of danger.

Mylordes, all this daie h . . . as calme as was possible so that I myght send no ship . . . this nyght before mydnyght. If ther blowe any wynde, I [have] appoynted sir Henry Sherborne with 10 sailes, and Wiseman [and] Walope with other 10 sailes to goo ouer. Sir Henry shall dra[we] by West Bolyn, and if the wynde woll serue hym to get betwene Boleyne and the galies, if they be abrode in the [see], as they war yesterdaie, and Wiseman shall come fro Ca[lais] warde along that shore to assaie what he cane do in like[wise].

And if this waie woll not serve, I cane se no waies howe t[o get] vnto them without liklihod of extreme daunger and parell, [onles] that I myght

---

[1] They captured 'a barke of Treyport' that we find among the King's navy (16 July–12 Aug. 1514).

haue 2 or 3,000 of suche soldyours as be nowe [in] Calies shepped in the haven there and so sent unto me, and to sett other 3,000 on land within 2 myles of Boleyn. With wiche company I think without gret daunger the said galays wold [be] put in grete daunger to be hade. Wiche I remyte to be deb[ated] and orderid after your wisdomys, besechyng you to advertise [me] of your further myndes in the premisses and I shall gladly folowe the same.

Also sir Thomas West is at Sandwiche w . . ., and I have commaunded hym to remayne there tell he k[nows your] further pleasures. May it therefore please you to certyfie [hym] howe he shall be ordered.

Also I have sent 2 good shipes [unto] Seland to waft the flete there.

I haue also apoynted and [ordered] to departe, when wynd shall serve, 9 good shipes to goo Nor[thward]. Wiche be sufficient, if the Ffrenchemen b . . . sailes. With Godes grace who kepe you.

Written in the Ma[ry Rose], in Dovour rode the 27 daie of May, at 7 at nyght.

Yours
T. SURREY.

108. *Thomas Lovell to the Bishops of Winchester and of Lincoln.*

(Calais: 5 June [1514]).

[Admiral Howard intended to revenge the burning of Brighton.]

. . . Ye wrote unto me that I shulde, oon the King's bihalve, commaunde all the capteynes that they shulde make noon attemptate nor excurse out of the pale: wherof they be not most gladdist nor best content to lyé still and maye do nothyng. . .

I had worde from mylorde Admyrall that he

intendid to have made landing here in these parties as yesterdaye or this mornyng for the revenchyng of the brennyng of Brighthenstone, but as yet I here of nothyng.

There rennyth a comyn brute still here that the Duc of Albany maketh preparacions for goyng into Scotland, and Richard de la Pole with hym.

(Brewer, i. 5151.)

109. *Thomas Lovell to the Bishops of Winchester and of Lincoln.*

(Calais : 23 July [1514].)

[French and Scottish ships in the Channel.]

Mylords, where this bochet with othres lettres conteigned in the same shuld have ben with your lordshipps two dayes past, so it is the passenger that caryed them wase chased over the sea and put in dangier, so that she wase glade to escape and constrayned to retourne with Cales roode this daye at afternoone, and the marryners say, so far as they can perceyve by them, they be bothe French saills and Scotts saills together, and now of late hathe gone and do goo often along the seas.

(Brewer, i. 5270.)

110. *Pandolfini, Florentine ambassador, to Florence.*

(Poissy : 24 July, 1514.)

[Prégent de Bidoux leaves for the Mediterranean in order to save the castle of Godefa at Genoa.]

Pregent, quale a' questi giorni era venuto qui, se n' è partito per il cammino de Normandia dove ha la sua armata. Che, al primo avviso d' Inghilterra, debbe con essa girare nel mare Mediterraneo per venire en Provenza, nel quale luogo, secondo mi è suto accennato da uno amico, credo che subito si armeranno tutti quelli legni che vi si trovano ; che, quando fussi il vero, non potrebbono essere per altro conto che per soccorrere la fortezza di Codifa.

(Poissy : 9 Aug.)

Il re di Francia in genere da me ricerco mi ha mostro avere grandamente a cuore le cose di Genova, mostrando essere al tutto risoluto volere soccorrere quello castello, dicendo avere disegnato mandarvi 16 o 18 galee, fra le quali saranno 4 galeoni, con le persone di fra Bernardino e Pregent, la persona del quale di già si trova en Provence.

(Poissy : 14 Aug.)

Sono gia 9 o 10 giorni che le galee di Pregent partirono di questi mari, girando alla volta de Provenza, dove disegnano trovarsi alli 4 o 6 giorni del futuro mese.

(Desjardins, *Négociations diplomatiques de la France avec la Toscane*, ii. 649, 653, 659.)

111. *French and Scottish ships moored at St. Malo.*

(About Aug. 1514.)[1]

[Christophe de Chanoy commissioner.]

Loys, etc. Nous voullons et vous mandons que la somme de 115*l.* 17*s.t.* à quoy se montent les parties que nostre amé et féal conseiller maistre Philebert Babou, par l'ordonnance et commandement de nostre bien amé Cristofle de Chanoy,[2] seigneur dudict lieu, par nous aussy commis verballement à ordonner et disposer de la despence neccessaire

---

[1] The English fleet was discharged in the beginning of August 1514 (Brewer, i. 5317).   [2] Cf. p. 76, note 3.

estre faicte pour les trois navires d'Escosse[1] et dis poser la Françoise d'Orléans,[2] la Petite Loyse de Hongfleur[3] au port et havre de Saint Malo pour icelle mectre en seureté et conserve[4] audict port, a payée baillée et délivrée comptant des deniers de sa commission à plusieurs personnes. . . .

(Bib. Nat., MSS. fr. 647, fol. 51.)

[1] Dougal Campbell, 'contremaître' of the Grand Nef d'Ecosse; Stephen Vallois, master.
[2] Also the nef de Dieppe (Capt. Jean Cinquart).
[3] Adenet Legendre, captain of the Petite Louise, died at St. Malo, 25 Sept. 1514 (Bib. Nat., MSS. fr. 26,114, n° 34), and was succeeded by Jean de Cantepye; master, Vincent Maria.
[4] In Sept. 1514 Louis XII. gave orders to send back to Scotland the three ships lying at St. Malo, and to send to the river Charente four other men-of-war then at Brest. But in December he gave counter orders to Christophe de Chanoy:

'Au moys de septembre [1514], nostredict feu seigneur et beau père ordonna que les trois gros navires d'Escosse qui estoient au havre de St Malo en nostre païs de Bretaigne, lesquelz il avoit fait venir pour luy donner secours et soy en servir en ladicte année seroient remenez et renvoiez audict païs d'Escosse, mesmement que les autres quatre navires qui estoient au havre de Brest en nostredict païs de Bretaigne feussent menez dudict lieu en Charente pour illec estre maréez et tenuz en meilleure seurecté qu'ilz estoient.

Pour la conduite desdictz navires audict païs d'Escosse et Charente, nostredict feu seigneur feist dresser ung estat, tant des victuailles neccessaires pour la provision des mariniers estant èsdits navires que pour les despences neccessaires estre faictes pour le nolléage des nefz qu'il convenoit prendre à Honnefleu pour porter lesdictes victuailles dudict lieu ausdicts havres de Brest et St Malo, où ledict seigneur les envoyoit. Lequel estat fut expédié et arresté, par l'ordonnance de nostredict feu seigneur, par vous ou aucuns de vous.

En ensuivant lequel estat et l'ordonnance dudict feu seigneur furent arrestées et prinses et par lordonnance du seigneur de Chanoy, cappitaine et conducteur général desdictz navires, trois nefz estans audict lieu de Honnefleu, c'est ass.' la nef nommée la barque Trinité de Guernezay du port de . . . [tonneaux, la barque] Gobiton du port de 30 tonneaux, appartenant à Guillaume Dudoyt, et une autre nef de Bretaigne appartenant à Allain de Bourson, du port de 80 tonneaux, et les victuailles neccessaires

112. *Sale of surplus victuals of the year* 1514.[1]

(Honfleur : 1 Jan. 1515.)

Ce sont les fraiz et sommes de deniers qu'il a convenu faire paier et délivrer tant pour faire remanyer, arrimer, visiter, livrer, remuer et transporter de lieu en autre les victuailles et provisions qui estoient en

pour l'advitaillement desdictz gros navires, en intention de les porter ausdict lieux de Brest et St Malo, ainsi que par nostredict feu seigneur avoit esté ordonné. Ce qui fut fait. La nef de Bretaigne, tantost après sa charge prinse et receue audict port de Honnefleu, partist dudict lieu et s'en alla au havre de St Malo, où illec ledict Allain de Bourson, maistre de ladicte nef, [print] bort, ainsi qu'il luy avoit esté commandé. Au moyen de quoy ledict Astremoyne Faure luy paia et bailla la somme de 100 l. pour le nolléage et victuailles de ladicte nef, en ensuivant ledict estat.

Et pour le regard desdictes deux autres nefz, elles ne partirent dudict port de Honnefleu, pour ce que, ce temps pendent que les chargemens se faisoient, seurvint lettres de nostredict feu seigneur audict seigneur de Chanoy, cappitaine dessusnommé, par lesquelles il luy contremanda que, si lesdictes nefz n'estoient parties pour aller audict pays de Bretaigne, il les tint audict Honnefleu toutesvoyes prestes à partir, quant nostredict feu seigneur luy ordonneroit et manderoit, et jusques à ce qu'il eust de ses autres nouvelles. En accomplissant ledict commandement, lesdictes nefz restèrent au port et rade dudict Honnefleu chargées, prestes et appareillées, comme dit est, par aucun long temps, sçavoir est ladicte barque Trinité par l'espace de trois moys, et l'autre nef par l'espace d'ung moys, actendant nouvelles dudict feu seigneur.

Lequel enfin manda et feist sçavoir audict seigneur de Chanoy que, pour aucunes causes seurvenues, il ne voulloit que lesdictz trois gros navires allassent en Escosse, ne les autres quatre navires en Charente, ainsi qu'il avoit paravant ordonné, et à ce moien qu'il n'envoyast porter aucunes victuailles en Bretaigne. A raison de quoy convint lesdictes victuailles descharger et remectre en leurs celliers et greniers dont elles avoient esté tirées et prinses. . . .'

The master of the Trinity received 200*l.t.* (12 men), and the master of the barque Gobiton 65*l.t.* (10 men) (Bib. Nat., MSS. fr. 25,720, n° 34).

[1] M. de Brézé, high seneschal of Normandy, gave licence to Harfleur to export to Ireland or Spain the corn stored in May 1514 (Rouen, 18 Sept. 1514) 'trop de blés, qui se sont tournés en empirance' (*Arch. Harfleur*).

la ville de Honnefleu demourez de reste de celles qui illec avoient esté faictes en dilligence au commencement de l'année dernière passée de l'ordonnance du feu roy Loys, dernier décédé (que Dieu absoille), pour l'advitaillement des armées qu'il ordonna lors estre mises sus par la mer, et en ce avoir quis plusieurs mises nécessaires pour la garde et conservacion d'icelles, que pour les loages des celliers, caves et greniers, où ont esté lesdites victuailles gardées depuis le 1er jour de janvier dernier passé jusques aux jours cy après déclarez qu'elles ont esté vendues et adevérées au prouffit du Roy nostre sire. Et ce par la déliberacion et ordonnance de Jehan de la Chappelle, commissaire dudit seigneur depputé en ceste partie, et par l'advis et oppinion de Jehan des Celliers, lieutenant général du viconte d'Aulge, et Laurens de Guenteville, grenetier du grenier à sel estably audit lieu de Honnefleu, à ce par le commissaire dessusnommé convocquez et appellez, comme officiers dudit seigneur estans et demourans en ladite ville de Honnefleu, en ensuivant le contenu ès lettres de commission d'icelluy seigneur.

Iceulx fraiz servans à l'acquit d'Astremoyne Faure, esleu du bas païs d'Auvergne, qui avoit esté commis à tenir le compte et faire le paiement de la despense desdites armées de mer, appellé par semblable avec ledit commissaire pour faire la recepte et tenir le compte des deniers qui sont venuz et yssuz de la vente dudit reste d'icelles victuailles. Desquelz deniers il a paié et baillé et délivré lesdits fraiz et sommes de deniers aux personnes cy après dénommées pour les causes et ainsi que s'ensuit. . . .

[Endorsed.] Deniers payez pour la garde des victuailles pour 113*l*. 17*s*.

(Bib. Nat., MSS. fr. 26,114, n° 101.)

INDEX

Abbeville, xx, 91, 94
Acciajuoli, Roberto, Florentine ambassador in France, letters from, 48, 108, 125, 129, 140, 144, 161, 200
Agnadel, 52
Aigues-Mortes, 196
Albany, Duke of, xlv, 198, 199, 206
Alderney, xxxii, 99, 100
Alencé, Jean d', 71
Alos, or Losa, Domingo, Spaniard, 77, 162
Alynson, W., 11
Andalousia, 42
Angers, xxxi, 72
Angoulême. See Valois
Anne of Greenwich, or Anne Galant, King's ship, 6, 96, 160
Anne, Queen of France, xxii, 47, 75, 92, 134, 138, 139
Anthony Montrigo, 115, 118
Antwerp, 94
Aragon, 43, 44, 46
Arran, Earl of, Scottish admiral, xliii, 188
Arras, 94
Arthur. See Plantagenet
Artois, 193
Ashe water, 163
Atclif, W., ix
Audeley, Sir J., xv
Auge, Pays d', in Normandy, 18
Aumont, M. d', letters to, 17, 18, 20, 21
Awerey, Oliv., 156

Babou, Philibert, 207

Badoer, Andrea, Venetian ambassador in England, 41; letter from, 193
Baillart, Jean, French captain, 93
Bainbridge, Cardinal, xii; letters to, 26, 57, 124
Baptist of Harwich, 97, 123, 127, 150
Barbara Iseham, x
Barbara of Greenwich, king's ship, 9
Barbelée, Jean, master of the Louise, 88, 90
Barclay, Richard, captain, xxxvii, 123, 130, 131
Barton, Andrew, vii to x, 8, 10
Barton, John, xliii, 75, 125
Barton, Robert, xvi, xvii, xliii, 27, 90, 93, 169, 178, 199
Bavarin, Antonio, Venetian consul in London, letters, &c., from, 52, 71, 108, 180, 188
Bayonne, 2, 19
Beachy Head, 151
Beaune, Jacques de, 138, 177
Bedell, carpenter, 105
Benlow, Richard, 61
Berenghier, Jacques, of Lille, xvi, 6
Bernardin, Fray, captain of French galleys, xxiii, 42, 91, 141, 150, 207
Bernay, 191
Berquetot, Regnault de, captain of the nef de Dieppe, xxv, xxviii, 54, 65, 66, 67
Bertheaume Bay, xvii, xxvii, xxxiv, xxxv, 133, 135
Berwick, xvi
Bessin, Adrien de, 68

212 INDEX

Béthune, French ship, xxiv, 51
Béthune, town, 193, 194
Beurat, 133, 135
Bidoux, Pierre de, his nephew, 140
Bidoux, Prégent de, captain of the French galleys, xxii, xxx, xxxi, xxxii, xxxiv, xxxvii to xl, xliv to xlvi, 51, 52, 58, 59, 71, 72, 75, 92, 98, 121 to 123, 124, 126, 140, 141, 142, 144, 145, 146 to 150, 154, 155, 159, 161, 172, 173, 198, 199, 200, 202 to 205, 206, 207; letter from, 132
Bigars, Louis de, s^r de la Londe, French captain, 55, 56, 93, 181, 182, 187
Biscay, 37, 38, 41, 72, 173
Blackheath, xv, 4
Blackwall, ix, 80
Blancbaston, Charles, of Dieppe, 180, 182
Blancs-Sablons, xxxvii, 146
Blois, xxiii, 51, 59, 76, 134, 139
Bohier, Thomas, 68, 69, 70, 201; letter of, 76
Bonde, W., 78
Bordeaux, 19, 20, 46, 47, 150
Boulogne, xliv, xlv, 20, 192, 193, 200, 201, 202 to 205
Bourben, Duc de, 24
Brabant, 91
Brandon, Sir Charles, lord Lisle, xxi, xxxiv, 107, 165
Bréhat, île, 197
Brest, xviii, xxiv, xxv, xxvii, xxviii, xxxii, xxxiv, xxxv, xxxvi, xli, xliii, 22, 46, 47, 48, 49, 52, 53, 57, 58, 59, 60, 61, 65, 66, 72 to 75, 91, 92, 98, 99, 104, 121, 122, 126, 127, 129, 130, 132, 133, 146, 150, 158, 163, 164, 165, 169, 176, 186, 209
Brézé, Louis de, comte de Maulevrier, High Seneschal of Normandy, 76, 77, 180, 183, 187, 190, 191, 197, 209
Brigandyne, John, captain, xxi
Brigandyne, Robert, clerk of the ships, 78
Brighton, xlv, 205, 206
Bristol, 97, 120, 164
Brittany, xvii to xix, xxii, xxiii, xxvii, xxix, xli, xliv, 1, 22, 24, 26, 27, 36, 37, 40, 41, 43, 45, 46, 47, 48, 49, 52, 53, 54, 63, 64, 71, 72, 125, 129, 140, 141, 154, 155, 158, 161, 166, 167, 168, 169, 173, 174, 183, 184, 186, 187, 189, 190
Brook, Sir Edward, xviii
Broughton, 4
Browne, John, painter, 81
Browne, Sir Wistan, captain, xv, 5, 33, 81, 150, 156
Brownhill, Robert, xvi, xvii, 27
Bruce, William, James IV.'s herald-at-arms, xliii, 125
Bruges, John, 131
Bucy, Sr. de, 24
Bull, Sir Stephen, xviii, xxxvii, 15, 36, 83, 146, 203
Burdet, Sir John, xv, xviii, 8
Burgo, Andrea di, 3
Burgundy, Admiral of, 91

Cadiz, vii
Caen, 73
Calais, xliii, xlv, xlvi, 1, 20, 21, 23, 41, 97, 130, 140, 141, 198, 199, 203 to 206
Calcout (Calcutta), 47
Campfer. See Vere
Campofregoso, Octavius, Doge of Genoa, 52
Candia, xv, 19, 41
Cantepye, Jean, French pilot, 74, 209
Carew, Sir John, 36, 50, 57, 58, 63
Carmerien, Guillaume, French captain, 38
Carrickfergus, xliii
Cartagena, xxiii, 37
Casenove, Guill. de, x
Castille, 43, 44, 46
Caudebec, 103
Caux, Chef de, 2, 18, 102, 103
Caux, Pays de, xx, 102, 103, 191
Cavalcanti, J., xxiii
Chacho, or Chathei, Gabriel de, Breton, 57, 63
Champeroux, M. de, 165
Chanoy, Christ. de, French captain, 76, 208, 209

INDEX

Chantrezac, Alain de, letters of, 17, 20
Charente, River, 21, 208, 209
Charles VIII., King of France, x, 47
Charles, Prince of Spain, 174
Charles, Sir. See Brandon
Charran, Alphonso, Spanish captain, xxxviii, xxxix, 119, 143, 147, 148
Cherbourg, 152
Cheyne, Thomas, captain, xxxix, xl, 145, 148, 149, 156
Chio, xv, 19
Christ of Lynn, King's ship, 82
Christopher, Davy, 8, 85, 97
Cinquart, Jean, French captain, 169
Claricha, or Claristanc, Breton, 55, 57
Clarke, W., 16
Claude de, Princess, xl, 134, 139
Clercy, Ant. et Jean de, 101
Clermont, René de, Vice-Admiral of France, xxii, xxv, xxviii, 2, 3, 17, 27, 29, 32, 33, 38, 54, 59, 65, 66, 67, 200
Cloge, John, master of the Peter Pomegranate, 68, 81
Cobham, Sir Edward, xv, xviii, 9
Coetanlem, Nicolas, 47
Coimbre, Duchess of, 46
Compton, W., xxxvii, 78, 104, 146
Concarneau, xlii, 69
Conflans, Antoine de, French captain, xxiv, 37, 51
Conquet, xvii, xxxvii, xl, 133, 137, 140, 145, 146
Convicts in Prégent's galley, 7, 195
Convicts wanted for the row-barges, 143, 151, 156
Cooke, captain, 11, 84, 85, 160
Coppelan, Gilbert, of Dieppe, 197
Cordelière, xxii to xxvii, 47, 48, 49, 60, 61, 62, 63
Cordelière, list of French killed, 54, 55, 57, 58
Cornangel, Breton, 63
Cornwall, Ric., captain, xl, 145, 148, 149
Corunna, xxiv, 199
Cotton, Sir John, 4

Cradock, Matthew, 19, 78, 85; his bark, 85, 97
Croix-Porzmoguer, 133, 135
Crozon, xviii, xli, 121, 123, 126, 140, 155
Crussol, Louis de, 51

Dacre, Thomas, Lord, letter from, 188
Darcy, Lord, vii
Dartmouth, xxvii, xxxiii, xxxvi, 53, 54, 87, 106, 152, 158
Daryllio, Juan, pilot, xxxiii, 118
Daunce, John, 36, 64, 78, 109, 110
Dawtrey, John, xv, xli, 4, 33, 64, 109, 110, 185
Delabare, Sir J., xv
Denmark, vii, viii, xxix, 27, 37, 46
Denmark. See Ships
Des Celliers, Jean, 210
Devereux, Walter, Lord Ferrers, xxxviii, 79, 95, 119, 141, 149, 150, 154, 156
Dieppe, xxvii, xliii, xliv, xlv, 17, 18, 73, 76, 90, 91, 93, 94, 103, 180 to 183, 193 to 195, 198, 199
Dinan, 22, 140
Dol, 141
Don, Sir Griffith, xv, xvi, xviii, 5
Dorset, Marquis of, xvii, xxviii, xxix
Dover, xlv, 15, 97, 130, 192, 203, 204
Downs, the, xxxiv, 15, 37, 83, 94, 98, 120, 176, 202
Dragon of Greenwich, King's ship, 9, 65
Draper, 164
Drepa, French captain, 54
Du Bouchage, Ymbert de Bastarnay, Sir, 24, 46, 184
Du Château, M., 134-5, 139
Du Chillou. See Le Roy
Du Pont, Mathurin, 21
Du Poulx, Barthelemy, 196
Du Quesne, Jean, 190

Echyngham, Edw., captain, xxxvi, xxxvii, 27, 84, 130; letter from, 145
Edinburgh, xvi, 26, 27, 74

Egecombe, Sir Piers, 165
Elderton, 16
Eldicar. See Ellerkar
Elizabeth, of Newcastle, xxxix, 156
Ellerkar, Ralph, captain of the Mary Jane, 61, 82
Eltham, 68
Emmanuel, King of Portugal, xxx, 42, 43, 44, 46, 58, 174
Escripture, d', Esquetat (?), 91
Estouteville, d', 190
Etaples, xlvi
Eu, 90, 91, 94, 195, 196
Exeter, xl, 159

Falaise, 191
Falmouth, xxix, xxxii, 99
Faulconer, David, xvi, xvii, 27
Faure, Astremoine, commissioner for the fleet of Normandy, 39, 191, 192, 210
Favri, Nicolo di, 58
Fécamp, 20, 103, 152, 195, 196
Ferdinand, the Catholic, King of Aragon, x, xi, xxi, xxiii, xxviii, xxix, xxx, xxxiii, 58, 161, 162
Ferrers. See Devereux
Finistere, Cape, 37, 38
Fioravanti, Lodovico, 176
Fitzwilliam, Sir W., xv, 126
Flags, xlvii, 198
Flanders, 106
Fleming, John, captain, 10, 68, 80, 95
Flodden, xliii
Florence. See Acciajuoli
Florentine, xv, 16, 17, 18, 19
Fontarabia, xx, 17, 20, 21
Forde, W., 3
Fox, Ric., Bishop of Winchester, xli, 165, 169 ; letters to, 49, 205, 206
Françoise de Dieppe, 178, 180, 181
Françoise d'Orléans. See Nef d'Orléans
Freman, Master of the Katherine Forteleza, 95, 160

Gabriel, Royal, xxxiii, 80, 98, 118
Galice, xxiii, 42, 46, 72, 164

Gascony, 1
Gates, Sir Geoffrey, xv
Gautier, Pierre, comptroller of the victualling of the French fleet, xxii, xxvii, 24, 25, 56, 90, 93
Gédoyn, Robert, French secretary of State for Finance, 24, 25, 56, 60, 175, 184, 187, 192
Genoa, xxii, xxx, 51, 196, 206, 207
Genoese, xv, 16, 17, 18, 19, 42
George of Falmouth, 8
Germany, 37
Germyne, 84
Gonson, W., captain, xxxvi, 7, 78, 104, 123, 189
Gonson, W., captain, letter from, 130 to 132
Goston, John, 10
Gradenigo, Francesco, 180
Graville, Louis de, Admiral of France, 99, 177, 184
Great Bark, King's ship, 82, 95, 128, 171
Great Nicholas, 130, 131
Greenwich, 86
Guelders, Charles, Duke of, vii, 1, 2, 26, 27
Guenteville, Laurent de, 210
Guérin, Raoulin, French captain, 39, 40
Guernsey, xxxii, 99, 101
Guinea, 47
Guines, 198
Guipuzcoa, 41
Guise, Comte de, 24
Gurk, Matthew Lang, Cardinal of, 60
Gurney, Thomas, captain, 10, 84, 156
Guyenne, xi, xvii, xx, xxviii, 17, 23, 27
Guyvarra, Don P. Belis de, 162
Gyldeford, Sir H., xxi, xxxiv, 107
Gyrdelar Head, 94

Haeze, Fr. de, xvi
Harfleur, 2, 17, 18, 73, 91, 93, 169, 195, 196, 209
Harper, captain, xxxvii, 127, 150, 154
Harward, George, x

INDEX 215

Havre, Le, 39
Hayward, or Haywarde, Henry or Hervy, master of the Regent, 13, 68
Henry VII., vii, 18
Henry VIII., vii to ix, x, xi, xvi, xvii, xix, xxi, xxii, xxiii, xxviii, xxix, xxxii, xxxiii, xliii to xlvi, 1 to 3, 17, 18, 23, 40, 41, 71, 189, 200; letters to, 42, 46, 72, 94, 121, 126, 154, 161, 188, 193; Henry VIII., letters from, 124
Henry, King's galley, 87
Henry-Grace-Dieu, xxxiii, 72, 77, 79
Henry of Hampton, 34, 96
Heron, John, 64, 111
Hogue, La, 190
Holland, 91
Honfleur, xx, xxvii, xxxi, xxxii, xlii, xliii, xliv, xlvi, 2, 17, 20, 39, 41, 56, 69, 70, 71, 73, 74, 75, 76, 88, 90, 91, 92, 99, 102, 175, 177, 180, 181, 186, 187, 189, 190, 191, 193 to 198, 210
Hopton, John, 7, 78 to 83, 97
Howard, Sir Edward, viii, ix, x, xii, xv to xxvii, xxxiii to xl, 4, 7, 12, 15 to 19, 22, 26, 27, 33 to 36, 37, 48 to 50, 61, 63, 80, 109, 129, 133 to 139, 141 to 145, 154 to 156, 162, 167, 168; letters from, 94, 121, 126
Howard, Lord Thomas, viii, ix, xl, xli, xlii, 109, 205; letters from, 154, 159, 163, 167, 202; letters to, 166
Husy, John, clerk of the Ordnance, 117

Ireland, xxiii, 42, 43, 46, 209
Iseham, John, captain, ix, x, xxxvi, 8, 123, 130, 131

James IV., King of Scotland, xvi, xxix, xxx, xxxvii, xliv, 18, 26, 27, 46, 69, 70, 75, 108, 124, 162, 176, 183, 184, 186
James, of Antwerp, 117
James, of Hull. See Mary James
James, of London, 41

Jenett, of Purwyn, viii, xxxix, 10, 64, 84, 95, 123, 156
John Baptist, or John Hopton, King's ship, xxxiii, 7, 81, 98
John of London, 13
Joubert, François, letter from, 172
Julius II., Pope, x, 26

Katherine, King's galley, 87
Katherine, of London, 160
Katherine Forteleza, King's ship, xxxiii, 80, 95, 96, 103, 105, 118, 161, 162, 176
Katherine Pomegranate, King's rowbarge, xii, xxii, 11, 34, 41, 78. See Sweepstake
Katherine Prow, 95
Katt water, 163
Kingston, Sir K., xv
Kirkcudbright, xxiii, 43
Knight, W., letter from, 22, 46
Knyvet, James, captain, xxi, 1, 12
Knyvet, Sir Thomas, captain of the Regent, xxi, xxv, 50, 52, 53, 57, 58, 63

La Bastie, M. de, French ambassador in Scotland, 188
Lacaille, Martin, 180, 182
La Chapelle, Jean de, 210
La Chastre, Charles de, commissioner of the ordnance in Normandy, 24, 175
La Chesnaye, Nicolas, 19, 20
La Chesnaye, Jean de, 196
La Fayette, captain of Boulogne, letters to, 200, 201
La Hay. See Ley
Lalemant, Jean, commissioner for the fleet of Normandy, 38, 39, 55, 56, 88, 90, 177, 178, 182, 190, 191
Lalo, Aloise de, xvi
La Londe. See Bigars
La Masure, Jean de, 195
Lamballe, 140
La Mothe, or La Motte. See Tocque
Lando, Piero, letters from, 60, 68
Languedoc, xx, xxi

La Pole. See Suffolk
La Primaudaye, Philippe de, comptroller of the victualling of the French fleet, xliv, 175, 179, 182
Lasagni, Genoese agent in France, 24, 51
La Sala, Fernando de, Spaniard, xxxiii, 77
La Thieuville, Jehannequin de, 18
La Trémoille, Louis II. Duc de, xvi, 17, 189, 196; letter from, 21
Laval, M. de, 133 to 139
Le Brun, Louis, Sr. de Sallenelles, captain of the Louise, 2, 59, 177
Leclouston, Adam, 173
Le Fevre, Jacques, 71
Le François, Grégoire, 195
Legendre, Adenet, French captain, 55, 68, 69, 70, 208
Leicester, viii
Leith, xliii, 176
Leonard of Dartmouth, 95, 96
Le Roy, Guyon, Sr. du Chillou, admiral of the French fleet, xxxi, xxxii, xxxiv, 73, 76, 77, 89, 99, 132, 133, 148, 170
Lespargne, French captain, 76
Lesse Bark, King's ship, 83, 95
Le Veau, Jean, Flemish ambassador in France, letters from, 1, 2
Levrière, 169, 180, 181
Lewes, John, 27, 156
Ley, or Loy, Simon de, Breton, 55, 57
Lezcano, Juan de, Spanish admiral, xxix, xxx, 41, 58, 59
Lincoln, Bishop of. See Wolsey
Lion, Robert Barton's ship, viii, ix, xliii, 93, 169, 178, 199
Lion of Greenwich, King's ship, 8, 34
Lisbonne, 42
Lisieux, 191
Lisle, Lord. See Brandon
Lizard, King's ship, xxxix, 84, 95, 97, 123, 124, 156
Lombardy, xxii
London, 185, 193
Longueville, Duc de, 2, 19
Losa. See Alos
Louis XI., x

Louis XII., x, xvi, xxii, xxiii, xxviii, xxix, xxx, xxxi, xl, xliii, 1 to 3, 19, 23, 24, 27, 37, 43, 47, 51, 56, 57, 59, 60, 71, 73, 75, 125, 162, 175, 183, 186 to 188, 191, 192, 200, 201, 207 to 210
Louise, French admiral's ship, xxiv, xxv, xxviii, xxxi, 50, 59, 88 to 90, 99, 177
Loveday, John, 27
Loveday, Walter, 160
Lovell, Thomas, letters from, 205, 206
Lucy, Sir Thomas, xv, xviii, 6

Magdalene, xxi, 34
Mailly, de, 90
Malaga, 52, 197
Margaret, of Topsham, xxi, 12, 64
Marguerite, of Savoy, xv, 92; letters to, 1, 2, 3
Maria de Loreto, xxxiii, 77, 86, 96, 118, 202
Marie de Clermont, 38
Marie de Honfleur, 173
Marseilles, xxxi, 196
Martinengo, Marco de, Genoese agent, 52
Martynet, 10
Martyr, Peter, 18, 41; letter from, 51, 58, 180
Mary Barking, x, 189
Mary George, King's ship, 6, 7, 81, 95, 96
Mary Howard, 7, 189
Mary Imperial, 120
Mary James, King's ship, xxi, xxiv to xxvi, 60, 61, 62, 82, 96
Mary John, King's ship, x, xvi, 6, 80, 83, 171
Mary Rose, King's ship, 3, 4, 36, 60, 61, 68, 80, 95, 96, 98, 107, 158, 166, 205
Maulevrier, Comte de. See Brézé
Maximilian, Emperor, 20
Mediterranean, xlvi, 47, 196, 206
Meynerde, Thomas, 16
Middelburg, xxxii, 99
Milan, 196
Montauban, Philippe de, 21, 22
Montcontour, 140

INDEX

Montivilliers, 103
Montmorency, Duc de, 18
Montreuil-sur-Mer, 20
Morlaix, 63
Morley, John, secretary of James IV., 46
Morton, Sir Robert, xv, 6
Morvilliers, Raoul de Lannoy, Sr. de, bailli d'Amiens, 46
Moussy, Regnaut de, vice-admiral of Guyenne, 2
Murray, bishop of, 125

Naples, xxiii, xxx, 47, 59
Navarre, xxviii, xxxiii
Nef de Bordeaux, 76, 176
Nef de Brest, xxii, 47
Nef de Dieppe, xxv, xxviii, 54, 65, 66, 76, 193, 194, 208
Nef de Morlaix, xxii, 47
Nef de la Rochelle, 92, 176
Nef d'Orléans, 55, 76, 208
Negropont, xxx
Nevell, Sir Edward, xv
Nice, 51
Nicholas Benley, 116
Nicholas Draper, 189
Nicholas, of Hampton, xxxv, 10, 83, 128
Nicholas Montrigo. See Sancho de Garra
Nicholas Reede, xxxiii, 7, 81, 96. See Great Nicholas
Norfolk, 3, 64
Normandy, xvi, xix, xx, xxii, xxiii, xxxi, xliv, xlvi, 1, 2, 3, 17, 22, 24, 25, 27, 40, 41, 46, 48, 72, 73, 100, 101, 158, 175, 176, 177, 181, 182, 183, 193, 196, 197

Ogilvy, James, 27
Ordnance, English, 120
Ordnance, French, xxv, xxx, xxxix, 2, 18, 24, 49, 50, 51, 52, 69, 70, 75, 76, 98, 136, 140, 147, 154, 155, 159, 200
Oxford, Earl of, xxviii

Page, Richard, 131
Palshid, Richard, 15
Pandolfini, Florentine ambassador in France, letter from, 206

Paris, 134, 139, 195
Paris, Etienne Poncher, bishop of, 24, 46, 184
Parliament, English, 1, 71
Parr, Sir W., xv
Pasqualigo, Lorenzo, Venetian consul in London, xv, xix, xxiii ; letters from, 16, 18, 36, 40, 63, 72, 185, 197
Péguineau, Martin, French ambassador to Scotland, 68, 69, 70, 74, 75
Pelle, Jean, 102
Pesaro, Francesco, letter to, 52
Peter of Fowey, 8
Peter Pomegranate, King's ship, x, 4, 5, 33, 68, 81, 104, 163
Petite Louise, xliii, 55, 68, 69, 70, 74, 169, 208
Phellips, Richard, 15
Picardy, xx, xliv, xlv, 17, 23, 141, 189
Piéfort, Jean, French gunner, 68, 69, 70
Piennes, de, 201
Pierdux, Joes, 90 to 95
Pirton, Sir W., xviii
Plantagenet, Arthur, captain, xxxv, 83, 127 to 129, 171
Plymouth, xxxii, xxxiv, xl, 98, 104, 105, 111, 119, 121, 122, 145, 151, 160, 161, 166
Pont-Audemer, 17
Ponynges, Edward, vii, 50
Port-Blanc, 197
Porte, Robert, 78
Portrieux, 132
Portsmouth, xvi, xxii, xxiv, 13, 14, 16, 34, 41, 60, 120, 121, 180, 202
Portugal, xxiii
Portugal, King of. See Emmanuel
Portuguese, 174
Porzmoguer, Hervé de, captain of the Cordelière, xvii, xxiii, xxv, xxvi, xxvii, 42, 54, 57, 63, 65, 66
Power, John, 8
Poyntes, Ant., captain, 83, 97, 163
Prégent. See Bidoux
Privateers, English, 19
Privateers, French, xxiii, xliv, 38, 41, 42, 43, 192, 197

Privy Council, of England, 202
Privy Council, of France, 19, 46
Provence, 207
Pucher, Baudouin, 193

Queenborough, xxxvi, 130

Ratclif, Lord, ix
Ravenna, xvi, 18
Regent, King's ship, x, xiii, xvi, xxi, xxiv to xxvii, 13, 14, 15, 33, 35, 36, 49, 50, 52, 53, 57, 58, 62, 63
Reprisal, letters of, 19
Rieux, Jean de, 140
Robertet, Florimond, French secretary of state for the finance, 33, 46, 71, 132, 200, 201
Robineau, Jean, 39
Rochelaise, xxiii, 74, 197
Rochelle, La, xx, xxi, 2, 46, 47, 154, 158, 173, 174
Rohan, Pierre de, 165 ; letter from, 98
Rome, 52
Rondelline, Adam, 196
Rose, French ship, xxiv, 51, 180, 181
Rose, King's galley or bark, 87, 171
Rose Henry, King's rowbarge, xvi, 11, 78. See Swallow
Rothwell, Roger, 171
Rouen, xxiii, 17, 20, 21, 68, 71, 73, 75, 76
Roussel, Philippe, xxiii, 42, 74, 99, 169, 170, 176, 177, 197, 198
Rousset, Jean, Prégent's lieutenant, 195
Rouville, Louis de, admiral of the French fleet, xliv, 183, 184

Sabyn, William, xxxvi, xxxviii, 9, 84, 104, 128, 146, 165 ; letter from, 141
Sabyn, ship, 9, 64, 84, 104
Sacre, 169, 180, 181
Saint Brieuc, 140
Saint Mahé, 169
Saint Malo, xxxiv, xliv, xlvi, 42, 91, 99, 121, 122, 140, 207, 208
Saint Matthew, Cape, 122, 129, 133, 134, 135, 137

Saint Michael, Scottish ship, 176
Saint Nicholas, island, 163
Saint Omer, 20, 132, 133
Sancho de Garra, 96, 115
Sandrin, Laurent, 194
Sandwich, 98, 202
Scarella, Andrew, 87
Scotland, vii, xvi, xvii, xxiii, xxxi, xlv, 17, 18, 26, 27, 42, 43, 68, 74, 75, 129, 169, 170, 176, 199, 206, 208, 209. See James IV., Ships
Séguier, Dominique, 140
Seine, river, xx
Seman, Peter, pilot, 95, 118, 171
Shelton, John, 132
Sherborne, Sir H., captain, xv, xviii, xxxix, 10, 82, 146, 149, 156, 204
Shipman, John, 120
Ships, Lists of, xiv, xxii, 47, 49, 64, 77 to 88, 109 to 121, 171, 172, 178, 183, 197, 202 ; Danish, xliii, 90, 92, 120, 170, 180; Flemish, xix, 36, 37, 106, 117, 151, 152, 174 ; French, 73, 74, 90 to 94, 98 ; Genoese. See Maria de Loreto. Portuguese, 37, 38, 42, 174 ; Scottish, xxix, xlii, xliv, 72, 73, 90, 92, 120, 167, 169, 170, 175 to 177, 180, 185 to 188 ; Spanish, xxii, xliii, 37, 38, 40, 41, 43, 50, 59, 104, 107, 114, 115, 117, 127, 130, 152, 153, 164, 167, 170, 195, 207, 208. See Gabriel Royal, Katherine Forteleza, Lezcano, Sancho de Garra
Sibille, 39
Sickness in the Fleet, 151, 185
Sirrea, Martin, pilot, 118
Smith, Myles, 3
Soome, John, 156
Southampton, xiii, xv, xvi, xxvii, xxix, 13, 14, 15, 16, 26, 52, 53, 54, 63, 68, 104, 108, 110, 121, 150, 153, 158, 163, 166, 167, 176, 185
Southwell, Sir Robert, 109
Sovereign, King's ship, xxii, xxv, 14, 34, 40, 41, 50, 79, 95, 96, 119
Spain, xxiii, xxix, 72, 209
Spert, Thomas, Master of the Mary Rose, 3, 68, 80

INDEX

Spinelly, Thomas, letters from, 46, 72, 75, 90, 99
Stanley, Bastard of, 201
Style, John, English ambassador in Spain, letters from, 42, 173
Suffolk, 64
Suffolk, Richard de la Pole, Duke of, 201, 206
Sussex, xliii, xlv
Swallow, King's rowbarge, 78, 84, 95
Sweepstake, King's rowbarge, 78, 85, 95
Sydney, Sir W., captain, xv, xxxix, 9, 82, 147, 149, 156
Symons, or Symonds, W., comptroller of the Navy, xlii, 117
Syo. See Chio

Taillevant, bark of the Louise, 89
Talbot, 201
Tavarant, N., 134, 139
Thérouenne, xliii
Thomas of Hull, xxxvii, 127
Thurcull, Richard, 131
Tocque, Charles de, Sr. de la Motte, French ambassador in Scotland, xvi, xliii, 27, 68 to 70, 74, 75, 169, 170
Tolly, W., 156
Toucque, 190
Tournai, xliii
Trade, the, xi, xvii, xl, xli, 122, 142, 146, 149, 153 to 158; interruption of, xxiii
Tréport, le, xlvi, 103, 195, 196
Trevanyon, or Trevynyan, Sir W., captain, xxxii, 8, 79, 127
Trinité de Honfleur, 196
Trinity of Bristol, 78, 97
Trinity of Wight 41
Turks, xxx
Tuthill, H., 13

Ughtred, Ant., captain of the Mary James, xxi, xxv, xxvi, 60, 61, 62, 63
Unicorn, Scottish king-at-arms, 75

Valois, François d'Angoulême, duc de, xx, 24, 139

Valtan, Pierre Louis de, bishop of Rieux, French ambassador in England, 3
Vangel. See Cornangel
Vaughan, Thomas, 15, 203
Vendôme, Comte de, 24
Venetian, xxxi, 52
Venice, 71
Vere, xxxii, 90, 93, 197
Veulettes, 102
Viart, Guillaume, 68
Vibert, Nic., 191
Vicquemare, Hector de, 175
Victualling, English ships, xxxiii to xxxvi, xlii, 11, 13 to 16, 104, 105, 153, 154, 166; French ships, 24, 25, 51, 56, 88 to 90, 175, 177 to 179, 209
Vincent of Fowey, 114

Wallop, Sir T., captain, xxxix, xl, xlvi, 145, 146, 148, 149, 156, 204
West, Nicolas, xxxvii, 125, 205
Westall, John, surgeon of the Regent, 63
Weston, Richard, 101
Whistles of Admiral Howard, xxxix, 134, 139, 145, 148
Wight, Isle of, xvii, xix, 22, 104, 165, 166
Wiltshire, John, 99; letter from 198
Winchester, Bishop of. See Fox
Wine sent to James IV. by Louis XII., 70
Wingfield, Sir Richard, letters from, 192, 193
Wiseman, 156, 164, 204
Wolsey, xxxiii, xli, 35, 79, 80; letters to, 22, 46, 103, 141, 145, 159, 163, 167, 192, 198, 205, 206; letters from, 26, 49, 57, 166
Woolwich, 80, 87, 98, 105
Wyndham, Sir Thomas, xviii, 5, 36, 81, 94, 104, 109, 110, 185, 204

Yelverton, Robert, 11
York, 61

Zealand, ix, xvii, 37, 91, 130, 131, 174

www.ingramcontent.com/pod-product-compliance
Lightning Source LLC
Chambersburg PA
CBHW031944230426

43672CB00010B/2046